The How to Grow and Cook It Book
of Vegetables, Herbs, Fruits, and Nuts

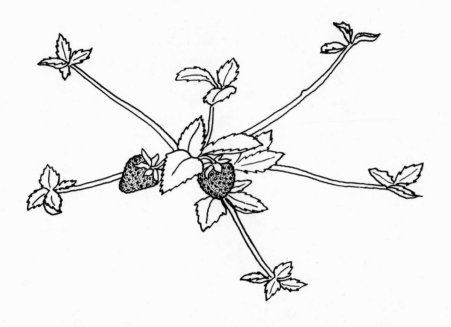

The How to Grow and Cook It Book of Vegetables, Herbs, Fruits, and Nuts

by Jacqueline Hériteau

Illustrated by David M. Hunter

Hawthorn Books, Inc., Publishers
A Helen Van Pelt Wilson Book
New York

For my father, Marcel Stephan Hériteau,
who put in my first garden
and taught me how to make French bread,
and for my husband, David Marvin Hunter,
who wanted to see it all on paper

Acknowledgments

Putting together the technical information required for the
book, as well as the recipes, has made me the debtor of almost
everyone I know who gardens and cooks. In addition, special
acknowledgments for help received must go to Walter W.
Washko, Agronomist, and David A. Kollas, Pomologist, of the
Cooperative Extension Service of the University of Connecticut;
to Alice F. Skelsey, of the Agricultural Research Service of the
United States Department of Agriculture; to the Stark Brothers'
Nurseries, of Louisiana, Missouri, for special help on the
fruit-garden section; to Mrs. Rhoades Robinson, who put the
extensive garden library of her Community Service, Inc., at our
disposal; to the New York Horticultural Society; to Sharon's
Hotchkiss Library, which sent far and wide for information on
missing subjects; and to Helen Van Pelt Wilson, an editor
who does much more than just edit books.

Contents

Acknowledgments   vii

List of Illustrations   xi

Introduction: Fresh from My Garden   xiii

1 Food Plants in Your Landscape   1

2 Soils for Top Production   11

3 Timing, Intercropping, Succession   16

4 From Seeds to Harvest   24

5 How to Grow Vegetables—
   Artichokes to Zucchini   33

6 Fine Vegetable Cookery—
   Artichokes to Zucchini   88

7 Sauces and Pastries   192

8 Agreeable Herbs to Grow and Use   203

9 Orchard Fruits and Berries for the Home Garden   210

10 Cooking and Serving Fruits   223

11 Bounty from Nut Trees   252

12 Cooking with Nuts   259

Appendix: State Agricultural Extension Services Addresses   272

Table I—Vegetables to Plant in Early Spring   274

Table II—Vegetables to Plant in Mid-Spring   276

Table III—Vegetables to Plant in Late Spring   277

Table IV—Vegetable Troubles and What to Do   278

Table V—Herb Planting and Use   284

Table VI—Fruit Planting and Spraying   286

Index   289

List of Illustrations

A small garden of choice vegetables and salad ingredients   2

An urban quarter acre in which attractive food plants provide both good land-scaping and productive crops   7

Suburban acre accommodates a large vegetable garden, fruit and nut trees, berry patches, and an herb garden.   8

A border garden of food plants and flowers   9

Dwarf apple in "Belgian fence" espalier   10

Compost pile   14

A large garden, 50 x 100 feet, has widely spaced rows to accommodate mechanical tillage and employs succession plantings to increase yield.   17

A small garden, 25 feet square, has closely spaced rows and employs intercropping and succession planting.   19

Seedlings in flat transplant best when cut apart to avoid loss of soil.   22

Pegs and string to keep rows straight   25

Double-digging   26

Seedlings of vegetables   28–29

Four ways to stake tomatoes   84

To make decorative cantaloupe halves   144

Seedlings of herbs   204

Cartwheel herb garden   205

Planting and pruning orchard fruits   214

Planting strawberries   216

Planting and pruning raspberry and blackberry bushes   219

Planting and pruning grapes   221

Introduction:
Fresh from My Garden

Travelers returning from France often praise the flavor of vegetables and fruit they have had, and give credit either to the climate or to the cook. It is possible that some plants, artichokes and pears for instance, prefer Continental weather, but others are not benefited by it. No apple abroad is as good as most American and Canadian varieties, and American sweet corn planted in France is a disaster. My French father tried it once at the Château de l'Enardière for love of my Scotch-Canadian mother, but only the chickens would eat the crop. Nor is it true that every cook in France is a Vatel or an Escoffier. Some cooks at home may take more pains with their recipes than some cooks here, but to my mind an important factor in the success of their concoctions is that most vegetables and fruits used abroad are garden-fresh.

Any weekday at 7 a.m. in my father's village in the Vendée, you will see Madame Albert, the cook at the Hôtel de la Plage, shopping the market stalls for the youngest carrots and the biggest bargains; she sniffs the cantaloupes, upturns mushrooms, nibbles string beans, and offers vociferous contempt to any farmer whose produce she suspects of being left over from yesterday. The Shrimp-Dressed Artichokes, the Petits Pois à la Française, and the Fraises des Bois Crème Fraîche which she serves you at noon were harvested at dawn.

In Les Sables d'Olonne my aunts Louise and Andrée, my uncles Roger, Robert, and Marc, and all their neighbors each have a small garden. Espaliered pears ripen against warm walls, leeks are transplanted three times in tense competition for the biggest, and grapes are learnedly pruned. The fruit my aunts serve and the vegetables they cook were either picked in the garden minutes before or brought from twice-daily trips to the market. These women are known for their cuisine and are most particular about the freshness of the ingredients. The fisherman has not been born who can sell an Hériteau a fish old enough to have a glaze to its eye!

Before frozen foods, the flavor of cooked vegetables in America was much better. A kitchen garden was a part of many suburban and most rural homes. Meals were certainly less varied than those that come from today's supermarkets. I can recall a year-long visit with my Canadian grandmother, Sadie Agnes Sutherland, when peas and tomatoes vanished with the first snow and we had to be content (and were) with variations on the winter theme of root vegetables and pickled produce—potato baskets filled with crisped perch, fluffy butternut pie, carrot cookies, bread-and-butter pickles.

The frozen-food counter represents progress, of course. When people exchange one way of life for another, they usually do so because the new way fills needs the old way did not. In the cold months I trundle my cart up and down the aisles weekly, grateful for the year-round variety of vegetables and fruit, however many days the poor things have traveled, however heavily sprayed with preservatives and gassed for color, however unripe when picked, however inferior to my taste are these necessarily mass-produced foods.

The generation that made a cliché of "She can't cook like mother could" spoke truth, but I blame the ingredients, not the cook. The flavor of peaches and corn and lettuce fresh from the garden is so astonishingly superior to that of produce available frozen or even fresh in stores that to anyone who likes to garden and is fond of food, growing his own seems a modest chore.

For instance, producing greens for a mixed salad, or the tomatoes, green peppers, and crisp wedges of Bermuda onion that make shish kebab, is easier mentally and physically than doing a good job on a medium-size flower bed. The art of growing food can be reduced to a few basic simplicities; once you have grasped them and the garden is established, the upkeep is not demanding.

Like green stamps at the supermarket, there are bonuses. All the jack-o'-lanterns our friends can use grow with no extra effort in the cornpatch, where the big pumpkin leaves shade the earth and inhibit weeds. Among the hills of corn are one hill each of popping corn and ornamental corn that belong to our children. In their enthusiasm to achieve their own harvests they learn about growing, about the seasons, and about man's relation to the earth, wisdom they would never acquire if I set them to pick beetles from the roses or pull weeds from the petunia bed.

Et puis, food costs being what they are now, growing your own lets you *faire des petites économies.*

Chimney Hill   JACQUELINE HÉRITEAU
Sharon, Connecticut

**The How to Grow and Cook It Book
of Vegetables, Herbs, Fruits, and Nuts**

1 Food Plants in Your Landscape

Where you plant and how much depends upon what space you have, how the area is landscaped, and what you like to look at. You can plant enough vegetables and herbs, fruits and nut trees on a third of an acre to feed a family of five and have some left over to sell. Along the Italian Riviera almost everyone does, and families grow the grapes for their table wine as well. Ask how they do it, and you will learn that a well-cared-for 25-foot row produces much more than a badly cared-for 50-foot row. And that's the truth.

HOW MUCH GARDEN DO YOU NEED?

The Vegetable Crop

A "big" garden is 50 by 100 feet. It includes such important perennials as strawberries, asparagus, and rhubarb, and supplies a family of six with fresh vegetables and enough to pickle, store, and freeze for the winter as well. A medium-size garden is 40 by 60 feet; without the perennials, it provides an average family (that now means four and a half people) with fresh vegetables throughout the growing season and also enough to store and freeze.

A garden 25 by 25 feet is small, but it will supply the average family with fresh vegetables and salad makings from late spring to early autumn. Use the Yield column of the Planting Tables at the back of the book to figure out how much of each crop these garden sizes can produce; this will help you to work out the size garden you require.

Before you decide to plant everything in the catalog, however, remember the Italian Riviera, where a flourishing 25-foot row yields more than a struggling 50-foot row. My first vegetable garden was 40 feet wide by 95 feet long, and it taught me this: Until you have

1

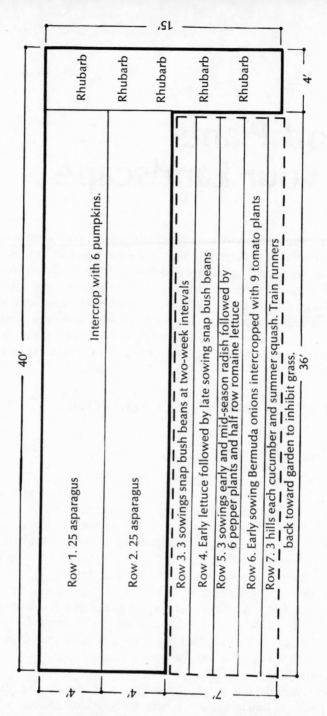

A small garden of choice vegetables and salad ingredients, designed to be increased by one new row each year, until the gardener finds he is giving it as much time and space as he can spare

the perennials in and going, and the weeds under control, a big garden can be a terrible chore. The best way to find out what size your garden should be is to start with a small plot, and add one row to it each year until it requires as much effort, time, and space as you are *happy* to give. Then keep it to that size. Since the perennials, once established, require no more care than flowering shrubs, begin with the two easiest ones, asparagus and rhubarb, and then add enough space for a salad garden.

For a family of five, plan on about 350 square feet for asparagus and rhubarb; ten asparagus plants and one rhubarb plant for each member. Add another 250 square feet and you can grow tomatoes, peppers, Spanish or Bermuda onions, early and late lettuce, several crops of green beans, a few late root vegetables such as beets or carrots or turnips, and a scattering of the herbs you use most. Then prepare for the row you will add next year this way: In the sod bordering the last row of the garden, dig six round holes 4 feet in diameter, and here plant squash and cucumber vines. The runners, trained back toward the garden, will discourage grass and weeds and make the new row much easier to dig up for planting the next spring.

Intercropping (or "companion planting") and succession planting make it possible to produce all these crops in very little space.

Intercropping. A glance at the Approximate Days to Maturity column of the Planting Tables at the back of the book will show that some vegetables produce their crops in as little as three weeks, others as much as five months. By combining the planting of small, fast-growing vegetables, such as radishes and lettuce, with taller, slow-to-mature species, such as cabbage and Brussel sprouts, one row can be made to yield two crops. You can also combine tall and short crops that mature at about the same time: corn, which grows to 6 feet, and pumpkins or squash, which hug the ground, or pole beans and onions.

Succession planting. The word "succession" here is used two ways: It can mean repeated sowings of one vegetable at intervals of two weeks so that the crops succeed each other in maturing. Radishes, lettuce, and bush snap beans, which mature quickly, are often planted this way. "Succession" can also mean the sowing of a second crop in a row after the first one has been harvested. For instance, carrots, broccoli, turnips, or early peas, planted at the very beginning of spring, are harvested and out in time to be followed by any crop that will have time to mature before cold weather sets in. See the Planting Tables for suggestions.

The Herb Crop

A small, formal herb garden is charming but not a necessity to the cook. For most herbs, one flourishing plant usually supplies enough for use fresh, some to dry for winter, and some to give away. (Garlic and onions go into the vegetable garden.) A plot 2 by 5 feet gives space enough for chives, tarragon, basil, thyme, sweet marjoram, summer savory, and a little parsley and dill. If you can fit the parsley and dill into the vegetable garden, the remaining herbs will fit handily into a window planter or a strawberry jar. All the herbs can be intercropped in the vegetable garden, of course, but they are handier close to the kitchen door.

The Fruit Crop

Fruit grows on trees, bushes, and vines, all of which are perennial and require little more care than your flowering shrubs. The exceptions are melons, which are annual vines; grape vines, which require trellising; and strawberry plants, which must go into the vegetable garden or in a separate bed of their own. Since they are so easy, the number you plant should depend on the amount of fruit you want to harvest and the space available. Here is a list of the yields you can expect from mature plantings of those fruits most important to the home gardener:

An 8-foot dwarf fruit tree yields 1 to 3 bushels (50 pounds to a bushel); semi-dwarfs, 12 to 16 feet tall, yield correspondingly more, 5 to 10 bushels. Plums yield 1 to 2 bushels. A 50-foot row of red raspberries yields from 10 to 50 pounds of berries, or about 1-1/2 quarts to a bush; purple and black raspberries yield slightly less; blackberries yield 1-1/2 quarts to a bush. Grapes produce about 15 pounds per vine; blueberries yield about 4 quarts to a bush; strawberries yield up to 1 quart to a plant.

One other factor must be considered in planning your fruit garden: cross-pollination. Most apples and pears require cross-pollination to set fruit. So do most plums. Most peaches and nectarines are self-pollinators, but not all. Sour cherries are self-pollinators, but most varieties of sweet cherries are not. A few kinds of grapes require cross-pollination, and so do a few kinds of strawberries. Cross-pollination improves the yields of blueberries. You must plan on two of each fruit that requires cross-pollination. This won't affect the space needed for the strawberry bed or for the grapes or blueberries, since you will want more than one plant or vine anyway, but if you have room for only two dwarf fruit trees, for instance, you must choose either two self-pollinators or a pair that can cross-pollinate.

The Nut Crop

Nut trees, with the exception of the almond and the pretty little hazelnut, are tall, handsome trees often grown for their beauty as shade trees rather than for their crops. This is particularly true in colder areas where trees hardy enough to survive the winter yield only nuts that are very difficult to crack. Newly developed early-bearing varieties produce nuts with thinner shells and will succeed in colder or warmer climates than their forebears could take, so more and more nut trees are appearing in home orchards. A single nut tree will provide upward of 2 bushels of nuts at maturity, more than enough for the average family. However, many varieties require cross-pollination, which means finding space for two in your grounds.

WHERE TO PLANT?

Essentials

All food plants require well-drained soil and full sun. A few herbs like a little shade at noon, and a few vegetables are more tolerant of shade than others. Cabbage, beans, broccoli, and leafy vegetables endure more shade than do tomatoes, corn, potatoes, cucumbers, melons, and root crops. A southern slope that offers protection from north winds is the preferred site, and a sandy loam which warms up quickly in spring is ideal. Avoid steep slopes where the soil will erode, and really low spots where late and early frosts settle. Keep the vegetable garden away from airless corners where pests and diseases prosper, and away from big trees that will compete with it for soil, moisture, and nutriments. If you can, locate the vegetables near your water supply and tool shed. If you live in a wooded area, locate food plants as close to the house as appearances will allow, to discourage hungry little animals.

These are the practical requirements of food plants, but unless you are planning to make truck gardening your business, another important consideration is how they will look from the living room, porch, or patio.

Aesthetics

Because many food plants are quite beautiful, fitting them into your landscape will not be difficult. A small garden of herbs is a delight, but all the herbs you really need can be planted to edge a flower bed, should there be no other place for them. Nut trees grow into stately specimens worthy of the front lawn. Fruit trees are as pretty as their ornamental cousins, the "flowering" fruit trees, and can be used instead. Espalier a pair of apple trees against a dull garage wall; set them in two's to border a garden path; or plant a miniature orchard to screen the vegetable garden.

The really small dwarf fruits can even be grown in planters on the patio, or as foundation plants. Low-growing varieties of blueberry make a handsome hedge that glows red in autumn. Grapes too can be trained low enough to make a hedge, or high enough to shade an arbor, a picture window, or a terrace.

On the other hand, cane fruits and rows of vegetables hardly contribute to the beauty of a small landscape. Though a tidy raspberry patch becomes a drift of snowy blossoms in spring, the rest of the season it is best hidden in a dip in the grounds, or relegated to the back property line, or a corner behind the garage.

Some vegetables, assessed purely for their ornamental value, are surprisingly attractive. In fact, I have always wanted to plant flowers in among the vegetables and herbs to see what could be achieved. Rhubarb and asparagus in their summer finery are striking. Rhubarb blooms in tall, shaggy, off-white spikes; asparagus feathers into delicate green ferns, and either is striking in or as a backdrop to the flower border. Tomatoes aglow with tiny red cocktail fruits are pretty enough to go anywhere; so are the shiny, pointed-leafed peppers, and the ornamental globe artichokes.

Vegetable crops that go in and come out a few weeks later leaving holes in the ground obviously belong in a garden of their own, along with such long-legged things as pole beans and cornstalks. I have hidden vegetable gardens behind evergreens, fruit orchards, rose hedges, and the garage. I have seen others concealed by stone walls, tall forsythias, or mixed borders of tall ornamentals such as phlox, helenium, and rudbeckia. One of the prettiest I have ever seen is a low-growing garden surrounded by dwarf apples espaliered in the method known as Belgian fence.

But of all the vegetable gardens I have known probably the one I love best is Aunt France's, which isn't hidden at all. You step from her kitchen door into a small grape arbor; beyond it, fenced on

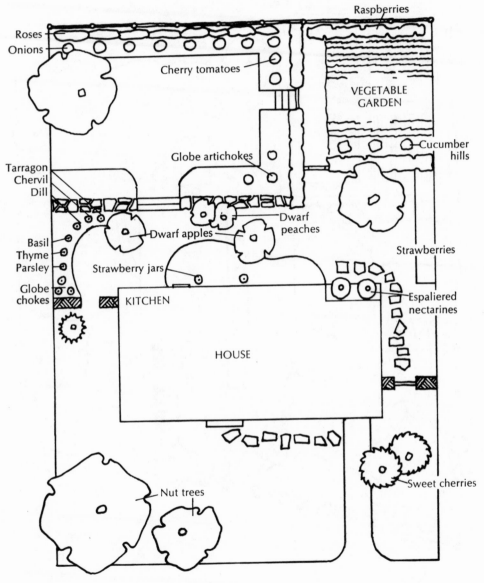

Roses
Onions
Cherry tomatoes
Raspberries
VEGETABLE GARDEN
Cucumber hills
Globe artichokes
Tarragon
Chervil
Dill
Dwarf peaches
Dwarf apples
Basil
Thyme
Parsley
Strawberry jars
Strawberries
Globe chokes
Espaliered nectarines
KITCHEN
HOUSE
Nut trees
Sweet cherries

SCALE: 1/2"=10'

An urban quarter acre in which attractive food plants provide both good landscaping and productive crops

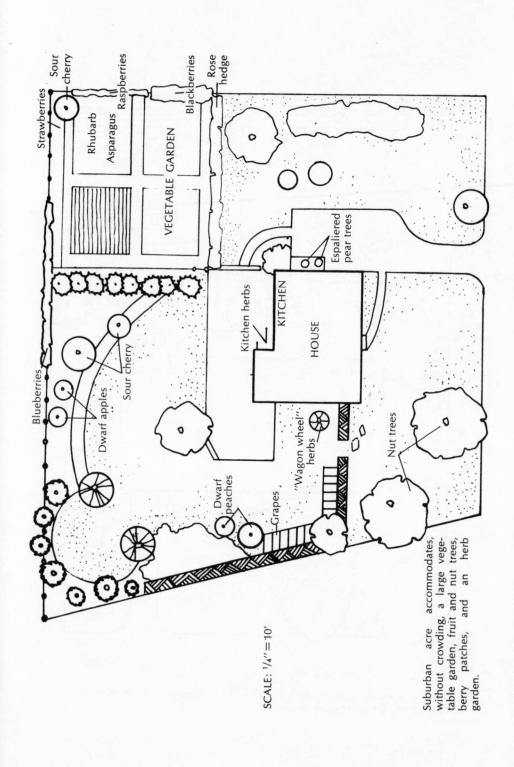

Strawberries

Sour cherry

Rhubarb

Asparagus

Raspberries

Blackberries

Rose hedge

VEGETABLE GARDEN

Espaliered pear trees

Blueberries

Dwarf apples

Sour cherry

Kitchen herbs

KITCHEN

HOUSE

Nut trees

"Wagon wheel" herbs

Dwarf peaches

Grapes

SCALE: 1/4" = 10'

Suburban acre accommodates, without crowding, a large vegetable garden, fruit and nut trees, berry patches, and an herb garden.

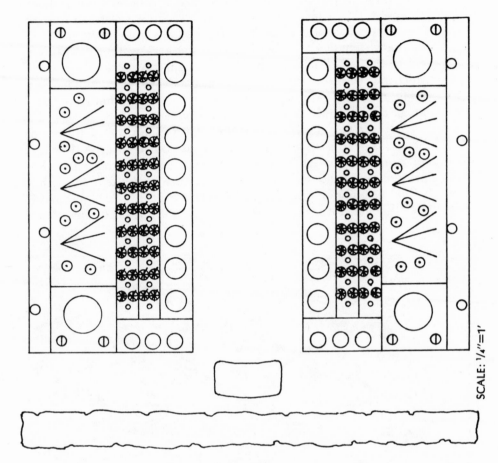

SCALE: 1/4"=1'

Border garden of food and flowers: Two balancing beds, 7½ feet wide and 15 feet long, rely on succession planting and intercropping to produce 5 vegetables, 2 perennial fruits, 7 herbs, and 3 or 4 types of flowers. Behind a front edging of everbearer strawberries are 2 rows 12 inches wider, in which early radishes are followed by cactus zinnias and low-growing white petunias; behind this is a row 3 feet wide with a rhubarb plant at either end and room for 3 staked tomato plants intercropped with romaine lettuce. The tomatoes were preceded by 3 rows of early lettuce. Herbs edge the corners of the row. Behind the tomatoes, a 12-inch row accommodates tall-growing helenium and 4 cucumber vines.

KEY:
○   Early radish
○   Helenium and 4
      cucumber vines
⊙   Romaine lettuce
⊕   Parsley, thyme, basil,
      chervil, tarragon, savory, chives
✺   Cactus zinnias and
      petunias
○   Dwarf marigolds or
      6 more strawberries
○   Everbearer strawberries
      18" apart
○   Rhubarb
⋀   Tomatoes

either side with 3-foot stone walls, is a vegetable garden about 80 feet by 150. A pair of gnarled pear trees grows in it and straight paths bisect it, and you can tell no weed has found a home there for years. Climbing strawberries cover the back wall of the garden, and to the left is a flower border belonging to the little house in which my cousin Arlette and her husband live. It is another way of life; probably most of us would rather have a swimming pool, but the garden of Aunt France is very nice indeed.

Wherever you decide to put your food plants, don't try to set them all out in the same year. Rather, as your landscape develops and you feel a need for more plantings, consider those that will give delight at the table as well as pleasure to the eye. My father is fond of pointing out that Rome wasn't built in a day, and that if it had been, the Romans would have had a terrible backache.

Dwarf apple in "Belgian fence" espalier

2 Soils for Top Production

What turns a butcher, a baker, an executive vice-president into a gardener? What makes a sophisticated woman dedicated to automation in the home root around in the earth with a hand tool, the sun freckling her neck and soil seeping into her shoes? Success. Success is what keeps the gardener going. Every minute seed that grows presents a day-to-day ovation to the person who planted it. When I burn a pie, all I need do to know life isn't a failure is trot down to the garden and count the beans that have sprouted since yesterday. When my son announces that Tommy's mother has a new car and looks younger than I do, I take a ruler and measure maturing apples.

What this chapter tells you about how to make plants grow may be a bore, but if you will grow it my way, your garden will produce lush crops *for many years to come*. The magic formula for real success is soil improvement. I once attempted to garden without it and lived to regret it—and I know.

HOW TO IMPROVE THE SOIL YOU HAVE

Structure, fertility, and pH reaction are three separate and distinct qualities of soil and should be clearly understood before a soil-improvement program is begun.

The *structure*, or composition, of soil governs its ability to admit and retain moisture, as well as the ease with which tender rootlets can grow and seek out moisture and nutrients. *Fertility* refers to the soil's content of the nutrients necessary for sturdy plant growth. The *pH reaction*, a term that refers to relative acidity or alkalinity, determines whether or not those nutrients will be in forms available to plants. A soil-improvement program that corrects structure, adds fertility, and provides the correct pH balance for food plants will

11

produce the good garden loam in which food plants thrive with minimal demands on your time and energy.

A soil-improvement program that takes into account only one or two of the requirements for good garden loam can be largely wasted. For example, two of the three requirements often can be provided simply by digging well-rotted manure into the soil; manure is humus and often is all that is needed to improve soil structure, and it is so high in plant nutrients that it is often all that is needed to create a fertile condition. However, like other organic humus, it is acid, and unless the soil's pH reaction is checked and other elements added to keep the acid condition from becoming extreme, this acidity may lock up nutrients so the plants cannot use them, despite the fact that they are there, and in well-structured loam.

Structure

As generally defined, good garden loam is composed of 1/3 humus, 1/3 sand, and 1/3 clay, a combination that makes the soil stick together in a crumbly fashion when damp. The word "friable" refers to this crumbly quality of loam.

Pick up a handful of damp, not wet, soil from your land and pack it as though to make a snowball, gently. If it is good garden loam, it will make a ball that will crumble readily under slight pressure. If it doesn't crumble easily, it probably has too much clay in it. Heavy clay soils won't dry and warm up readily to become workable in early spring; tender plant rootlets have a tough time fighting their way through; and once clay soil has dried out, it sheds water that should be penetrating down to the plant roots.

When the opposite problem exists, and the soil won't ball but crumbles loosely in your hand, then it contains so much sand that water runs right down through it, leaving the soil dry and plants thirsty shortly after watering. Furthermore, the quickly draining water takes with it minerals and nutrients the plants vitally need.

The way to improve deficient soil is to add whichever desirable elements are lacking: to clay soils, add humus and "sharp" sand, a sand which has a particular structure, and is neither "dead" sand nor sea sand, neither fill nor gravel; to sandy soils, add humus and rich muck or clay soil. How much of what? Your local Agricultural Extension Service upon request will send a booklet explaining how to provide them with a soil sample they can analyze for you. Addresses for Extension Services for the whole country are listed in the back of this book. The other way to find out what your soil needs is to test it yourself.

Cover a test patch 2 feet square with a 1-inch layer of the element or elements you think are missing. Mix it thoroughly to a depth of 18 inches, and try the snowball test. Make sure the soil is neither wet nor dry, but damp. Keep adding the missing element, a 1-inch layer at a time, until the soil becomes friable. Keep a record of how much has been added so you will know how much to order.

You can import a whole gardenful of soil, 18 inches deep, and deposit it on the back yard, but it is an unnecessary expense when a few yards of humus and sand or clay can be dug in when you are preparing the garden for planting. You would be amazed at the willingness of farmers to deliver a load of well-rotted manure to your garden if only you have the courage to knock on their doors and ask. If you have neither farmers nor courage handy, garden centers and many nurseries sell compost or humus of some type, soil, and loam. A few also sell sand, or you can find it through sand and gravel dealers. Make sure you get sharp sand.

Fertility

There is an ideal way to do anything, and the ideal (but not the only) way to provide fertile humusy soil for food plants is this:

In the fall turn the sod of your garden site 18 inches under, with a plow or a spade and plant on top of it a cover crop of rye, alfalfa, clover, sweet vetch, or other legume. Just before the crop matures, turn it under (that's what cover crops are for) along with a 1-inch layer of manure combined with 1 pound of superphosphate per bushel of manure. During the winter it will all decompose. In spring add a 1-inch covering of well-rotted manure or compost and mix that into the top 18 inches of soil. Use this soil as your source for all garden plantings. If rotted manure or compost isn't available in quantity, just a little of it mixed into the furrows in the vegetable garden, or in with the soil for planting trees or cane or bush berries, is almost as good.

Any one of these procedures will do much to improve soil fertility, but if none is possible have your Agricultural Extension Service recommend a complete fertilizer (nitrogen-phosphorus-potash) and add it at the rate of 50 pounds for each 2,500 square feet. Or dig in dried manure at the specified rate. If you have done your homework and provided well-structured friable soil, tell yourself that

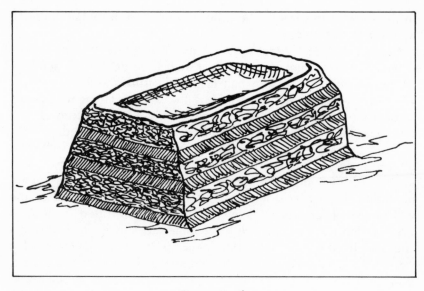

Compost pile

the chemical fertilizers will do a good job for you. And promise the garden compost next year.

The compost pile. Given eighteen months to three years, any organic matter left to the weather will rot and become crumbly black compost. Therefore you can make a compost pile of almost any organic matter, and you should. One of the side benefits of a compost pile is that it provides a place to dump garden refuse, dead sod, pulled weeds, grass clippings, and so on.

A compost pile is not attractive, so build it out of sight. Mark out a 4-foot square and dump onto it organic refuse from the garden, the grounds, and the kitchen until you have a concave layer 6 inches deep. Do not include diseased materials or large bones or thick twigs. Cover this layer with a layer of manure or with a layer of soil to which you have added 1 pound of your garden fertilizer. Make this second layer 3 inches deep. Water the pile and repeat the layers until the compost is 5 feet high, or until cold weather. Make a depression in the top sufficient to collect a puddle of rain water or snow. Turn it once before frosts, leaving it concave as before, and let it sit until spring. Each spring begin a new compost pile, and in time you will have a succession of compost crops.

PH Reaction, Acidity and Alkalinity

With all this digging in of material your soil will be light, fluffy, and fertile, all of which will be of little use to the plants if the soil is either too acid or too alkaline. The symbol pH stands for "potential of hydrogen." The relative acidity or alkalinity of soil is always expressed in terms of this symbol. Neutral is pH 7. Lower readings are increasingly acid. Higher readings are increasingly alkaline.

The pH reaction of soil determines to a great extent the availability of most plant nutrients. Food plants flourish in slightly acid soils with pH readings of between pH 6.0 and pH 6.8. Most American soils have a pH of between pH 6 and pH 7. A depleted soil becomes increasingly acid. Lime "sweetens" soil, and most vegetable gardens require applications of lime every three to four years. To increase acidity of alkaline soils, ammonium sulfate is added. The rate at which either lime or ammonium sulfate should be added depends on your soil's pH reading.

The Agricultural Extension Service will give you a pH analysis on request, or you can test the soil yourself with one of the inexpensive soil-testing kits available at garden centers.

I can imagine what Mr. Bartlett, the farmer who lived up the road from us in Plainfield, Vermont, would say to all this. All he does to his garden is add manure yearly and a casual handful of lime now and then. But we can't, all of us, Mr. Bartlett, get manure!

3 Timing, Intercropping, Succession

The best way to forget you can't garden in February is to make a planting plan for your vegetable garden. I make several rough drafts, for my mind changes as each new catalog lands on the snowy doormat. You discover that artichokes, which you gave up growing, can be had in a new hardy variety, and you must make room for them. Or the children (ages eleven, five, and three) announce they are going into the popcorn business to pay their way through college, and a row of cauliflowers on which hung plans for intercrops and succession plantings is dumped in favor of college futures.

HOW TO PLAN THE PLAN

Once you have decided the size your garden will be, rule out a sketch of it, then make a list of the vegetables you want most. Check Tables I, II, and III at the back of the book and beside each vegetable on your list make a note of its days to maturity and the space (between rows and between plants in the row) that will be required in the garden to produce the yield you want. Check the tables again to see what fast-growing crops could precede, succeed, or be planted with the ones you have already chosen (see "Intercropping" and "Succession Planting" in Chapter 1, page 3), and make a list of these, with their days to maturity. Now pencil your lists into rows ruled on the garden plan, along with the time they go into the garden and the time they come out. That's all there is to it, except that you have probably chosen more than you have room for, and will have to juggle.

Row				
1. Sweet corn	} Early	Sweet corn	} Mid-season	3'
2. Sweet corn		Sweet corn		3'
3. Sweet corn		Sweet corn		3'
4. Sweet corn		Sweet corn		3'
5. Sweet corn	} Late	Sweet corn	} Late	3'
6. Sweet corn		Sweet corn		3'
7. Tomatoes (staked)				4'
8. Tomatoes (staked)				4'
9. Tomatoes (staked)				4'
10. Early potatoes				3'
11. Early potatoes				3'
12. Pepper		Eggplant	Chard (Swiss)	3'
13. Lima bean (bush)				3'
14. Lima bean (bush)				3'
15. Lima bean (bush)				3'
16. Snap beans (bush)				3'
17. Snap beans (bush)				3'
18. Broccoli				3'
19. Early cabbage				3'
20. Onion sets		Rows 16 through 31 can be replanted after harvest with such crops as: endive, cauliflower, Brussels sprouts, spinach, kale, beets, cabbage, broccoli, turnips, lettuce, carrots, and late potatoes		3'
21. Onion sets				2'
22. Carrots				2'
23. Carrots				2'
24. Beets				2'
25. Beets				2'
26. Kale				2'
27. Spinach				2'
28. Peas				2'
29. Peas				2'
30. Lettuce } seed early	Lettuce } 2 wks. later	Lettuce } 4 wks. later		2'
31. Radish	Radish	Radish		2'
32. Strawberries				2'
33. Strawberries				3'
34. Asparagus		Rhubarb		3'
35. Asparagus				3'
				4'

100'

50'

A large garden, 50 x 100 feet, has widely spaced rows to accommodate mechanical tillage and employs succession plantings to increase yield.

One way to acquire space in the garden for an extra vegetable or two is to set rows close together. Row widths are planned according to the size of the vegetable at maturity. In really big gardens rows are set 2 to 3 feet apart so that a mechanical cultivator such as a rototiller can be used to keep the weeds under control. You don't need a rototiller to handle a smaller garden, since weeds are easily controlled by mulching, and so rows can be closer together. The most space-saving system of row spacing is one popular among farmers in New England, who often sow vegetable rows close enough so that the tops of the mature vegetables meet across the rows, thus shading the soil beneath and inhibiting weeds.

When your drafts have given way to a clean final plan, make two copies: one to keep handy to the garden, and the other to keep clean in a file. Next year the clean copy will tell you without soil smudges and water wrinkles where the brassicas were and the cucurbits (which must not be followed by sowings of any plant belonging to these groups, respectively), and where the peas were so you can take advantage of the nitrogen this legume deposits in the soil. Last year's plan also answers questions like, "How many tomato plants weren't enough?" and "How many squash were too many?"

In the garden file keep a log, or diary, recording when things were planted and when they matured, and the interesting things they did. Monsieur Bertrand, a peasant who once rented me an ancient stone cottage overlooking the Mediterranean, wrote up his log every night. From fifty years of keeping a log (he always wore a sea cap though he had never been to sea) he could say with almost infallible accuracy what was going to happen next in the garden and how to prevent or promote it.

Here are some excerpts from my log which you may find handy:

1. Plant perennials together at one end of the garden to avoid roadblocking the rototiller.
2. Don't plant tall things like corn and staked beans between the sun and smaller plants; plant in gradations of height with the lowest on the south side.
3. Don't forget the corn has to be planted in blocks, for it is wind-pollinated from one plant to another.
4. Rotate crops to discomfit bugs and diseases that breed in the soil and attack only certain kinds of vegetables.
5. Remember to get two crops from each row by intercropping or succession planting. Early-maturing crops are: beets, 55 days;

Bush snap beans, follow with romaine lettuce
Staked tomatoes intercrop lettuce, onion sets, or radishes
Early broccoli, follow with 2 rows late carrots
Early carrots, follow with Brussels sprouts
Onion family, follow with 2 rows late lettuce
Pepper plants
Swiss chard or kale, half row lettuce
Early beets, follow with fall or winter squash
Early beets, follow with fall or winter squash
Early bush peas, follow with 2 sowings bush beans
Summer squash, follow with fall turnips
Summer squash, follow with fall turnips
6 hills cucumber

Small garden, 25 feet square, has closely spaced rows and employs inter-cropping and succession planting.

bush beans, 48 days; chard, 50 days; cress, 20 days; cucumbers, 53 days; kale, 55 days; kohlrabi, 55 days; leaf lettuce, 40 days; early peas, 55 days; radishes, 22 days; scallions, 40 days; spinach, 42 days; summer squash, 50 days; turnips, 35 days. Late crops to sow for winter storing: late carrots, celeriac, celery, onions, parsnips, pumpkins, rutabaga or late turnips, winter squash.

Seed Varieties

When you can, choose disease- and insect-resistant varieties to avoid possible problems. All catalogs offer good seeds but not the same strains and varieties of seeds, and no one variety is the best for every section of the country. Choose varieties advertised as "best for the home gardener": These are the delicious vegetables the commercial gardener cannot grow because they are not suitable for shipping. Catalogs sometimes offer varieties that can solve gardening problems; for instance, carrots do best in soil free of rocks, but some varieties offered have been bred which do well in rocky soil.

The best advice you can get on which variety will be most successful in your garden is from your Agricultural Extension Service, or from a gardening neighbor with a gourmet palate.

Seeds for many species of vegetables are available in varieties labeled "early," "midseason," or "late." Early varieties are those that prefer spring weather and, usually, mature most quickly. Midseason varieties are those that do well through summer heat, and mature more slowly. Late varieties are, of course, the slowest to produce crops, and are those to plant when you want vegetables for winter storage.

WHEN TO PLANT

Advice on this subject must vary almost from neighbor to neighbor, so many factors are involved. Gardens in Florida have been planted and harvested before Northern gardens are put in. Valley people plant later than hillside dwellers because frosts settle in valleys. Clay soil cannot be worked as early in spring as sandy soil because it keeps winter cold and moisture longer. Again, the most accurate information available is from the Agricultural Extension Service, or from a gardening neighbor. However, some pretty accurate generalizations are possible:

The Vegetable Tables at the back of the book have been compiled according to planting times: early spring, mid-spring, and late spring. Early spring is defined as "as soon as the ground can be worked." This means as soon as a handful of soil squeezed into a ball in your fist crumbles readily under pressure from your thumb. Seeds sown before this state is reached may rot before they can warm up enough to germinate. And by working the soil too early you will probably compact it and ruin its crumbly structure. Mid-spring is three to four weeks later. Late spring means when the temperature has reached 70 degrees and is fairly stable.

Most vegetables are cool-season crops that do best in temperatures ranging from 55 to 70 degrees. Some vegetables tolerate some frost. Among them are cabbage, Brussels sprouts, kale, broccoli, kohlrabi, turnips, spinach, beets, parsnips, onions, and asparagus. Others will be damaged if late frosts nip them when they are reaching maturity: lettuce, peas, cauliflower, celery, carrots, artichokes, white potatoes, endive.

Some vegetables are definitely warm-season crops and are easily damaged by frost; in fact, they prefer 65- to 80-degree temperatures: muskmelons, cucumbers, squash, pumpkins, beans, tomatoes, peppers, sweet corn. Others require temperatures above 70 and a long growing season: sweet potatoes, watermelon (although some varieties have been developed which mature quickly), eggplant, and okra. These are crops more easily grown by Southern gardeners.

If yours is a short growing season, take advantage of the fact that many vegetables can be started indoors and transplanted: asparagus, beets, broccoli, Brussels sprouts, celery, Swiss chard, cabbage, cauliflower, eggplant, endive, kale, kohlrabi, leek, lettuce, onion, parsley, peppers, rhubarb, tomatoes. A few others can be started indoors but must be sown individually in 3-inch peat pots and planted pot and all because they do not transplant well: lima beans, cucumbers, gourds, melons, sweet corn, watermelons.

HOW TO START SEEDLINGS INDOORS

Sow seeds indoors four to eight weeks before they can be set out—four weeks for fast-growing crops, six to eight weeks for slower crops. Fill the flats or peat pots with garden soil and cover with 1 inch of spaghnum moss; do not enrich the soil or plants will grow leggy. Sow the seed in the spaghnum moss, water gently, cover with plastic or glass to preserve moisture, and place in a warm room to germinate. When the seedlings are up, place them in a sunny window, uncovered; keep cool-weather vegetables in the coolest room in your house and keep warm-weather vegetables in temperatures above 70 degrees. If the plants yellow, let

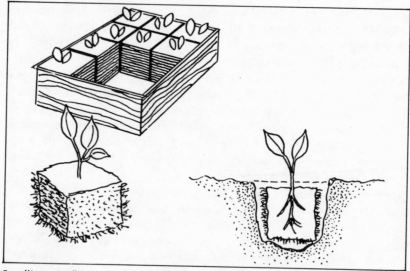

Seedlings in flat transplant best when cut apart to avoid loss of soil. Plant an inch below indoor level and water well.

them dry a bit, then water with ammonium nitrate at half strength.

A week before planting time let them dry somewhat, then place the flats outdoors in increasingly sunny locations to harden off the seedlings. Bring indoors if the temperature drops.

To transplant seedlings, loosen the soil in roomy holes in the garden deep enough to bring plants to 1/2 inch below their indoor levels, pour in 1/2 cup of starter solution, and before it seeps away, dip the seedlings into the bucket of starter solution, place them in the hole, and firm the soil. Be sure the top edge of the peat pot is 1/2 inch below ground; otherwise the pot acts as a wick and draws moisture away from the plant's roots.

When you can, transplant just before a rain; it gives the seedlings a real boost. If you don't have time to harden the plants off before you set them out, protect them with paper bags or bushel baskets for their first few days in the open.

Many gardeners transplant seedlings grown indoors three times; this produces stockier, stronger plants. Frankly, I haven't the patience for it. I am opposed to extra labor of any kind. I start indoors only a few large plants, such as tomatoes, green peppers, melons, cucumbers, and eggplants. I can't see how having lettuce or spinach a little earlier justifies fiddling around with the planting and transplanting of dozens and dozens of seedlings. But then, I have never had to.

About being in a hurry: Wherever you live, there is always a favorite crop or two you want in or out before the weather does something or other: I want the tomatoes to ripen early (they are 95 cents a pound this week in Lakeville, and this is July!) and the peppers to ripen before frost, and the melons. In the Cannes garden, we wanted the tangerines to ripen before Christmas frosts got to them. You can increase the warmth available to plants set out early, and protect them from frosts at the end of the growing season, by placing canopies of clear plastic over them. The canopies can be anchored by sawhorses or earth-filled bushel baskets, or stapled to stakes. But as a general rule you cannot get vegetables to flourish before the weather tells them it is safe to do so. As my friend Maro Chapman, who has been a farmer in Connecticut all his life, observes: Put them out too early, and they'll just sit there and sulk!

4 From Seeds to Harvest

A garden expresses the gardener. Some gardens expose wide rows of earth meticulously weed-free between neat drills of vegetables, and display tomatoes, beans, and peas on tall, tidy stakes. Any such garden belongs to an experienced, orderly gardener who likes to work hard. I am not opposed to order, or even to hard work when it is profitable, but for the beginner whose soil is full of last year's weed seeds waiting to germinate and who has never staked a pole bean before, there are easier ways to do things— and I suggest you try them. There is always time to work harder if the garden you get as a result of working less hard doesn't satisfy your particular personality.

GETTING THE SEEDS IN

Tools

A rototiller is invaluable for digging and cultivating a really big garden. If yours is going to be less than really big, you will find that a few simple tools are all you need. Here is my list:

- a square-ended hoe and a pointed hoe for planting and cultivating
- a rake for smoothing
- a four-tined fork for digging (you may prefer a spade; David does)
- a long 2 by 6 plank to walk on between rows and keep the earth less compacted
- a long string attached at either end to a pointed peg 6 inches high to help keep the garden rows straight
- a trowel for transplanting chores
- a plastic bucket for starter solution
- a rain-making type of watering device attached to several lengths of hose and a peanut butter jar to measure how much water you have put down

and a wheelbarrow for toting it all

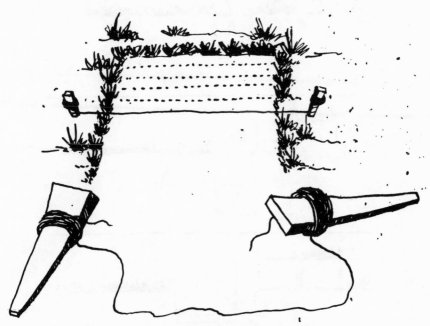

Pegs and string to keep rows straight

The plank stays in the garden. I also have a flat-bottomed wicker basket for harvesting, a few sheets of clear plastic to shelter crops from frost, and a few old bushel baskets for the same purpose.

Digging the Garden

Digging the garden with a rototiller saves some backbreaking work once the garden is established. It is not a good idea if you are placing a garden where a garden has never been before. We rototilled chopped sod into our Westport garden and discovered that an insidious weed called witchgrass or quackgrass propagates from slivers. I filled a very large depression at the bottom of the garden with the witchgrass and soil I pulled from that garden by hand (the only way to get it out) over the next five years. Unless you can get a good-sized tractor to turn the sod so far under it can't come up, you had better either remove the sod by hand or dig it 2 feet under by hand. Once the sod has been removed you can rent a rototiller if the extent of the job warrants it, or double-dig the soil, adding the materials needed to improve it as you go (see Chapter 2, pages 12–13).

Sowing the Seeds

When the garden has been dug, reformed into good soil, and fertilized, leave it in its lumpy condition until you are ready to plant, and then rake smooth only the rows you are about to plant. If you rake it all smooth with the thought that it will all be ready, you will be sowing seeds among almost-germinated weeds. Never work the garden when it is wet.

With your planting plan handy, measure off the row you are going to sow, drop the 2 by 6 plank down along it, and stake your string at either end of the row. Draw either your square-ended hoe or the pointed hoe down the row under the string to create a furrow the depth and width required for the seed you are about to plant. (I sow carrots and beets in very wide furrows and I use the rake to create those.) Now walk back up the row dropping seeds into the furrow at the specified rate (see Tables I, II, III), and then go back down it again using the back of the rake or else the square-ended hoe to draw earth back over the seeds; use the flat of the tool to tamp the earth gently but firmly over the seeds.

Information on transplanting seedlings is in the previous chapter.

The depth at which seeds should be planted often perplexes the beginner. If you have no specific instructions, plant them so they are covered by soil to no more than three times the seeds' thickness. An excellent system is to make furrows twice the depth at which the seed is to be planted, and then to half fill the planted furrows with finely pulverized soil. As the seedlings grow, wind and water will fill the furrow with soil, and the plants will have a deeper, firmer rooting than had they been planted at the surface.

Under the instructions for growing individual vegetables you will see that corn and cucumbers, and many of the larger vine vegetables such as winter squash, are planted in "hills." To plant in hills means to plant seeds in groups of four or six, and to allow several feet between groups.

Double-digging fluffs soil to 18 inches. Remove sod first, "spank" it to loosen earth, then bury at the bottom of the hole. Spread a layer of sand, humus, or soil to be added to the area and mix well into the top 18 inches.

SEEDLINGS OF VEGETABLES

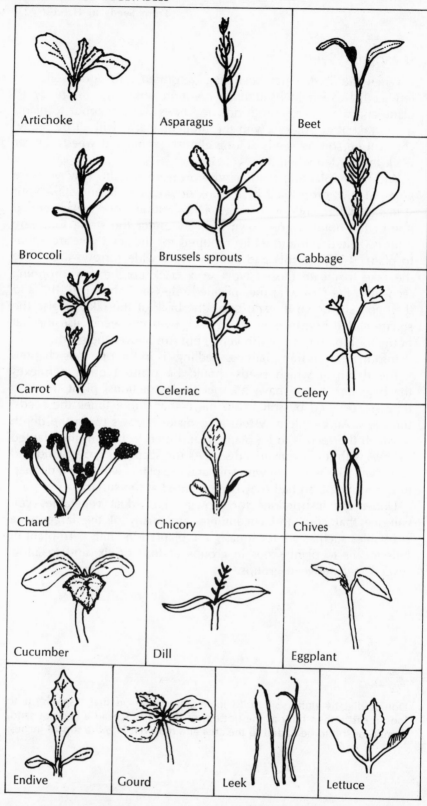

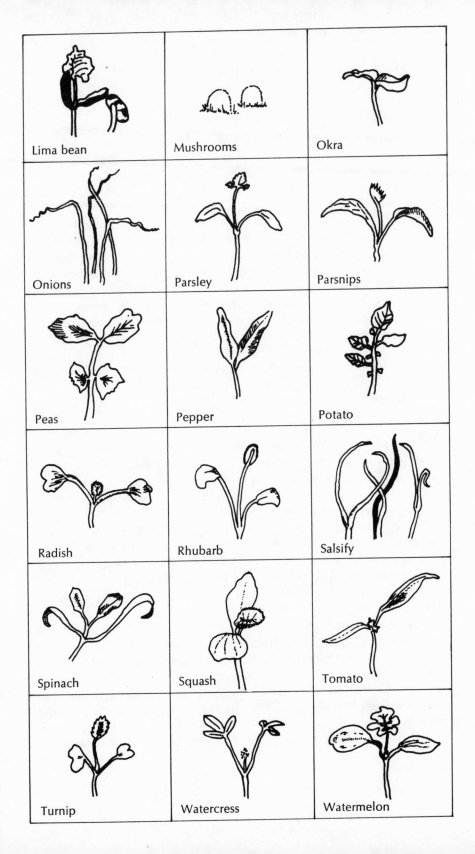

Lima bean

Mushrooms

Okra

Onions

Parsley

Parsnips

Peas

Pepper

Potato

Radish

Rhubarb

Salsify

Spinach

Squash

Tomato

Turnip

Watercress

Watermelon

HELPING PLANTS TO PROSPER

Watering

In France we always watered rows after they were sown to help the seeds to germinate, and I still do. The other time it is important to water is when plants are beginning to mature their crops, particularly crops high in moisture content such as tomatoes, cucumbers, melons, squash.

In-between watering will be required depending on whether you have mulched the garden, since mulching keeps the soil moisture from evaporating. Unmulched gardens should be soaked by the clouds or by the hose once a week. Between 1 and 1-1/2 inches of water will get moisture down the 6 to 8 inches necessary for most vegetables. If you use a sprinkler system, you can measure the water applied by setting a straight-sided, wide-mouthed glass jar (peanut butter jar will do) in the middle of the garden and letting the sprinkler run until the jar contains an inch and a half of water. Shallow watering is bad; plant rootlets grow toward the moisture area and since the surface of the soil dries out first, the rootlets are destroyed by the first dry spell.

Weeding and Mulching

Weeds are much less prolific when they have been controlled for three or four years, and if you mulch the garden from the outset, there is no reason ever to have to deal with them except in a minimal way. There are several ways to mulch:

The most effective way to mulch the garden is to plant your seeds between strips of black plastic or in slits cut into black plastic. The drawback is that this method eliminates intercropping and makes succession planting more difficult to work out.

Another method is to plant rows so close together that the tops of the mature vegetables meet; this keeps the sun from reaching the soil, and few weeds can grow. Until the plants are fairly close, you will have to do some cultivating between rows.

The method I prefer is to mulch closely spaced rows with a 12- to 14-inch-deep coat of organic material. This not only keeps weeds out, but it also adds humus as the bottom layer decays. This can either be dug into the garden in the fall, or left on as a year-round mulch. A year-round mulch is great, but it has drawbacks. When I first heard of handling a garden this way I covered mine with the only organic mulch available in quantity, autumn leaves. When the asparagus failed to appear in spring I learned that soil buried deep under leaves all winter long is still cold enough in May to make ice cubes, given time. Unless the mulch is a loose-packing, light one such as salt hay, 6 to 18 inches is enough. Use a year-round mulch, but in the fall dig it into those rows where very early crops will go; peas, for instance, and onions. In the spring, pull it away from the perennials, asparagus and rhubarb. Since organic mulches decompose on the underside, they must be topped every year with a new coat.

There is another "must" associated with organic mulches: They require nitrogen to decay and will compete with the crops. Add a complete fertilizer to the soil at the rate of 3 pounds of 5-10-10 to each 100 square feet organically mulched. Mulches of leaves, wood chips, or manure are also acid; keep a check of the soil pH. If you plan to use leaves, let them dry, then grind them up with a rotary mower; otherwise they cake in waterproof layers, shedding rain and harboring bugs.

Keeping Your Plants Healthy

Vegetables grown in good garden loam seem immune to most plant troubles, but occasionally you may hit a trouble spot; the Vegetable Troubles Table at the back of the book discusses them. When spraying or dusting with any pesticide, remember that the food underneath the applied poison is going to be set on your table and eaten. *Follow the manufacturer's instructions closely,* and if you can avoid spraying, do.

A few health rules followed will help to keep troubles away:

1. Design the garden and its surroundings for good air circulation.
2. Don't water on muggy, overcast days.
3. Keep vegetable debris on the compost heap or in garbage pails. Burn any suspect matter.
4. Rotate crops.
5. When you run into trouble, make sure to buy disease-resistant varieties next time.

Flourishing good health and a clean garden won't save a carrot from a hungry rabbit, of course. Keep furry friends away with a chemical repellent or use an organic one, such as dried blood, which also adds nitrogen to the soil. Other deterrents are a 6-foot-tall fine-meshed wire fence buried 2 feet underground, a good mouser, and a noisy game-chasing dog. To keep birds from the berries use netting.

HARVESTING AND STORING CROPS

Beans and peas, tomatoes, peppers, New Zealand spinach, and many other crops will produce over a much longer period if you keep the maturing fruits picked. The advice on growing specific vegetables, in the next chapter, indicates which ones to keep picked. Experience brings a kind of instinctive sense about which to treat this way.

There is an excellent bulletin, "Storing Vegetables and Fruit," available from the U. S. Government Printing Office. If you want to do a very professional job of preparing storage places, write for it to: U. S. Department of Agriculture, Washington, D.C. 20250. It is the Home and Garden Bulletin No. 119. The Department stipulates that your request be on a postcard and that you include your address and zip code.

You might also be interested in "Jellies, Jams and Preserves," Bulletin No. 56; "Home Canning," No. 8; "Home Freezing of Fruits and Vegetables," No. 10.

We have found that our garage makes a satisfactory storage place. We place root crops in barrels or wooden boxes with half an inch or so of damp sand between layers. Once a month in the winter we pack an inch of snow on the top layer of sand. Cabbages and cauliflower keep well wrapped in several sheets of newspaper and stacked two deep on airy shelves. We store apples in barrels here, too, each wrapped in a scrap of paper, and pears. Grapes and peaches keep for many weeks in an old refrigerator reserved for them.

Now that we have gone through the list of things that a gardener must do to produce and preserve crops, you can understand my lack of interest in extra work, such as staking tomatoes. Nothing really has to be staked. Delicious peas grow on bushes; they don't have to cling to chicken wire to taste good. Exquisite green beans grow on bushes. Snow peas, which are a pod pea, do not, but you can do without them until your garden is well under control. Tomatoes do not need to be staked to produce, and most professional growers do not stake theirs. The yield is somewhat less for unstaked tomato plants, so compensate by planting a few extra. The smallest garden has room for that, and it will save you a great deal of fuss.

5 How to Grow Vegetables — Artichokes to Zucchini

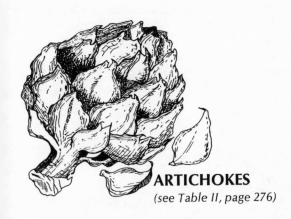

ARTICHOKES
(see Table II, page 276)

The globe artichoke is a handsome perennial most successful in mild coastal regions. Because the French believe it is good for the liver, we tried hard to grow artichokes in our Westport garden. Unfortunately, the Shrimp-dressed Artichokes and the Purée of Artichokes au Beurre Noire we had looked forward to were few and far between, and we finally gave up. This plant will succeed in humid areas just south of Connecticut. In the South, crops are produced in spring; farther north, in late summer. Catalogs are now offering new hardy varieties that are worth a try if you love artichokes.

33

Planting and culture. Plant in trenches 8 inches deep, lined with 1 inch of compost or manure; or work the bottom 2 inches of soil in the trench until friable, and mix in a handful of 5-10-5. Plant roots 5 to 6 inches below the surface, cover with soil, tamp firmly. When plants are 4 inches tall, mulch heavily to preserve moisture. Cut away all but six of the suckers that develop at the base when plants reach 8 inches and transplant the suckers to make a new row. Cut plants back to the ground in the fall. In cool areas, protect them through winter with an inverted bushel basket filled with dry leaves.

Fertilizer. Halfway through the growing season, apply a small handful of compost or fertilizer to each plant; repeat after harvest.

Harvesting. The thickened bracts which surround the developing flowerhead, and the fleshy base from which the flowers arise, are the edible part of the plant. Several of these floral envelopes are borne on branch ends of tall stems. Cut away with 1 inch of stem when artichokes are the size of an orange.

Freezing. If you have a crop of any size, freeze a few artichokes so you can make Francesca's Marinade for your Christmas parties. Select very young artichokes that have not yet developed a hairy choke. Cut away the stem and two or three rows of leaves. Scald in boiling water—1-1/2 pounds of artichokes to 4 quarts of water—for 4 minutes. Chill in running water for 3 minutes, drain, pack, and freeze.

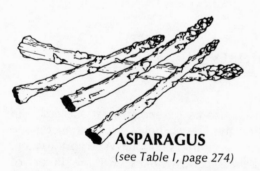

ASPARAGUS
(see Table I, page 274)

If you think store-bought asparagus is good, just wait until you taste some fresh from your garden, cooked quickly in lots of boiling water, and served *au naturel* with lemon butter! Or cut into strips and stir-fried, Chinese fashion, in a little oil. Incidentally, these are opposite-pole recipes. At one extreme you toss the vegetables a few at a time into enough boiling water so that the boiling never stops; at the other extreme is stir-frying, where no water is used. The first method is French, the theory being that if enough water is used at a boil the vegetables are seared and lose none of their natural juice. The second method is the one used in Chinese and Japanese cooking. These methods have two things in common: very quick cooking and delicious results.

Asparagus is a perennial. The young stalks are harvested in early spring for about six weeks. Then the spears are allowed to grow into tall feathery "ferns" pretty enough to backdrop flowers. Ten plants per family member provide enough for fresh servings and some to freeze. A bed started from seed should not be picked until the fourth year, so buy 2- or 3-year-old roots instead; these can be harvested the second year and will produce for five to twelve years. Volunteer seedlings will provide new roots to enlarge or renew the bed. Select only rust-resistant varieties such as Mary Washington or Martha Washington.

Planting and culture. A sandy loam will warm quickly in spring and give an earlier crop; feed it well, since the asparagus will be there for many years. In early spring dig trenches 4 feet apart and 10 inches deep. Mix soil from the trenches with 1/3 its volume of sand; line trench floors with 1 inch of manure or compost or dried cow manure; cover with 4 inches of the sand soil. Spread roots 18 inches apart on a hump in the trench floor; cover with 2 inches of soil. As the asparagus grows, fill in the trench. In August or in early spring transplant 1-year-old seedling roots to a new row.

Fertilizing. In early spring work in a handful of compost or 1 tablespoon of garden fertilizer around each plant. Just before spear growth starts, work in 1/2 ounce of nitrate of soda per plant. After the cutting season, rake 1 pound of nitrate of soda in for every forty plants.

Blanched asparagus. If you prefer asparagus blanched (white), set rows 7 feet apart. In early spring ridge earth up around the plants so spears can grow 6 inches without breaking ground. When tips show, cut the spears 6 inches below ground. After the harvest, spread the ridges to land level. This is the way they are often grown in France. I prefer the green, unblanched asparagus.

Harvesting. Break asparagus spears close to the ground as they reach a height of 6 to 8 inches. If you fail to keep the bed picked, the spears will shoot up into ferns and end your harvest. When production slows visibly, let the ferns grow.

Freezing. Wash asparagus, cut to fit freezer containers, and save tough portions for soup. Blanch 1-1/2 pounds at a time in 4 quarts of boiling water for 3 minutes, chill in running water 3 minutes, drain, pack, freeze. Asparagus freezes beautifully.

BEANS
(see Table II, page 276)

The flavor of just-picked, pencil-slim green beans is enough to turn almost anyone into a dedicated gardener. When you tire of them tossed in butter, try stir-frying and experiment with the herb butter. I marinate leftovers while still hot in Oil-and-Vinegar Dressing and serve them in an oniony salad the next day. Wax beans are best in cream, the old-fashioned way; try the Kentucky Wonder Appetizer with any of the edible shell beans when they are still young enough to use as snap beans.

Happily you can plant the bean crop in successions that will last all season. Beans, wax or green, come in bush and pole varieties. Bush varieties mature in about eight weeks; pole varieties mature in nine to ten weeks, require staking, but produce for a longer period. Many varieties of pole beans can be used as snap beans, as fresh shell beans, or dried for winter. Pole limas are a delicious warm-climate crop. Gardeners in colder areas must use the bush varieties of limas. (From my garden log: Plant marigolds and savory among beans to repel beetles. Till coffee grounds into bean rows six days before planting to ward off fusarium wilt.)

Planting and culture. Plant bush and pole beans as soon as the weather warms. Limas go in when the apple blossoms fall. Sow pole beans after July 1 only if a long summer lies ahead: sown late, they won't produce for twelve to fourteen weeks. Drop bush beans 3 inches apart in furrows 1-1/2 inches deep, cover with 1 inch of fine soil, tamp. When seedlings are 3 inches high, thin to stand 5 inches apart. Plant pole beans in hills 2 to 3 feet apart, 6 seeds to a hill; thin to 4 seedlings. Plant limas eye down.

Fertilizing. When pole and lima bean blossoms appear work 1 tablespoon of 4-8-4 or a handful of compost into each hill. Bush beans growing in well-prepared garden loam will not require further fertilizing.

Harvesting. Keep snap beans picked and the plants will keep producing. Snap beans are finest when 6 inches long and cooked the minute they reach the kitchen. Wax beans are best after they turn a buttery yellow. Pole beans to be served as snap beans must be picked before they begin to swell out; when the pods become round, shell and serve the beans fresh. When shell-bean pods yellow, they are ready to be shelled for drying and storing. Never disturb bean plants when the leaves are wet; you will knock off the blossoms that are the coming crop.

Freezing. Cut snap beans into 1-inch diagonals, blanch 1-1/2 pounds at a time in 4 quarts of boiling water for 4 minutes, chill in running water 4 minutes, drain, pack, freeze. Very thin beans require 3 minutes.

Storing. Shell the beans on a dry day and spread on screens in an airy place such as the garage or a well-ventilated attic. They will dry in about three weeks depending on the weather. Store in old mesh (onion) bags in a dry room.

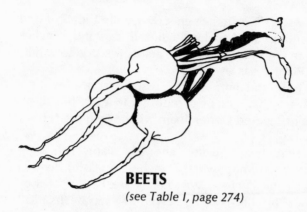

BEETS
(see Table I, page 274)

Fresh young beets are as sweet as fresh corn on the cob and almost as good. At the market in Les Sables huge beets such as I have never seen here are sold skins on and smoked tender. Gabrielle, who was my son Kris's *petite bonne* when he was small, often brought these back from the market to make a dish I call Gabrielle's Beets. In America I make it with winter-stored beets. Borscht is another good dish from winter beets, and very easy to make. Tiny new beets should be cooked my mother's way, served with sweet butter and fresh ground salt, or with sour cream with a touch of dill or sweet marjoram.

Sow two beet crops. In early spring sow a short row of an early variety that crops in forty-five days; it will provide delicious cooking greens as well. In early summer sow a longer row of a late variety to provide baby beets for summer's end and big sweet beets for winter storing.

Planting and culture. Beets do well in garden loam worked 6 to 8 inches deep: they will be fibrous if the loam is too sandy. As soon as the soil warms in spring drop 3 seeds to an inch in furrows 12 inches wide and 1 inch deep. Cover with 1/2 inch of fine soil, tamp. When seedlings are big enough to eat as greens, thin plants to stand 2 inches apart. Harvest the larger beets as plants become crowded.

Harvesting. I pull crisp beet leaves from the plants when I need cooking greens; it doesn't harm the beets as long as enough leaves are left to nourish the plant. Beets are finest when they are 3 inches around.

Storing and freezing. Leave winter beets in their rows until hard frosts are expected, then dig and layer in damp sand in a cool place. Or boil beets until tender, skin, dice, pack, freeze.

BROCCOLI
(see Table I, page 274)

For family meals in France we often treat broccoli the way we do asparagus: We sliver it into asparagus-like stalks, cook until just tender in a little water and serve with Lemon Butter Sauce. It is a particularly appropriate way to handle the second half of the broccoli crop, which produces smaller heads. Try your favorite asparagus recipes on fresh-from-the-garden broccoli. You will be surprised how successful they are.

To gardeners, broccoli offers an advantage its white cousin, cauliflower, does not: a second, bonus crop which is produced after the first crop has been harvested. Both these vegetables, and Brussels sprouts and cabbage as well, belong to the genus *Brassica*. All are rather similar in flavor, need cool weather to succeed, and have similar growing requirements. Never plant any *Brassica* where a relative was the preceding crop, as they are all subject to the same insects and diseases.

Plant an early crop of either broccoli or cauliflower for late-spring harvesting, and a late crop of either cabbage or Brussels sprouts for fall.

Planting and culture. If you have twelve to fifteen growing weeks ahead by the time the ground can be worked, sow seed directly outdoors. Drop at the rate of 1 package to a 50-foot row in furrows 1 inch deep, cover with 1/2 inch of soil, tamp. When plants are 3 inches high, thin to stand 18 inches apart. In cooler climates, start seeds indoors four to six weeks ahead and transplant to the garden as soon as the ground can be worked. Set 18 inches apart in the row and a little below indoor planting levels.

Fertilizer. Just before the broccoli head matures, work in a tablespoon of 4-8-4 to encourage the second crop.

Harvesting. Harvest when the heads are about 3 inches across.

The flavor is better before the florets begin to separate. Cut 5 inches of stem with the head to encourage side shoots. In the Vendée they say broccoli cut in the early morning has better flavor, but I am prejudiced in favor of harvesting just before cooking.

Freezing. Wash, trim away outer leaves, soak 1/2 hour in 1 quart of water with 1/4 cup of salt; rinse, split lengthwise, peel tougher portions of stalk. Scald 1-1/2 pounds at a time in 4 quarts of boiling water 4 minutes, chill in running water 4 minutes, drain, pack, freeze.

BRUSSELS SPROUTS
(see Table I, page 274)

My French aunts treat Brussels sprouts with a respect these miniature cabbages are never given in America, perhaps because they usually are well aged when purchased here and have a strong cabbage flavor. Aunt France does them in cream, a trick she learned from an aunt in northwestern France. I love the tiny fresh sprouts cooked very quickly in just a little water and served with melted butter and snips of dill fern. Cream of Sprouts Soup will surprise you with the delicacy of its flavor. Try the Brussels Sprouts Milanaise on the most confirmed sprouts-hater you know.

See Broccoli.

Harvesting. The sprout buds develop in the axil of big leaves on the main stem. Breaking off the lower leaf where each sprout is beginning to form hastens the crop. Pick sprouts when they are 1 to 1-1/2 inches around, and cook at once.

Freezing. Pick and cook all the sprouts that are mature, use whatever you need for the family meal, and freeze the rest sealed in plastic bags.

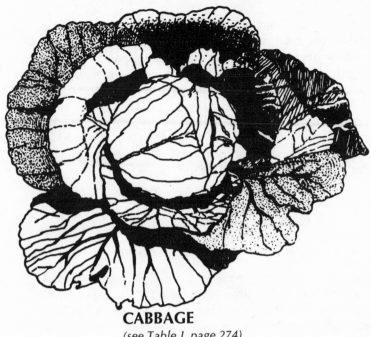

CABBAGE
(see Table I, page 274)

The flavor of home-grown tender green cabbage has little in common with that of commercial cabbage and is more versatile than you suppose: It makes a delicate soup or a hearty soup with dumplings, and even a pie!

There are many varieties of cabbage that produce crops both early and late. Early green cabbage has the most delicate flavor, to my mind. Some people prefer the handsome crinkled Savoy. Red cabbage is a must for shredding into summer salads, and the Chinese or celery cabbage makes some wonderful Oriental dishes. All except Chinese cabbage can be started indoors for earlier crops. (From my logbook: Dust the ground and the leaves around the cabbage head with flour when young heads are forming, to foil caterpillars. Plant onions with cabbages to deter the same pests.)

See Broccoli.

Harvesting. When heads are solid, cabbage is ready; if not harvested they will burst. Cabbage you are not ready to use can be left in the field for a week or so if you yank them hard enough to break the roots but not hard enough to pull up. To harvest, slice the head from the stem, then dispose of the plant in the interest of sanitary gardening.

Storing. Cooked cabbage and cole slaw both freeze well, but you should make your own sauerkraut at least once: If you don't like it, it is probably because you haven't learned to soak it before using. To store fresh cabbage, pull it up by the roots when the weather has turned cold and hang it upside down in a cool place such as an unheated garage. A week or ten days later cut away the stem and outer leaves, wrap the head in several layers of newspaper, pack loosely into a barrel or a box and store in a cool place. If winters are not severe, you can store cabbage layered in hay in the garden row. Cover with a plastic sheet to shed rain.

CANTALOUPES
(see Table III, page 277)

Cantaloupe is the name given to a kind of muskmelon which was first grown at an Italian castle called Cantalupo. The true cantaloupe is rarely grown in America, being small and quickly perishable, but the name is loosely used for other varieties of muskmelon with netted skin. The related honeydew and casaba melons are for gardeners with sixteen to seventeen weeks of warm growing weather, but several varieties of delicious and hardy "cantaloupes" will ripen in Northern gardens. Start seedlings indoors, set out after temperatures reach the 70's, and protect from early frosts with plastic canopies.
See Melons.

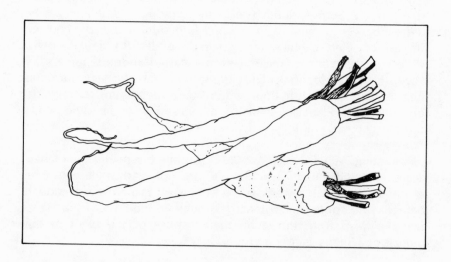

CARROTS
(see Table I, page 274)

If you think carrots are for people with deficient night vision, that is because you have never had tender new baby carrots cooked in heavy cream. Or Glazed Carrots with Lemon. Or Carrot and Raisin Salad, which is a favorite even of children. Carrots are more versatile than you might suppose. My Vermont farming neighbor, Mrs. Bartlett, made carrot marmalade, a preserve I assumed was an old American recipe until I ran across it in the bible of French cooking, *Larousse Gastronomique!* Carrot cookies, however, I am sure are American, and they are delicious.

The carrot chop is an easy one, as long as you keep crabgrass from going to seed in or near the vegetable garden. Carrots can be planted in succession from early spring through early summer. Seeds are slow to germinate, so plant early radishes with the carrots to mark the rows. (From my logbook: Mix fine unused coffee grounds with the tiny carrot seeds to help sow them evenly; the perking-coffee grounds also keep maggots away. Work wood ashes into the carrot row six weeks before sowing to deter cutworms. Keep celery away from carrots.)

Planting and culture. Carrots grow knobby in rocky ground and fibrous in soil that is too sandy. A fine, deeply worked loam is necessary to produce handsome straight carrots. Scatter seeds as soon as the ground can be worked over a 12-inch-wide bed 1/2 inch deep. Cover seeds with 1/4 inch of fine soil, tamp. Weed the bed when the carrot ferns are up. When ferns are 4 inches high thin and cook the thinnings; they are superb! Thin again when carrots become crowded.

Harvesting and storing. Pull the largest carrots as needed to leave space for smaller ones to grow. Mature crops can stay in the ground with a mulch for protection until just before a hard frost. Or you can dig carrots in early autumn, break off the tops, and store layered in damp sand in a cool place. Moisten the top layer of sand monthly to keep the carrots from drying out.

CAULIFLOWER
(see Table I, page 274)

Fresh cauliflower is a glamorous vegetable and should be used for exciting recipes, not buried in a tasteless white sauce. Try it in a shrimp salad, in a gratinée with a crisp collar of spicy watercress, or go Oriental with the Beef, Cauliflower, and Snow Peas recipe.

Cauliflower is another member of the *Brassica* group, and in the interests of a healthy garden it shouldn't be planted where a relative grew just before. Sometime try purple cauliflower, a late variety which makes a show-stopping centerpiece for buffets. (Alas, it turns green when cooked!)

See Broccoli.

Blanching. Blanching cauliflower heads improves the flavor, so when the heads begin to form, tie the outside leaves over the head with raffia or soft rags.

Harvesting. Cauliflower is ready two to three weeks after the head has been covered. Cut the head where it meets the main stem, pull up the rest of the plant and dispose of it.

Storing and freezing. Cauliflower will keep for several weeks when the whole plant is pulled up and hung upside down in a cool dark pace. To freeze, break head into 1-inch florets, and proceed as for freezing broccoli. But save some to make cauliflower pickles!

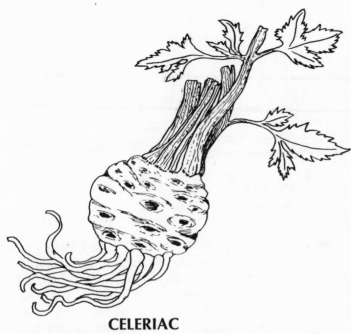

CELERIAC
(see Table II, page 276)

Celeriac, or celery root, is the celery-er celery, and if you think of celery as a delightful flavor rather than as a crisp decoration, you should grow celeriac. Crisp young roots, raw, make a marvelous hors d'oeuvre, and cooked, celeriac perks up the flavor of almost anything from soup to mashed potatoes. Celeriac stores well and is less fuss to grow than its long-legged cousin. Started in early spring from seed, celeriac matures in 120 days. One package produces about 400 plants, which may be more than you want unless celery is your favorite flavor.

Planting and culture. As soon as the ground warms, drop seeds in watered furrows 2 inches deep, cover with 1/4 inch of fine soil, tamp. When seedlings are 2 inches high, thin to 6 inches apart. As the plants grow, rake soil up against them until they are mounded 2 inches high.

Fertilizing. After thinning, work a handful of 4-8-4 into the row.

Harvesting and storing. Use roots as they get to be 2 inches around; at maturity they are about 4 inches across. Pull celeriac up by the tops, clean off side roots, twist off tops, and store layered in moist sand in a cool place.

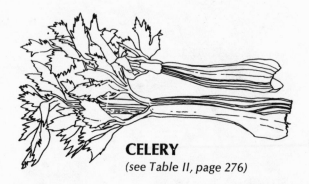

CELERY
(see Table II, page 276)

A few fresh celery stalks poached with milk and butter make one of the finest soups I know, with hardly more effort than it takes to open a can. Try the Braised Celery recipe, too: When it has the flavor of the garden-fresh vegetable, it is one of the best of all accompaniments for beef roasts.

Celery isn't as simple as the carrots-beans-beets garden staples because it must be bleached or it will be bitter. However, it is easily grown even in colder areas and, mulched in trenches in the garden, keeps well through fall.

Planting and culture. Avoid sowing celery in clay soils and work a handful of garden fertilizer into the row before you plant. If you have seventeen to twenty growing weeks ahead, when all danger of frost is past, sow celery outdoors in watered furrows 2 inches deep; cover with 1/4 inch of fine sand, tamp. When seedlings become crowded, thin to 6 inches apart. In cooler regions start seeds indoors; when the weather is settled, transplant to the garden 6 inches apart in the row. When plants are 8 inches high, blanch by hilling soil up against outer stalks at a level just above the heart of the plant. Hill every ten days until plants are 12 to 18 inches tall.

Fertilizing. A tablespoon of a quick-acting nitrogenous fertilizer per three plants added just before hilling will benefit peaky celery.

Harvesting and storing. Cut celery as needed 2 inches below ground and trim away outer stalks. Hilled celery will withstand light frosts. To store for winter, pull celery up by the roots and stand closely packed in a trench 2 feet deep. Covered with a mulch 2 feet deep, it will keep well into freezing weather.

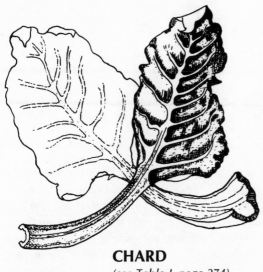

CHARD
(see Table I, page 274)

Swiss chard is a member of the beet family, but it looks more like rhubarb with white or red stalks. Where spinach presents difficulties, chard is grown for the leafy green part of the plant, but devotees of the vegetable prefer the succulent stalk and prepare it like asparagus. The large ribs are excellent stuffed, too.

Kale is another green used as a spinach. Try chard and kale along with spinach to discover which suits your palate and your garden best. One advantage of chard over spinach is that the leaves can be harvested from the time the plant matures until frost kills it, whereas true spinach offers only one crop.

Planting and culture. As soon as the ground can be worked in spring, sow seeds in furrows 2 inches deep, cover with 1/4 inch of fine soil, tamp. When plants are 3 inches high, thin to stand 4 inches apart. Thin the row again when the plants are 7 inches high. The thinnings are delicious in salads or braised in butter.

Fertilizing. If the plants look peaked in midseason, work a handful of 4-8-4 into the row.

Harvesting and freezing. To harvest, just give outer leaves a sharp twist; don't strip the plant, however. Even before the plants are mature you can steal a few outer leaves now and then. Before freezing, wash leaves well. Pull leafy part from the stalk, scald 1-1/2 pounds at a time in 4 quarts of boiling water for 3 minutes, chill in running water 3 minutes, drain, pack, freeze.

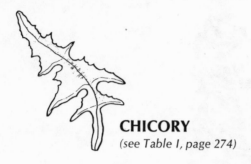

CHICORY
(see Table I, page 274)

Chicory is a slightly bitter salad green closely related to endive. It matures in about sixteen weeks and is grown commercially for its roots, which are the "chicory" added to some varieties of coffee. Small bundles of the dark green leaves are sold in specialty markets. With a garlic dressing it makes a strong, refreshing salad. The root can be dug and braised or boiled like parsnips. When the leaves are blanched in the field by banking, as for celery, the crown of whitened leaves is often called witloof. For this purpose also, roots are often forced in a dark cellar during winter months to produce a crisp white heart of leaves less bitter than those grown outdoors.

See Lettuce *and* Endive *for culture.*

CORN
(see Table II, page 276)

Sweet corn, ornamental corn, popcorn, and corn for cattle and for starch are all grown about the same way, but sweet corn is picked when it is tender ("green") and the others are allowed to ripen before they are harvested. No corn from the supermarket or even your favorite roadside stand can compare with that picked in your own garden, and cooked and eaten before the half-hour is out.

To ensure a continuous supply through late summer, plant early, midseason, and late varieties simultaneously, or plant 2 rows of an early hybrid every ten days. Honey and Cream Sweet Hybrid has been our favorite for years. Plant a hill or two of popcorn for the children (try the Crackerjack recipe) and a hill of ornamental corn for the Thanksgiving table. (From my logbook: Use the children's fall catches of fish to prepare next year's corn rows; 1 fish to a

hill. Mark the planted fish with stakes. Try starting corn earlier under plastic canopies; this method has produced good crops early under experimental conditions.)

Planting and culture. Plant corn when the apple blossoms fall, in a well-drained location. Corn requires cross-pollination, so sow it in blocks of short rows. Drop seeds 5 to a hill, in holes 1 inch deep, 8 inches apart in hills 3 feet apart, cover with 1/2 inch of fine soil, and tamp. Scatter 1/2 package of pumpkin seeds through the corn-patch to act as a mulch. When corn is 4 inches tall, thin to 3 plants per hill. Corn seeds germinate more quickly if watered after sowing.

Fertilizing. When you thin the seedlings, add a tablespoon of 4-8-4 to each hill; when the tassels appear, add another.

Harvesting. Harvest when the silk begins to turn dark brown. Ripe ears are usually plumped out but some skinny ears also are ripe. When you have pulled back the silk on unripe ears a few times you will develop a feeling for which are ready. Never pick corn until you have set the cooking water to boil. Harvest popcorn and ornamental corn when the ears are fully ripe, and hang by the stripped-back husks in a garage or attic to become bone-dry. It will take several weeks.

Freezing. Corn frozen as soon as it is picked has an excellent flavor but is not crisp. Use only small ears for freezing on the cob. Husk, brush away the silk, scald 1-1/2 pounds at a time in 4 quarts of boiling water for 5 to 7 minutes, depending on size, chill in running water 5 minutes, drain, pack, freeze. Scald larger ears 5 minutes, chill 15 minutes, then cut the kernels from the cobs, pack, and freeze.

GARDEN CRESS
(see Table I, page 274)

If you like to use watercress as lavishly as I do but haven't a quiet and unquestionably pure little stream to grow it in, try a small sowing of the annual garden cress in the lettuce rows. It looks and tastes like watercress, grows readily in the spring and early summer, is ready in twenty days, and can take the place of its glamorous cousin in many recipes and as garnishes for grilled meats and roasts.

See Lettuce *and* Watercress.

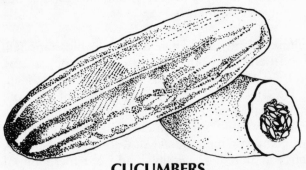

CUCUMBERS
(see Table II, page 276)

What would summer be without cucumbers? When you raise your own you can use them lavishly to make that wonderful icy, limp cucumber salad so good with sour cream! It took me some time to discover that the cucumbers for pickling can be used for the table if they are allowed to grow larger than pickling size, and that the cucumbers grown for the table can be pickled if picked smaller. This is not true of the tiny gherkins, which spend a great deal of time getting to be 2 or 3 inches long and really are for pickling. Making pickles is a lot easier than you think until you try it.

Cucumbers are a cucurbit (melons, squashes, gourds), and though very easy to grow, are susceptible to wilt and mosaic blights spread by the cucumber beetle; to avoid trouble never plant any cucurbit where a family member was the previous crop. I plant onions with my cucurbits to deter the beetle, with some success. Choosing wilt-and-mosaic-resistant varieties helps, too. Six hills will supply the average family with enough cucumbers to serve fresh and for modest pickling projects.

Planting and culture. Cucumbers planted in the garden are apt to run all over the neighboring rows; if you have the space, sow cucumbers in round hills cut into the sod a few feet from the last garden row. They are heavy feeders, so add an extra handful of compost to the soil in each hill, or a small handful of your garden fertilizer.

If you are willing to wait seven or eight weeks for your cucumber crop, sow seeds outdoors after the weather has become warm. Sow 6 seeds to a hill in 1-inch holes, cover with 1/2 inch of fine soil, tamp. Thin to 4 seedlings when plants are 3 inches high. For earlier crops, start seeds indoors, 2 to a 3-inch peat pot. Cucumbers do not transplant well. Thin to 1 seedling when 3 inches high, and plant outdoors when the weather warms, 4 pots to a hill. Sow a few seeds in the hills at the same time: if the growing season is long you will have succession crops. Mulch well, and water thoroughly when cucumbers begin to mature; avoid wetting the foliage.

Fertilizing. Keep cucumber vines picked to encourage production. They taste best when they are 5 inches long and before the seeds toughen. Harvest only when plants are dry.

Freezing. Slice peeled cucumbers wafer thin, scald for only 20 seconds, plunge into cold water, drain thoroughly, pack, freeze. They won't be crisp, but they will be good in salads and you can use them to make the Gorgeous Cucumber Soup, too. But save some for pickling!

DANDELION
(see Table I, page 274)

The dreadful dandelion is a delicious perennial. I have never cultivated it because my lawn always has. In Vermont, dandelions grew in the tall grass of a field opposite the house, and my father blanched them by tying the outer leaves together with a bit of wool. The inner leaves then became pale, and the flowers, too. We used them in salads dressed with oil and vinegar and two cloves of garlic. We also made dandelion wine and cooked the greens, which were very welcome as the first spring crop. Catalogues offer varieties for the home garden. Since it is a perennial, the crop won't be ready for harvest until the second spring. Try the Dandelion Wine recipe when your neighborhood has a big crop to offer.

Planting and culture. *See* Lettuce.

Fertilizing. Add a handful of garden fertilizer to the row if the plants look peaked in midseason. In my opinion this is unlikely to occur.

Harvesting. *See* Lettuce. I have heard of dandelion roots being forced in the cellar, as chicory is, but I have never heard of the roots being eaten. David says they can be roasted and will make an imitation coffee.

EGGPLANT
(see Table III, page 277)

Eggplants are such a culinary delight that even the Northern gardener, for whom they present some problems, should grow them. You have never tasted anything better than the baby fruit, fresh-picked, pared, sliced 1/2 inch thick, tossed in beaten egg and breadcrumbs, and fried in butter or olive oil! When they are a little larger, make Turkish Caviar to spread on cocktail crackers. It's a guaranteed conversation piece, and so is Gay's Eggplant Salad.

Eggplant is a member of the potato-tomato family, and like tomatoes can be set out only when the nights have warmed. They require nine to eleven weeks to mature; in cool regions start them indoors and protect them at the end of the summer with plastic canopies. Early Beauty Hybrid is a variety that matures in about nine weeks. To avoid problems, don't plant eggplant where tomatoes were growing the year before.

Planting and culture. In areas where the weather has definitely warmed by the first of May, sow eggplant outdoors in furrows 1 inch deep, cover with 1/2 inch of soil, tamp. When seedlings are 3 inches high, thin to stand 18 inches apart in the row. In cooler areas sow indoors in flats and keep at a temperature between 70 and 75 degrees. After June 1 plant outdoors 18 inches apart in the row. If the plants become yellow and spotted, they may be short of water. Some Northern nurseries offer started plants at the end of May.

Harvesting. When fruit is about 4 inches in diameter and a glossy purple black, it is ready to harvest. Protect with mulch or a plastic canopy toward the end of the season in cooler areas. If you suspect a frost, pick the plants clean and store the fruit in a cool dark place to ripen.

Freezing. Peel and slice 1/3 inch thick, drop into 1 quart of water containing 1/4 cup of salt to prevent discoloration. Scald 1-1/2 pounds at a time in 4 quarts of boiling water for 4 minutes, chill in running water 4 minutes, drain, pack, freeze. Or make the ratatouille for Ratatouille Pastry, and freeze it.

ENDIVE AND ESCAROLE
(see Table I, page 274)

Endive and escarole are much confused and often called by each other's name. Strictly, they are slightly different forms of one plant, *Cichorium endivia*. Chicory is another species of the same genus. Endive is a flat, ruffled salad green with a crisp golden heart. Escarole is a broader-leafed variety of it. Belgian endive is the forced and blanched shoots of either endive or escarole. In France it is used as a vegetable; braised it makes a marvelous quiche; and someday I am going to force endive so that I can have an unlimited supply of it! In America, Belgian endive is too expensive to use in anything but salads. Any variety of endive is as easily grown as lettuce and a delicious crisp addition to your salad bowl.

See Lettuce.

GARLIC
(see Table I, page 275)

Aioli is one of the famous dishes of southern France. Strictly speaking, it is not a "dish" but rather mayonnaise made in a bowl in which 4 large cloves of fresh garlic have been ground with a pestle. The aioli is then served with a heaping platter of mixed fish that have been poached in a stock (made with a pinch of thyme, a bay leaf, and a small onion) for 20 minutes. For it to taste as it does in Cannes, it should be made with fresh garlic—and that is reason enough for planting a row of garlic in your vegetable garden. Have you ever tasted Garlic Soup? Made with fresh garlic, that, too, is exquisite. And then there is garlic butter.

Planting and harvesting. Garlic does best in a not too rich soil. Catalogues offer "mother sets," but I prefer to buy large-cloved garlic at the grocery store for planting: divide the cloves and plant as onion sets. Each one grows into a large garlic head which then divides into cloves. The children help me to braid them into bunches and we store some in the cool attic, and a few in the kitchen.
See Onions.

GOURDS
(see Table II, page 276)

Every garden should have one or two plants of ornamental gourds; they make the Thanksgiving centerpiece, delight the children, provide small gifts for friends, and are easy to grow. Gourds are vines, and I have seen them used very effectively as screens along garden fences. Gourds are planted after the weather warms, along with the squashes; but my children, who are in charge of gourd production, usually start them indoors in 3-inch peat pots toward the end of April, and set them out in June. Gourds do not transplant well from flats. They are cucurbits and must not be planted where a relative was the previous crop.
See Squash.

HORSERADISH
(see Table I, page 275)

If yours is a small garden, horseradish isn't something to bother with, and, too, this perennial can become a pesky weed. But sometime try a bit of it in a secluded corner for the fun of using it freshly grated in an iced or a hot sauce. Commercial or prepared horseradish is simply pickled with a little vinegar and can be made in minutes. Add prepared chili sauce to it, and you have made a delicious shrimp cocktail sauce.

Horseradish is propagated by small sets, or roots, which are planted in early spring and furnish large roots in fall.

Planting and culture. Plant the pencil-size roots in trenches 12 inches deep and set them 2 feet apart. Plant at a slight angle so that the upper end of the root is 4 inches deep. Cover with soil. When the shoots are 2 inches tall, remove the soil from the upper part of the root, rub away all but the top shoot, and replace the soil.

Harvesting. In early fall dig the roots, trim away rootlets, wash and dry. If you leave a few roots in the ground, they will provide next year's crop. If you leave a few in the ground and forget it, your yard will be full of horseradish in a few years.

Storing. Layer in damp sand, or simply leave in the ground, and dig as needed through cold weather.

JERUSALEM ARTICHOKE
(see Table I, page 275)

Jerusalem artichokes are the small knobby root of a species of American sunflower that is a perennial and will grow almost anywhere. In the South they are used for pickles, or thinly sliced as a salad with vinegar, salt, and pepper. They are delicious cooked as new potatoes are, in their skins, then scraped and served with melted butter. They become stringy when overcooked. The flavor faintly resembles that of the globe artichoke, and their texture is reminiscent of water chestnuts. In France, we call them *topinambours;* Italians call them "sunflower artichokes," and it is the Italian word for "sunflower," *girasole,* which English later corrupted into "Jerusalem." The flowers are pretty in a corner of the garden, and the tubers have the added virtue of being starchless. If your catalogue doesn't offer roots, look for fresh tubers at a specialty food market in autumn, divide them into eyes, plant, and mulch well, for next year's crop. It is safer, in cooler areas, to plant root divisions.

Planting and culture. There is just one crop a year, which must be planted as soon as the ground can be worked. In Southern areas, plant in late fall. Set cut pieces of the tuber 2 inches deep and 18 inches apart in hills of 6.

Harvesting. Dig Jerusalem artichokes in fall after the top growth ceases. A few tubers left in the ground can be dug in early spring or allowed to start a new patch for later harvest.

KALE
(see Table I, page 275)

Kale is a spinachy, vitamin-loaded species of the genus *Brassica*, closely related to cabbage. It is grown for salad and boiling greens where spinach presents difficulties, and is marvelous as a creamed casserole. There are spring cropping varieties which are sown in early spring and mature in about eight weeks, and late varieties which grow through the summer and provide greens through fall and into early winter with a little protection. The thinnings of either crop create a whole new dimension for leafy lettuce salads.

Planting and culture. *See* Broccoli.

Harvesting. When the leaves become bright green and crisp, twist off outer leaves as required. Leaves left on the plant too long become dark green, tough, and bitter.

Storing. Kale can be frozen (*see* Chard) or covered with salt hay or straw and left in the garden until winter frosts.

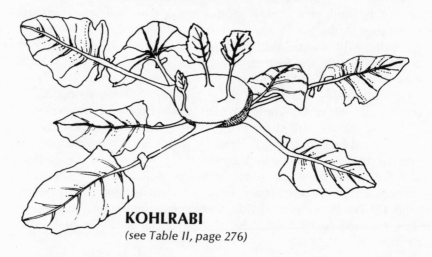

KOHLRABI
(see Table II, page 276)

Kohlrabi tastes like a delicious delicate turnip with cabbage overtones, and looks like a fat flying saucer with stemmed leaves shooting up from the base. It is extraordinarily crisp and very good served raw in 1/4-inch-thick sticks with a Bagna Cauda. A cupful of kohlrabi slivered into matchstick strips makes a wonderful addition to a mixed salad or can be added to an Oriental dish instead of water chestnuts. The strips retain their crispness even when cooked. A hardy member of the *Brassica* group, kohlrabi can be grown either as an early spring vegetable or as a fall crop, and matures in less than two months.

Planting and culture. As soon as the frost is out of the ground, sow seeds in furrows 1 inch deep and cover with 1/2 inch of fine soil. When plants are 3 inches tall, thin to stand 6 to 8 inches apart. Thinnings may be transplanted if you have extra space.

Harvesting. The thickened base of the stem is the edible portion, and it is best when 2 to 3 inches in diameter. Slice it just below the bulb, and pull up and dispose of the rest of the plant.

Freezing. Very young kohlrabi freezes well. Cut off the tops, peel, dice into 1/2-inch cubes, scald 1-1/2 pounds at a time in 4 quarts of boiling water for 3-1/2 minutes, chill in running water for 3 minutes, drain, pack, freeze. Thawed and boiled tender, it is a wonderful side dish for corned beef. (Corned beef is best cooked in a stock with sweet marjoram, bay, thyme, onion, and celery leaves, and should rest 2 hours in the liquid after the cooking is finished.)

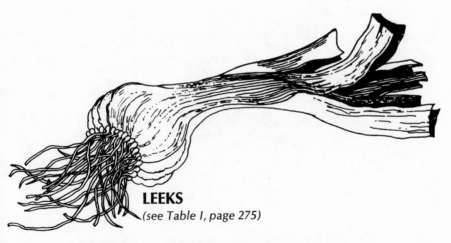

LEEKS
(see Table I, page 275)

Leeks are a kitchen, garden, and market staple in France, and impossible to get along without if you like French cooking. Well, almost impossible—you can use onion if you are stuck. A leek looks like a huge scallion, has the growing requirements of the onion family, and when fresh tastes like a sweet delicate onion. It makes one of the world's truly great soups, Gauloise, which you may call Vichyssoise. Since they are expensive and hard to come by in America, they are worth finding space for. They can stay in the ground until quite late in the fall with a light mulch.

See Onions.

Planting and culture. Sow seed in early spring. In France, the growing leeks are transplanted twice, this way: Thin to half the row when the seedlings are 2 inches high, and transplant the thinnings to another row. When the tops are as plump as straws, cut the tops back halfway, move the leeks to a trench 12 inches deep, and space them 12 inches apart. As they grow tall, fill the trench, ridging the earth against the lower portion of the stalks to blanch them. I find all this a lot of work, and grow small but nice leeks by planting 1 package in early spring, thinning at 2 inches high to stand 6 inches apart in the rows, and then gradually hilling to 3 inches high at the end of the summer.

Harvesting and storing. Use thinnings as scallions. Dig enough leeks when the weather cools to make quarts of Gauloise Soup for freezing. Before hard frosts, dig the remaining leeks and layer in moist sand in a cool place, or trench in the garden, as celery.

LETTUCE AND SALAD GREENS
(see Table I, page 275)

Have you ever had lettuce thinnings in soup? Or mixed with romaine and tossed in a cream and vinegar dressing? These dishes are reason enough to plant lots of lettuce, but there are others. Lettuce and other salad greens are delicious scantily cooked, chopped with butter and coarse salt, and served with corned beef, smoked tongue or ham, and even with hot dogs. And the more kinds of greens you grow the more interesting your salads will be. Among my favorite combinations are crisp romaine with oak-leaf lettuce and spinach; escarole and cress with cucumbers or beets; buttery Boston lettuce with escarole thinnings and parsley. At home, the salad dressing and the herbs that go into it are chosen to complement the main meat course, since the salad is served with it, and at family meals on the same plate. We use salad as Americans use the second or side vegetable. The main vegetable is most often served as a separate course before the entrée and after the soup or hors d'oeuvre, one reason so much attention is given to the preparation of vegetables.

Salad greens divide into three groups: the lettuces, the bitter chicory-endive-escarole types, the peppery cresses. One of each in the garden provides a succession of crops from early spring to late summer or early fall. The earliest crops are the leaf, then the loose-heading, lettuces, ready in forty to fifty days. They bolt when real heat arrives. Crisp tall romaine, or cos, lettuce planted at the same time matures in about twelve weeks, and given a little shade by the cornpatch will stand up well to summer heat. The endive-escarole types mature in about ten weeks and can be planned for early or late crops. Garden cress is ready in twenty days, and is a cool-weather crop to be planted in early spring or late summer. If you are short of space for all the salad greens you would like to grow, look for space among slower-growing vegetables, such as late cabbages or Brussels sprouts, or onions. If you want early, early lettuce, most varieties can be started indoors and transplanted.

Planting and culture. Sow seeds thinly over companion planting beds, or sow thickly in furrows 4 inches wide and 1/2 inch deep. Cover with 1/4 inch of fine soil, tamp. As seedlings grow, thin often to keep rows from becoming crowded, and to furnish your salad bowl.

Harvesting. Head-lettuce varieties, such as Boston and Bibb and iceberg, and the escarole-endive group are severed from the root at the base. Pick side leaves from looseleaf lettuce types and also from endives, escarole, and dandelions as needed. Pick branches of cress as needed.

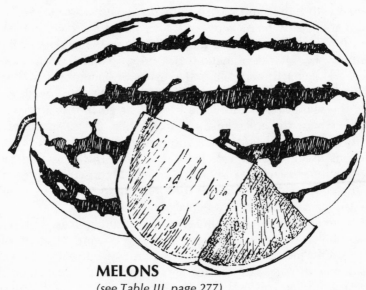

MELONS
(see Table III, page 277)

In France, muskmelons with a bit of salt or pepper are used as an hors d'oeuvre. The Italians go a step further and wrap cantaloupe in *prosciutto,* a paper-thin sliced smoked ham, and this is one of the great things to do with cantaloupe. For cocktail parties, skewer cubes of chilled cantaloupe inside slices of American or Italian prosciutto, and serve heaped on a pretty plate. There is no end to the delicious combinations of melon and fresh fruits; I have listed a few among the melon recipes, but most any combination from your own garden will be delicious. Marinate the macédoine in 1 tablespoon of Kirsch or lime or lemon juice if the flavor seems a little flat.

Melons for the home gardener divide into two basic groups, watermelons, and muskmelons, which include cantaloupe and honeydew and casaba types. Culture for both groups is essentially the same. All melons are native to warmer climates and do beautifully in Southern gardens. North of Philadelphia the new hybrids are more reliable. Though smaller at maturity, they ripen several weeks before the others. Where possible, choose wilt- and mosaic-resistant varieties and do not plant where any member of the cucurbit family grew before.

Planting and culture. If you can expect ten to twelve weeks of growing weather after the temperature has reached 70, sow seeds outdoors 6 to a hill, in holes 1 inch deep. Cover with 1 inch of soil, tamp, thin to 4 seedlings when plants are 3 inches tall. For earlier crops, start seedlings indoors, 2 to a 3-inch peat pot. Thin to 1 seedling when plants begin to crowd the pot, and plant 4 to a hill. Be sure the weather has really warmed, otherwise they will sulk. Melons produce both male and female flowers; the stem of the female flower is slightly thickened below the ovary, which becomes the fruit. The petals of the male flower drop off. My father pinches off the male flowers (calyx and petals) just after they have blossomed, on the theory that this preserves the plant's strength. Keep melons watered as they begin to fill out; slip the hose under the foliage to avoid wetting it.

Harvesting. Melons are at their best when vine-ripened. Muskmelons are ripe when the stem parts from the fruit with a slight pull. Ripe watermelons have a dull thudding sound when thumped that is hard to describe. Practice with the supermarket melons, if the manager will let you!

Freezing. Freeze only fresh, well-ripened melons. Pickle those that don't ripen before frost. To freeze, cut peeled, seeded melons into 1-inch chunks or balls, and gently pack into freezer containers. Stir 2 cups of sugar into 1 quart of water until it dissolves and the water is clear. Pour syrup over containers to cover fruit, leaving 1/2 inch of head room, cap, and freeze.

MUSHROOMS

Big beautiful white mushroom caps, peeled and stemmed, make wonderful appetizers or hors d'oeuvre stuffed with an herbed (tarragon or sweet marjoram) sour-cream mix, or crab meat shredded into mayonnaise. They are wonderful sliced into salads dressed with oil, vinegar, lemon juice, and a bit of fresh tarragon. I peel mushrooms only on special occasions and usually do no more than to sprinkle them with the sink spray and rub clean with paper towels. Mushrooms freeze beautifully, sealed into paper bags, and though they darken, they are good for cooking for months to come.

All of which is of little relevance to the home gardener who doesn't have a basement or shed where the temperature remains between 55 and 65 degrees and where he is willing to deposit composted horse manure, the medium in which mushrooms are generally grown. Catalogs offer spawn and send instructions for mushroom culture, but the composted manure is up to you. Mushrooms can also be grown in unheated buildings on this compost: The culture is spread on the growing medium in late summer and allowed to freeze through the winter; it will then produce fine crops in spring. I was cheered recently by the information that mushrooms have been successfully grown outdoors from catalog-purchased culture. The growing medium was horse bedding from a stable and the spawn was sown in later summer. Crops appeared following rains the next year and continued to flourish for several seasons after that.

Storing. Dry bumper crops between window screens in a dry warm place, store in mesh bags in a dry room, and use for soups, stews, and in scrambled eggs.

NEW ZEALAND SPINACH
(see Table II, page 277)

OKRA
(see Table III, page 277)

Okra is a Southern belle who flourishes where early hot summers allow her to mature quickly. Okra is also called "gumbo," as is a thick soup in which okra is often featured. New Orleans Fresh Crab Gumbo is typical of the way okra is used; try it the next time you go to the shore. Chicken Brunswick Stew is a delicious way to use fresh okra. And the baby pods are absolutely delicious boiled until tender and served with Hollandaise Sauce, or fried in half-inch rounds in deep fat, as French-fried potatoes, sprinkled with salt, and served very hot. Okra is best if it is chilled, stemmed, covered with boiling water for 1 minute, then drained before using.

Planting and culture. Sow seeds in furrows 1/2 inch deep, cover with 1/2 inch of damp soil, tamp. Water often until seedlings appear. When plants are 3 inches high, thin dwarf varieties to stand 15 inches apart, larger varieties 24 inches apart.

Fertilizing. If plants are peaked, apply one tablespoon of 4-8-4 as a side dressing to each plant after thinning.

Harvesting. Gather pods no more than 2-1/2 to 3 inches long. If the stem won't cut easily with a knife, the okra will be too tough to eat. Use at once.

Freezing. Just-harvested okra freezes well. Wash and rinse the pods, cut off the stem but avoid cutting into the seed pod, or the sticky juice will flow out. Scald 1-1/2 pounds at a time in 4 quarts of boiling water for 3 minutes, chill in running water 2 minutes, drain, pack, freeze.

ONIONS
(see Table I, page 275)

If you don't think the kitchen onions are worth finding space for, do make room for the big Bermuda or Spanish onions that are so good in shish kebab and salads. I use them in a variation on shish kebab that my friend Mary Buchanan brought back from Greece; it is a shish kabab in miniature, used as an appetizer with cocktails. And, of course, onion rings! Grow scallions and bunching onions to sliver into Chinese dishes or to serve with Chinese meals, and plant shallots because they are expensive, and nothing takes their place in Sauce Béarnaise or any fish sauce. Shallots and scallions can replace each other in recipes like the exquisite Beurre Sablais, but scallions won't dry and keep all winter as shallots will.

Planting and culture. The familiar red or white kitchen onions are usually raised from "sets," which are underfed onions harvested the summer before; some catalogs offer the big Bermudas or Spanish onions as seedlings to set out. Chives, a perennial of the onion family, are sold in clumps at garden centers. Seed for shallots is hard to find, so buy half a pound at the grocery store and plant these as onion sets. Onions can be raised from seed.

Onions are heavy feeders: add 1 pound of 4-8-4 with extra humus to every 20 feet of row. When frost is barely out of the ground, plant onion sets, garlic cloves, shallots, pointed tip up, in holes 1 inch deep, 8 inches apart, and cover with 1/2 inch of soil. Tamp firmly, as night crawlers somehow dislodge some sets. Plant onion seeds early, in furrows 1/2 inch deep, cover with 1/4 inch of soil, tamp. When they reach scallion size, raid the row often for the salad bowl, until plants stand 5 inches apart for smaller varieties, 10 inches apart for larger varieties. Plant some of the onion crop among cabbage, squashes, roses, or anything else that has a following of insects. Big onions and garlic send up hollow stems, like larger chives. Flowers are borne at the top of the stems and become bulbous fruits which carry the seeds. Bend these tops over when a few have bent by themselves; this is nature's signal that the onions are about ready to harvest. Harvest ten days later.

Harvesting and storing. On a sunny day pull up onions by the roots, or dig them up with a spading fork, and strew on the garden to cure until the tops dry out, or until rain threatens. When dry, rub off the soil, braid by the stems into bunches 18 inches long. They will keep in a dry cool place, and even in the kitchen, until spring sets them growing. Chives and perennial bunching onions will winter over in the garden without difficulty.

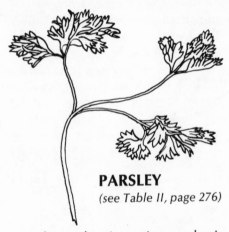

PARSLEY
(see Table II, page 276)

From the cook's viewpoint, parsley is an herb, not a vegetable, but we use so much of it that I grow two plants by the kitchen door for quick raids and a whole row in the vegetable garden in order to have enough for parsley soups, for stuffings and salads and garnishes, and to freeze for winter. Once you have tasted Sizzled Parsley Garnish done in clarified butter on a lovely slice of fresh sole, you may become an addict, too!

Though a carefree crop, this plant is slow to germinate. This is not really a problem, because parsley is a biennial, coming up with a generous crop the second spring and keeping you supplied until the new crop is ready for picking. It has some ability to repel bugs, or so I believe, and is pretty when bunched with dwarf yellow marigolds, another plant bugs don't like. In giddier days I planted them together in a circle around the cabbages.

Planting and culture. Soil must be fine for parsley seeds, which are not strong enough to fight their way through big clods of earth. Sow seeds before July 15, and where summers are very hot much earlier; make furrows 1/2 inch deep, and cover seeds with a scant 1/4 inch of fine soil. Tamp gently. Mark the row with a sowing of radish seeds on either side. I have soaked parsley seeds overnight and planted in damp earth at high noon, and I think that hastens germination. Keep lightly mulched through winter. When seedlings are 3 inches high, raid the row until plants stand 8 inches apart.

Harvesting. Break parsley stems from the plant and it will keep on producing, providing you don't strip it completely.

Freezing and storing. Wash, cut away tough portions of stems, dry on paper towels, seal into plastic bags, freeze. To store, dig up the plant and hang upside down in an airy place. When it is crackling dry, crumble off the leaves, discard stems, and store leaves in tightly capped bottles. See Chapter Seven.

Winter supply. Plants taken up and potted before frost will linger for many weeks, even months, in a sunny window. Indoor plants last longer however, when grown from a few seeds planted in early July in a large clay pot which is then set into the garden soil, and brought indoors when frost threatens.

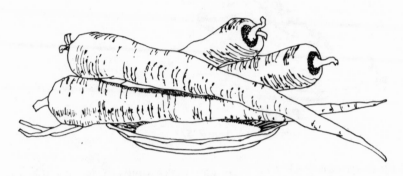

PARSNIPS
(see Table I, page 275)

If you grow no other root vegetable, do grow parsnips! Dug after the first frost they are crisp, sweet, and so delicate it is almost too bad to have them any way but *au naturel* with a little butter and a few drops of lemon juice. If you have a sweet tooth, you might try them *à l'orange.* Parsnips are a breeze to grow, and stay in the ground right through winter, one reason they were such a prominent part of the winter stock before refrigerators. My Canadian grandmother added them to delicious little cakes. The French side of the family taught me to use them in beef stews and to substitute them for carrots in vegetable soup occasionally.

Planting and culture. Since parsnip roots go straight down 8 to 12 inches, organic matter and nutrients have to be worked down to that level. As soon as the ground can be worked in spring, sow seeds in a furrow 1/2 inch deep, cover with 1/4 inch of soil. Germination is slow, so mark the row with a planting of radishes. When parsnip seedlings are 3 inches high, thin to 3 inches apart.

Harvesting and storing. Dig whatever roots you want to use from late summer through fall. When a hard frost threatens, cover the row with old newspapers or an organic mulch, and wait for the first thaw, when you can claim your early parsnip crop.

Freezing. Wash, peel, slice into 1/4-inch strips, scald at once (to avoid discoloration), 1-1/2 pounds at a time in 4 quarts of boiling water for 3 minutes, chill in running water for 3 minutes, drain, pack, freeze.

PEAS
(see Table I, page 275)

Only garden-fresh tiny peas can make petits pois into the exquisite sensation in flavor that they should be, and only the pods of home-grown peas are fresh enough to make pea soup as the English do. For that matter, only home-grown snow peas are perfect in flavor. In spite of which, I had an aversion to growing peas as long as I had to wrestle with the great roll of chicken wire we used to support them. Then I discovered bush or dwarf peas, which are a shade less prolific than the climbers, but are no more trouble to grow than bush snap beans. Snow, or sugar peas, really should be wire-staked, but some varieties grow no taller than 3 feet, and those I let scramble on 2-foot piles of mulch or bales of hay.

Peas can be planted so early that you should prepare their row in the fall; then you don't have to wait for the ground to become workable in spring. The earliest peas are smooth-seeded varieties not quite as sweet as the wrinkle-seeded types. (Extra sweetness wrinkles seeds, did you know that?) Wrinkle-seeded go into the ground two weeks later. I wait and plant those because they really are better, except for soufflés or purées. A sowing of peas in late summer will produce a fall crop if your climate offers a late fall and a frost-free September. Plant peas after a rain if possible; they come up much more quickly.

Planting and culture. Peas are legumes, which have the peculiar ability to add nitrogen to the soil, so when the crop is over, turn the old vines under, and plant a shallow-rooted crop on top. Plant peas almost before the frost is out of the ground in trenches 4 inches deep and 2 inches wide. Drop the seeds 3 inches apart in the row and cover with 1 inch of fine soil. Fill the trench around the seedlings as they grow. The more orthodox manner of sowing peas is to cover them with 2 to 4 inches of soil, but I find they germinate more quickly my way, and as long as the trench is filled gradually they are well anchored. Plant later varieties 2 inches deep in furrows 3 inches deep. Peas do not transplant. Don't mulch early peas; the weeds are not underway yet and the mulch keeps the earth from warming.

Harvesting. Pick peas of the smooth-seeded varieties before they are really plump; they are best then. Pick the sweeter varieties and snow peas when they are quite young, or they will toughen.

Freezing. Shell tender young peas, sort into uniform sizes, scald 1-1/2 pounds at a time in 4 quarts of boiling water for 2 minutes, chill for 2 minutes, drain, pack, freeze. Add a sprig of mint, scalded 10 seconds, to a few of the packages. Cut edible pod peas into 1-inch pieces, blanch 3 minutes, chill 3 minutes, drain, pack, freeze.

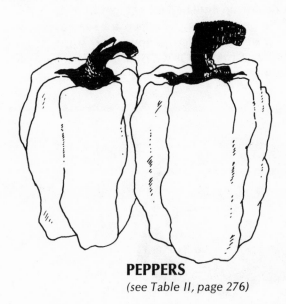

PEPPERS
(see Table II, page 276)

In their native tropics, peppers grow as shrubs. In cooler climes, they are grown as annuals. The small hot varieties go into pickling and such recipes as Mexican Chili; the large sweet, or bell, peppers, are the ones so good stuffed. These turn red when ripe, but in New England they rarely get that ripe, and are just as good harvested green. Sweet peppers mature in sixty to eighty days, and keep producing till frost kills the plants. They won't flourish if the temperature falls below 70 degrees. I start seeds indoors in May and set the young plants out toward the end of June, pampered under clear plastic canopies to try for an early August crop. About eight pepper plants will supply an average family. When the crop is overflowing, make Stuffed Peppers Provençale and freeze a few for winter. If you can, reserve enough to make Green Pepper Relish.

Planting and culture. Peppers do best on a sandy soil. Start seeds indoors, two to a 3-inch peat pot about six weeks before the outdoor temperature normally becomes a constant 70. Thin to one seedling per pot, and set out in rows 18 inches apart.

Fertilizing. When plants are beginning to set fruit, work a tablespoon of 4-8-4 in around each plant, and water it.

Harvesting. Peppers can be picked at almost any stage, but the very tiny ones are not much good. Gather any large ones, to keep the plants producing. Shelter with clear plastic canopies through the early frosts and hope for an Indian-summer crop.

Freezing. The last of the pepper crop will keep for several weeks in the crisper. Freeze extras: Cut seeded peppers into strips, sauté in butter 3 minutes, pack, and freeze. Or wrap in foil to exclude all air, seal into plastic bags and freeze. Defrost and cook before using.

POTATOES
(see Table I, page 275)

Have you ever had Potato Nests? This was Grandmother Sadie Agnes' gala specialty, but I have never seen it on American menus. In France, potatoes are treated with the respect due this most versatile vegetable. One excellent dish is Pommes de Terre Sautées, which is made from tiny fingerling potatoes that you buy already scraped. German fingerling potatoes, if you can find seed for them, are ideal for this recipe, but tiny potatoes just dug from your potato row are almost as good. Small gardens do not have room for a real sowing of potatoes, but one row will furnish enough for some delectable dishes with that home-grown flavor. Old winter potatoes that start to sprout in spring can be cut up, 2 eyes to a piece, and planted. For a real crop, buy disease-resistant treated seed potatoes from your dealer.

Planting and culture. Potatoes do best in sandy soil, rich in humus, and prefer rows where peas were the crop before. Don't plant potatoes in recently limed soil or where ashes or fresh manure have been dug in. As soon as the frost is out of the ground plant potato pieces eyes up 18 inches apart in trenches 4 to 6 inches deep and cover with 2 inches of soil. When seedlings are 5 inches high, hill the earth up around the plant to a depth of 2 inches. When the vines die down or are killed by frost, they are ready to dig.

Harvesting and storing. Harvest potatoes from the time the vines begin to die until they are dead. Dig for potatoes carefully to avoid spearing them with the spading fork, and work each hill well. Children are very good at this: they find the ones impatient grown-ups overlook. Cure the potatoes in the garden for a day, then pack into bushel baskets and store at about 50 degrees in a dark place with some humidity.

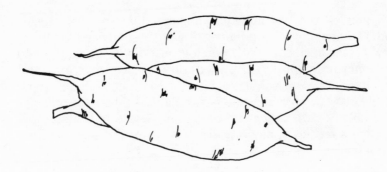

SWEET POTATOES
(see Table III, page 277)

We think of sweet potatoes as orange, yams as pale yellow, and Irish potatoes as white, but only Irish potatoes are potatoes. And they are not Irish. They came from South America to Italy about four centuries ago, thence to England, and the English brought them to Ireland. The sweet potato is the tuberous root of a perennial vine of the Morning Glory family. True yams belong to another, largely tropical family, are almost white, and are hardly ever available even in specialty stores. Some forms of sweet potatoes are often popularly called yams. Sweet potatoes occasionally succeed in gardens as far north as Connecticut, but they really belong farther south. The adventurous Northern gardener who can't find seed potatoes for sweet potatoes in seed catalogs might try cutting up fresh sweet potatoes from the grocery store for sprouts—that is, if he can find any in late spring.

Planting and culture. Sweet potatoes need light soil and four to five months of warm weather to produce a crop. The tubers are propagated by planting sprouts forced from cut-up tubers on a hotbed; the forcing is begun four to five weeks before planting time. The sprouts are then broken from the old tuber and transplanted to the garden when the weather has thoroughly warmed. They will have rootlets on the lower part of the stem. Plant 5 inches deep and 1-1/2 feet apart in ridges 12 inches high. Harvest the crop after frost has killed the tender tips of the vines.

Fertilizing. Sweet potatoes do best on fertilizers high in phosphorus and potash and medium to low in nitrogen.

Freezing. Harvest as potatoes; bake at 375 degrees until tender, mash, pack, freeze.

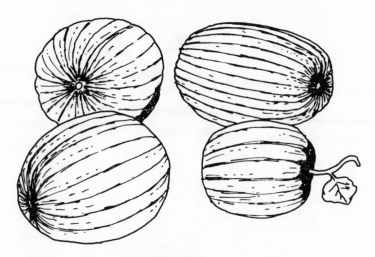

PUMPKINS
(see Table II, page 277)

Pumpkins provide such handsome crops in exchange for so little attention that most home gardeners grow them. Fresh, ripe pumpkin baked in wedges, or boiled in a little water, mashed and served with butter, salt, and pepper, makes a delicious vegetable; cooked strained pumpkin you have grown yourself makes a superior pie, and brings moisture and flavor to nut breads. Grow your pumpkins scattered through the corn patch to act as a mulch, or sow them casually near or on the compost heap; they will even climb fences with a little help. They come in all sizes; the smaller ones mature earlier, and are better for eating; the larger ones take longer but make fabulous jack-o'-lanterns. One package plants five hills, more than enough for most families. The pumpkin is a cucurbit; don't plant where another cucurbit was the previous crop.

Planting and culture. *See* Squash.

Harvesting. In Connecticut, pumpkins mature between September 1 and October 1. They are green when young, and turn orange as they mature. Protect them from frost if they are to be left in the field, or pick the crop and let it ripen piled on doorsteps as decoration or in the garage. Do not bring them indoors, as they will soften.

Freezing. Bake until soft, scoop out interior, remove seeds, mash, drain, freeze in quantities measured for pie recipes. Wash and dry the seeds, bake in buttered pans in a 250-degree oven, salt. Children like to nibble the inner seeds.

RADISHES
(see Table I, page 275)

Crisp, tiny, frost-hardy radishes are almost the first crop of the season, and a delight to eat with French bread and butter. Radishes come in early, midseason, and late varieties, are ready in two to three weeks, and are trouble-free until warm weather, when mine get wormy. Plan to intercrop 2 or 3 packages of the early ones among slow-to-germinate seeds to mark the beds; and try one package of large white radishes, which don't mind a hot summer. The big winter radishes are delicious peeled and sliced into narrow strips, either in a salad, or with mayonnaise, hard-boiled eggs and cubes of ham as an hors d'oeuvre. Use them for Chinese Beef and Radishes.

Planting and culture. As soon as the ground can be worked, sow early radishes broadcast over a shallow bed and cover with 1/4 inch of fine soil. If the seedlings are crowded, thin them. Later and larger varieties require more room; sow in drills 1/2 inch deep, cover with 1/4 inch of soil, tamp. When seedlings appear, thin to 1-1/2 inches apart, and try thinnings in the Greens with Sour Cream recipe.

Harvesting. Pull radishes whose shoulders appear through the soil. Keep ripe radishes harvested; they get tough and woody left in the ground past their prime.

Storing. Store the winter crop right in the row until hard frost, then pull and store layered in damp sand in a cool place.

RHUBARB
(see Table I, page 275)

Have you ever tasted really fresh pink rhubarb cooked in its own juice, sweetened just enough to be slightly sour and dolloped with whipped cream? If you have, you will agree that every garden should have its rhubarb patch. Once established, rhubarb will go on for eight or nine years and more, with little care. Started from seed it can be harvested only two years later, so order roots from your nursery man; these can be harvested next year. Allow one plant per family member so there will be enough for Barbro's Swedish Soup, and for pies, marmalades, and jams.

Planting and culture. In a permanent location in your garden dig holes 3 to 5 feet apart each way and about 10 inches deep. Mix a small handful of rotted manure, compost, or dried manure into the soil at the bottom of each hole, and cover it with 2 inches of loam. Set the rhubarb root so the crown is 4 inches below the surface, water, fill the hole with loam, and tamp gently. When the plants are eight years old, in the fall after the tops have died, dig up the roots, divide, giving each section 2 or 3 good buds, and replant in a new location. My friend Maro Chapman, a farmer, urges me to prevent the majestic panicle of white rhubarb flowers from developing, in order to keep the plant producing, but cutting it has never changed my rhubarb's behavior. At some point it stops being good, about when the weather warms, in fact.

Fertilizing. In the fall, work a small handful of compost or rotted manure in around each plant, or mix in 2 tablespoons of your garden fertilizer.

Harvesting. Harvest rhubarb in early spring as soon as the plant has grown a full stand of stalks. Grasp large stalks on the outside of the clump, yank, twisting slightly, and it will come clear of the base. Do not cut stalks.

Freezing. Rhubarb freezes well. Remove the leaves and 2 or 3 inches of the green stalk beneath the leaves, wash the stalks, drain, cut into 1-inch pieces, pack—allowing 1/2 inch for expansion—seal, and freeze. Thaw before cooking.

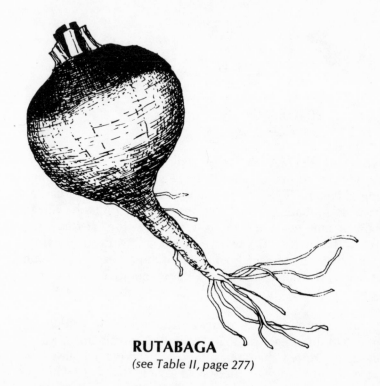

RUTABAGA
(see Table II, page 277)

Rutabaga and turnip are not the same vegetable, though closely related. Both are members of the cabbagy *Brassica* group. Without rutabaga, I don't think that I could make my favorite vegetable soup. It is a combination of about 1 cup each of celery, potato, carrot, and rutabaga diced and tossed into 2 quarts of water in which 1/2 cup of onion and 2 tablespoons of butter have simmered. By the time the potato has slightly thickened the soup, about one hour later, the whole has a delicate flavor. But without rutabaga it isn't the same. There are a few recipes in which the white turnip and the yellow turnip, as rutabaga is often called, are not interchangeable, but only a few. I plant rutabaga for a fall turnip crop not only because of the soup, but because it also keeps very well over winter.

Planting and culture. *See* Turnips.
Harvesting and storing. Harvest as you do turnips. Dip cleaned rutabaga in melted paraffin and store in a cool place. Or store, undipped, in a cool place with good air circulation and some humidity.

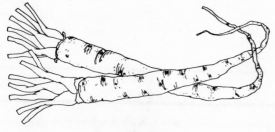

SALSIFY
(see Table II, page 277)

The next time you think "same old vegetables," buy a package of salsify seed: It has a faintly oystery flavor and is delicious used in carrot or parsnip recipes. Try it in Mock Oyster Soup, which is an old favorite in colder climates; use cooked in salads, too. Aunt Andrée sometimes uses the crisp young leaves in salads; the children often steal strips to eat raw while I am making dinner, and we all like it raw dipped into Bagna Cauda.

Salsify is an annual root crop, planted as soon as frost is out of the ground. Like parsnips, it can be left in the ground over winter and dug in the spring.

See Parsnips.

SHALLOTS
(see Table II, page 277)

Shallots are tiny members of the onion family that look like garlic cloves, but are larger and have a faint garlic overtone. Theirs is a more delicate flavor than any of the other onions, and they are used in French cooking for particularly refined sauces and stuffings. They are expensive to buy and well worth growing yourself. Seed is hard to find, so I have learned to buy shallots at the grocery store and plant them the way onion sets are planted.

See Onions.

SPINACH
(see Table I, page 275)

Nothing, not kale and not Swiss chard, and none of the boiling greens, really is quite as good as spinach just picked in the garden, wilted in a little boiling water, chopped with butter, and served with coarse salt. Spinach stir-fries beautifully, too. And no other green quite replaces fresh spinach leaves in a mixed salad.

But not all gardens grow it successfully: It has a hankering for "muck" soils that isn't easily thwarted! In the rich clay bottomland of our Vermont garden, spinach bolted so quickly it wasn't worth growing. In our sandy Westport garden it went to seed at once. Now I plant New Zealand spinach, which is almost as good, matures in ten weeks, needs less washing, produces happily through the summer, and replaces tips as they are harvested. To have the best of all possible worlds, plant one package of true spinach as soon as the ground can be worked, one package of New Zealand spinach in mid-spring for the summer supply, and another package of true spinach in August for a fall crop. True spinach is ready in six to seven weeks. (Even if you don't like store-bought spinach, do it. It really is different when it is fresh.)

Planting and culture. Spinach can be started indoors for an extra-early crop, if you want to go to that much trouble. New Zealand spinach germinates more slowly than true spinach, so soak seeds for forty-eight hours before planting. Drop 6 to 8 seeds per foot in a furrow 1/2 inch deep, cover with 1/4 inch of fine soil, tamp. Mark New Zealand spinach rows with lettuce seeds or late radishes. When the seedlings are 3 inches high, thin true spinach to stand 4 inches apart; thin New Zealand spinach to 6 inches apart.

Fertilizer. Feed a handful of nitrate of soda to New Zealand spinach when the plants are half grown.

Harvesting and freezing. True spinach is cut from the roots. New Zealand spinach is broken from its branches 3 inches from the top. You can pick some side leaves from true spinach for salads. You should not harvest much from New Zealand spinach until it is flourishing. New Zealand spinach will go on until frosts kill the plants. Spinach freezes well. Follow the instructions for freezing chard, but scald only 2 minutes.

SQUASH
(see Table II, page 277)

If everything else in the garden goes wrong, the squash and the ornamental gourds will come through. And that's good, because one of the joys of life is summer squash (yellow, marrow, or zucchini) only 5 inches long sliced into rounds, scantily cooked . . . well, have a look at the Jane Yamamoto recipe and at the Zucchini Salad. Squash you grow yourself is really very good. Furthermore, summer squashes produce crops in a month and a half, and if you keep the bushes picked they go on producing until frost. Fall and winter squashes planted in mid-spring are ready in late summer, but they are vines and must be tucked away where they won't overrun the garden. Half a package of yellow squash (I prefer the straight-neck) marrow, or zucchini is enough for the average family. Plant butternut rather than acorn squash for fall eating, if you are planning to have pumpkin as well; pumpkin and acorn have rather similar flavor and consistency. The butternut is sweeter and mealier. For winter, plant Blue Hubbard; it grows so big that you need only a few, and keeps until after Christmas. Two gourd vines for ornamental purposes is more than enough, too. Squashes are cucurbits and must not be sown where a relative was the previous crop.

Planting and culture. After the ground has warmed, plant bush varieties of summer squash in drills, dropping 2 seeds to a foot in a furrow 2 inches wide and 1 inch deep. When plants are 3 inches high, remove every second seedling. Plant fall and winter squashes, which are vines, in hills 5 feet apart, 6 seeds to a hill, and thin to 4 seedlings. Or plant 5 feet apart in a row. Or intercrop winter squashes with corn or Brussels sprouts or cabbages. Start ornamental gourd seed indoors in peat pots, 2 to a pot, thin to 1 seedling, and plant outdoors 5 feet apart.

Fertilizing. Winter squashes respond to 1 tablespoon of 4-8-4 worked into the ground around each plant after the vines begin to run.

Harvesting. Pick the summer squashes when they are 5 inches long and while the skin is tender enough to break with a fingernail. At the end of the season let a few zucchini grow to 2 feet long, peel, slice 3/4 inch thick, dredge in flour, and fry in olive oil. If you like them that way, let a few more grow and store them; they will keep some weeks in a cool place and extend your harvest after the vines have been frostbitten. Leave fall and winter squash on the vine until the stem shrivels; pick before frosts, or mulch through early frosts. Gourds can be picked any time after the shells have hardened.

Freezing. Summer squash freezes well cut into 1/2-inch slices and blanched 1-1/2 pounds at a time in 4 quarts of boiling water for 3 minutes. Cook double portions of fall squash for meals and freeze the second portion sealed into plastic bags.

TOMATOES
(see Table II, page 277)

Tomatoes succumb to the slightest frost. This means you must pick the late ones green and make tomato relish and piccalilli, or fry them sliced with bacon for breakfast. Or, if you don't want to make any of those things, cover the tomatoes with plastic canopies to see them through the early frosts and into Indian summer.

Usually one plants too many tomatoes, and a good way to get over the feeling of frustration this causes is to make Too-Many-Tomatoes Soup; or blend them in the blender, strain out the pulp, and make Bloody Marys with the juice, and meat sauce for spaghetti with the pulp.

North of Philadelphia plan to set out tomato plants; south of Philadelphia, but not in the midwestern cold belt, tomatoes can be started from seed outdoors. Provide a succession of crops by planting a few of the tiny cherry tomatoes, which ripen first, a few of the standard reds, which ripen in midseason, and a few of the glamorous, acid-free yellows and the pinks, which are all slow to produce but very good to eat. About 8 tomato plants provides enough to serve fresh for the average family; 12 to 18 provides extras to freeze. Try for earlier crops by opening the holes for tomatoes several weeks before they are to be planted, mixing sand into the soil, and letting it all warm; then put in the plants under clear plastic canopies.

Planting and culture. For earlier tomatoes, start seedlings indoors four to six weeks before the weather is due to warm, and transplant to the garden in rows with 3 feet of space all around; 2 feet if they are to be staked. Or sow seed outdoors as soon as the ground has warmed, if you are willing to wait eight to twelve weeks for your first crop, and if your climate allows. Drop seeds 1/2 to an inch in a furrow 1/2 inch deep, cover with 1/2 inch of soil, tamp. When seedlings are 4 inches high, thin to stand 2 to 3 feet apart and transplant the seedlings. When plants are setting fruit, keep well watered.

Pinching. At home we believe you get tomatoes sooner if you pinch and prune the vine this way: Remove suckers at the base of the plant as they develop, and those between main stem and branches. Keep fruit-bearing twigs nipped back to one leaf above the second fruit-spur.

Fertilizing. The earliest crop I ever got came from plants whose row had been enriched by the addition of the cleanings from enormous fish catches the autumn before. A small handful of compost or 4-8-4 worked in around the plant when they have doubled their planting size seems to produce more fruit more quickly. Mulch tomatoes to keep the plants weed free and to preserve moisture.

Staking. There are innumerable ways to stake tomatoes: on chicken wire nailed to stakes, or on tepees made of 3 5-foot

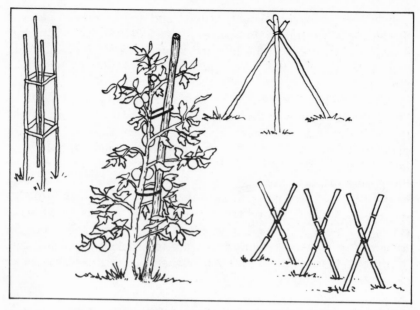

Four ways to stake tomatoes

poles, or surrounded by square structures of lathing with horizontals. The point is to have something strong near the plant to which the main stem and heaviest branches can be attached or on which they can lean. The prettiest way I know to stake tomatoes is to drive a row of 10-foot by 2-inch bamboo poles 18 inches into the ground on either side of each tomato plant in the row and at a slant so they can meet and be tied at a point 4 feet above the tomato seedlings. You end up with a row of X's and tie the tomato branches as they develop to the lower halves of the X's. The simplest staking system is to drive a stake 2 inches wide by 6 feet long into the ground 18 inches, just behind the tomato seedling, and tie the main stem and larger branches to it as the plant develops.

Harvesting. Tomatoes are best when picked dead ripe and just before they are to be used. Keep the plants clear of ripe tomatoes so their energy can go into maturing new fruit. Don't pick tomatoes when the leaves are wet. When nights turn cool, cover the plants with old newspapers, old sheets (or new sheets if you feel strongly about it), or with clear plastic canopies. If you can ward off the first batch of frosts you often can pick tomatoes through Indian summer.

Storing and freezing. If a frost touches the tomatoes they will be spoiled. Dig up plants bearing fruit that is turning from dark green to a whiter green, and hang upside down in a cool dark place; in a few weeks they will ripen. Or wrap picked tomatoes touched with white in tissue paper and let ripen in a cool dark place. My friend Mr. Silvio, the carpenter, freezes firm, ripe tomatoes raw wrapped air-tight in tinfoil, and sealed into plastic bags. Few of the really dark green tomatoes will ripen, and it is best to use them for prepared relishes. Or make very thick Italian meat sauce for spaghetti using your favorite recipe, and freeze it.

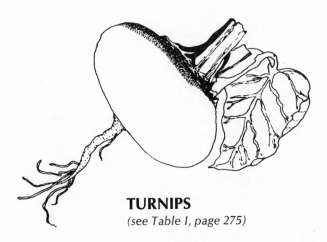

TURNIPS
(see Table I, page 275)

Baby white turnips, just 2 to 3 inches around and fresh from your garden, are an early-spring crop to delight in. The flavor is mild and sweet, the texture crisp, and it has nothing in common with that dreadful bitter vegetable you were served as a child. It is a cold-weather crop that can go into the ground as soon as the soil is workable; early varieties are ready in thirty-five days. A second crop can be sown between July 10 and August 1; the late varieties mature in sixty days or less, and can be stored for winter. You may prefer the yellow rutabaga for storing. The turnip is a *Brassica* and should not be planted where a relative was the previous crop. I dig ashes from the fireplace into the turnip row to put off worms.

Planting and culture. Sow seed in the garden as soon as the soil can be worked, in furrows 1 inch deep, cover with 1/2 inch of soil, tamp. Thin seedlings to stand 2 to 6 inches apart when they are 3 inches high. See above for second crop.

Harvesting. Turnip greens of varieties such as Foliage or Shogoin can be eaten as greens in thirty days after planting; the root is ready in seventy days. Early varieties can be pulled in twenty-five to thirty days, and later varieties in about sixty. Pull the largest first to leave space for others.

Storing. Store fall crops layered in damp sand in a cool damp place. To freeze, cut off tops, wash, peel, dice, or slice into 1/2-inch rounds, scald 1-1/2 pounds at a time in 4 quarts of boiling water for 3 minutes, chill in running water 3 minutes, drain, pack, freeze.

WATERCRESS
(see Table I, page 275)

Wonderful watercress will grow by the side of a slow-moving stream, and spread profusely through the years once well started. It is dangerous to gather it for eating unless the stream is definitely known to be unpolluted. The sprigs should be picked, or broken off at the tips, not uprooted. Propagation succeeds best by root divisions or cuttings. Any fresh bunch of watercress from the grocery store can be rooted easily in wet sand in a sunny window, and transplanted to your pure stream in early spring. It will also grow indoors for a little while in its rooting bed, but sooner or later white-flies get to it.

Planting and culture. Water and a mucky stream bank are the imperatives for watercress. If the bed dries out in midsummer you will lose the planting. Separate the rooted cress into small bunches, and plant at root level in holes 3 inches apart at the very edge of the water.

Harvesting. Watercress is at its best in early spring. Pick tips 3 to 4 inches long, leaving a few leaves below to nourish the root.

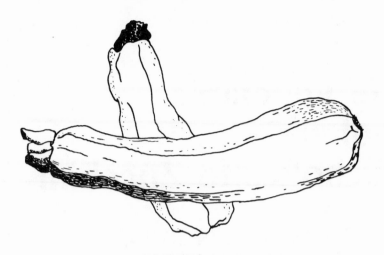

ZUCCHINI
(see Squash, and Table II, page 277)

The Italian word for squash is *zucca,* and the diminutive, *zucchino,* is the name for a quite small form of the vegetable marrow—a distinct botanical form, not just immature or baby marrow. Like another squash, the cucumber, zucchini should be picked at the right moment; in markets one sometimes finds them too old or too dry and fibrous. They are another vegetable which is definitely superior when home-grown and -gathered.

Zucchini are a comparatively recent addition to the American diet, were virtually unknown to our parents and grandparents, and have become very popular for their delicate flavor and texture, attractive color, and ease of preparation. Still, few cooks do more than boil them briefly or sauté them in a little butter. They deserve a more imaginative response. The Italians make them the chief ingredient of a canapé spread. They are excellent in salads; giant zucchini can be scooped out, stuffed, and baked, with the skins on. For a different light main dish or lunch, try Zucchini with Meat Sauce.

6 Fine Vegetable Cookery — Artichokes to Zucchini

Once you have tasted vegetables just picked in your own garden, you will have difficulty being satisfied with any vegetable, however good, you can buy. But to retain the delicate flavor and nutritional value of garden-fresh vegetables, you should cook them at once, and quickly, and only until barely tender. Overcooking ruins flavor and destroys the food value.

FIVE BASIC METHODS

There are five basic ways to prepare fresh vegetables. Most recipes, including soufflés, gratiné dishes, and aspics, are an elaboration of one of these.

1. Bake vegetables in their skins, on an oven rack or shallow pan, or peel them and bake in a covered dish.

2. Slice or cut them, peeled or unpeeled, into narrow strips, and serve raw with a dressing.

3. Boil them the French way in a quantity of water.

4. Boil them the American way in a minimum of water.

5. Stir-fry them the Chinese way in a little oil.

Many vegetables can also be French fried, a variation of stir-frying, but with a lot of oil or grease instead of a little.

I think the flavor of beans, peas, asparagus, and a few other vegetables is enhanced by the French method. Drop the vegetables into boiling water, a handful at a time, so that the boiling never stops. Or use so much boiling water that all the vegetables can be dropped in at the same time without checking the boiling. The French theory is that vegetables are seared by the heat of the water and so retain flavor and nutritional value. How true this actually is I do not know, but no cooking that produces such good-tasting results can be devoid of value.

The American method is the one currently recommended by home economists, and I prefer it for vegetables containing a lot of moisture, such as squash and tomatoes. Place a pan containing about half a cup of boiling water over medium heat, add the vegetables, and cook uncovered until they render their own juices, then cover and simmer gently until tender. You must watch them or they will burn. Ideally, no water will remain in the pan by the time the vegetables are tender.

To keep their color, green vegetables like peas and beans cooked either the French or the American way should be left uncovered all the time they are cooking. Never use iron utensils for green vegetables or tomatoes. Shake drained, boiled vegetables over heat to evaporate any remaining drops of water; otherwise the butter or the sauce you add will be watery. Leave the pan lid a quarter off cooked vegetables if they are to sit on the stove for a while before serving. If you cover the pan tightly, the vegetables will go on cooking; and steam, condensing on the lid, will make the sauce watery. I cook green vegetables until barely tender, drain, cover partially with the lid, and let them finish cooking in their own heat for 5 to 15 minutes.

Cook vegetables by whatever method appeals to you, but whatever you do, don't nullify the love and effort you have put into growing the vegetables by overcooking them!

STIR-FRYING

Walter Ian Fischamn, a writer who lives in a remodeled mill near us and is a demon cook, introduced me to the Chinese method. He prefers vegetable oil to olive oil. When I grumbled over the vegetables I burned in my early efforts to stir-fry, he said that anyone who can make cream sauce without lumps can learn to stir-fry in a try or two, and he was right.

Stir-frying is easiest if you have a wok, which is a cast-iron concave vessel available at Oriental specialty shops. But you can also stir-fry in an electric fry pan or a heavy skillet with sloping sides.

Leave leafy greens whole, or tear very large leaves into large pieces. Cut away thick stalks. For four servings, use 2 cups uncooked vegtables. Cut tender vegetables, such as scallions, green beans, and mushrooms, into small, straight pieces, 1-1/2 inches long, by 1 inch wide, if the vegetable allows it, by 1/16 inch thick, or about the thickness of a matchstick. Harder vegetables such as carrots, and those with long stalks, such as asparagus, cut on the diagonal. Using a very sharp knife, cut the vegetable on a very long diagonal about 1/2 inch from the top, roll halfway around, and repeat, until it has all been cut. The principle behind stir-frying is that the thinner the pieces the more quickly they will cook, so when in doubt, err on the thin side.

Heat 2 or 3 tablespoons of oil in a wok, an electric fry pan, or a slope-sided skillet until very hot but not smoking. Use either olive oil or vegetable oil, but remember that olive oil adds a distinct flavor of its own to the flavor of the vegetable. Drop the vegetable in all at once, and quickly toss to cover with oil, then keep tossing and stirring until cooked tender. Salt to taste. Leafy vegetables cook until wilted, then a minute or two more. Thicker vegetables require 3 to 4 minutes.

ASPICS, SOUFFLÉS, AND GRATINÉ DISHES

Then there are the dishes that do not call for a specific vegetable but can be prepared with almost any kind you prefer or happen to have. These include Vegetables in Aspic, Vegetable Soufflé, and au gratin preparations too seldom attempted but excellent variations on the vegetable theme.

VEGETABLES IN ASPIC

2 cups jellied stock
2 cups cooked vegetables
Carrot, parsley, or shrimp for
  garnish

Watercress or lettuce
Vinaigrette Sauce

1. Skim any fat from the top of the stock, and melt it. You need a firm jelly, so reduce the stock a little if it seems too liquid. Measure 2 cups.

2. Put a cooked carrot, or pretty sprigs of parsley, or tiny shrimp in the bottom of a small glass bowl for decoration. Add the cooked vegetables (with boneless morsels of meat or fish if you wish). Gently pour in the liquid stock and refrigerate until it jells.

3. Set the bowl *briefly* in a pan of hot water to loosen the gelatine. Then turn it out onto a bed of watercress or lettuce. Serve with Vinaigrette Sauce.

Serves four to six.

VEGETABLE SOUFFLÉ

1 cup cooked vegetable
1/4 cup butter
1/4 cup flour
1/3 cup vegetable water

1/3 cup cream
3 eggs, separated
1 egg white
Salt and pepper

1. Preheat oven to 325 degrees.
2. Cook and drain the vegetable and reserve the liquid. Shake the vegetable dry over heat. Mash through a ricer or rub through a sieve, keeping as light as possible.
3. Melt butter in an enameled saucepan. Stir in flour, then add vegetable water. Stir in cream and simmer, stirring for 5 to 10 minutes.
4. Beat egg yolks until thick. Beat egg whites until stiff but not dry. Pour a little of the hot cream mixture into the egg yolks, then stir the yolks back into the sauce until smooth. Fold in the egg whites, vegetable, and seasonings. Turn into a buttered 6-cup soufflé mold and bake 30 to 45 minutes.

Serve with a tablespoon of soft butter melted over the top, or with a Hollandaise or Béarnaise Sauce or Lemon Butter, or with a plain Béchamel with minced parsley. Or vary your vegetable soufflé by adding half a cup of slivered roasted almonds.

Serves four to six.

SCALLOPED VEGETABLES AU GRATIN

2 cups vegetables
Salt and pepper
4 tablespoons butter
1/2 to 1 tablespoon minced onion
4 tablespoons flour
2 cups light cream, warmed

Salt and pepper
1/2 cup bread crumbs
1 tablespoon butter
1/2 cup grated Parmesan or
    Swiss cheese

1. Preheat oven to 375 degrees.
2. Slice vegetables into small pieces, cook until tender, drain thoroughly and shake over heat to dry. Season lightly to taste.

3. Melt butter in an enameled saucepan; sauté onion until translucent. Stir in flour, then cream. Simmer, stirring, for 5 to 10 minutes. Season to taste.

4. Butter a baking dish. Cover the bottom with a little of the sauce, then arrange alternate layers of vegetables and cream sauce, ending with a layer of cream sauce. Sprinkle with bread crumbs, dot with butter, and sprinkle cheese over all. Bake 25 to 35 minutes, or until well browned. If necessary, place briefly under the broiler to brown.

Serves six to eight.

CLARIFIED BUTTER FOR SAUTÉING

An invaluable aid to the cook is Clarified Butter. It is a luxurious, wasteful distillation of butter in which food can be sautéed for a long period without burning. In some parts of France oil, or oil and butter are used, but Vendéen cooks pride themselves on an "all butter" cuisine. In the process of clarifying, the curds and whey, which burn easily, are removed; the oily liquid that remains sautés vegetables and meats to an exquisite golden brown and gives them a flavor oil, or oil and butter cannot equal.

Cut 1 stick (1/4 pound) of butter into small pieces and heat slowly in a small enameled saucepan until the butter foams. Skim off the foam and remove the pan from the heat. Strain the oily yellow liquid on top of the pan into a small crock. Now you have clarified butter. Freeze the milky residue for use in soups and sauces.

FINE GARLIC BUTTER

Garlic butter is a marvelous dressing for hot vegetables. It will keep for a week or more in the refrigerator, ready to give a party flavor to boiled vegetables or plain grilled meats at a moment's notice.

6 cloves garlic	1/4 teaspoon salt
1 quart boiling water	1/8 teaspoon pepper
1/2 pound (2 sticks) butter	1 tablespoon minced parsley

1. Drop the unpeeled cloves into the boiling water, bring back to a boil, and boil 5 minutes. Scoop out, peel, and rinse the cloves under cold water. Return to the water, boil for 30 seconds, drain, and dry. Pound to a smooth paste in a mortar.

2. Mash the butter into the garlic, a forkful at a time, until the mixture is creamy. Beat in salt, pepper, and parsley. Shape into a roll, and cover with wax paper. Store in the refrigerator until firm.

3. Cut rounds off the roll and melt over grilled meats, fish, hamburgers, or omelets as they finish cooking. Add to boiled potatoes, or drop into soups before serving. Or mix with 1 stick of butter and use for garlic bread.

Makes 1/2 pound.

MY FAVORITE ALL-PURPOSE STOCK

The experienced cook always likes to have on hand a constant supply of good stock. Dissolved bouillon cubes are a substitute, of course, but why settle for something inferior when you daily throw out many of the ingredients that can go into the making of excellent stock? With the exception of charcoal-broiled bones and mutton bones, any leftover meats and bones combined with the herbs and flavorings make fine stock. The gelatine that the cooking extracts from the ingredients is highly nutritious. You can intensify flavor by pouring half a cup of hot water into the bottom of a pan in which meat has roasted or sautéed, scraping, and adding this thinned-out pan gravy to the stock pot. You can add more beef or chicken bouillon cubes to strengthen the flavor. Reduce the stock to make a wonderful aspic with vegetables.

1 pound beef and bones	1/2 teaspoon marjoram
1 pound chicken bones and meat	1 stalk celery and leaves
Chicken giblets	2 sprigs parsley
1 pound veal bones and meat	1/2 teaspoon dried chervil
1 carrot	1 tablespoon salt
1 bay leaf	6 peppercorns
1/2 teaspoon thyme	3 beef bouillon cubes
1 onion stuck with 4 cloves	

1. Place all ingredients in cold water to cover. Bring to a boil and simmer for 4 hours. Strain, reserve the meat, discard the bones and herbs.

2. Serve the meat and soup stock for a meal with a crisp garden salad and French bread and butter. Store the remaining strained stock in the refrigerator. It will jell and a coat of congealed fat will form on top. Skim off the fat before using the stock.

Chicken Stock: Use mainly chicken bones and meat, with the herbs and flavorings.
Veal Stock: Use only veal bones and meat, with the same herbs and flavorings.

MY A TO Z RECIPES

Every vegetable can be cooked by one of the basic methods. Over the years I have tried, devised, and modified many recipes for garden-fresh vegetables, and have kept a growing and changing recipe file. Here are my favorites and others which my guests and my family enjoy. They are arranged alphabetically for specific vegetables, and include also some recipes for pickles, preserves, side dishes, hors d'oeuvre, and a few special sauces.

The section following this one gives recipes for combinations of vegetables, and the next chapter lists recipes for frequently needed sauces and pastries.

ARTICHOKES SERAPHINA'S WAY

At family meals in France we serve the artichokes and stems in soup plates propped on inverted forks so the bottom of the plate forms a receptacle for the sauce. Hollandaise Sauce is usually served at formal meals instead of Lemon Butter Sauce.

6 large globe artichokes
1 tablespoon salt
Lemon Butter Sauce

1. Wash, slice off stem ends, and stand artichokes upright; remove bottom row of leaves. Pare away woody outer skin of stem; reserve stems.

2. Stand artichokes in a kettle small enough and deep enough so they have to be squeezed in to stay upright. Then they won't bobble around as water boils. Cover with cold water, add salt. Bring water to a rapid boil, uncovered, throw in the stems, and cover. Cook at moderate heat 45 minutes. To test, gently pull one of the inner leaves. If it comes out, turn off the heat. If not, cook another 4 to 5 minutes.

3. Let the artichokes mellow in the water 15 minutes, then

drain. Serve with Lemon Butter Sauce, on dinner plates, as a first course, or as a separate vegetable course. Reserve the stems for salad. Serves six.

Artichokes Vinaigrette: Drain and chill cooked artichokes, add a little Vinaigrette Sauce, and serve in a soup bowl with more sauce. This is a good way to use leftovers.

SHRIMP-DRESSED ARTICHOKES

This is a substantial dish. I usually serve only Butter Biscuits, a chilled rosé wine, a chilled dessert, and coffee with it.

4 large globe artichokes	1 tablespoon butter
1 cup heavy cream	1 tablespoon flour
1/2 cup dry white wine	Salt and pepper
2 teaspoons strained lemon juice	8-ounce can tiny cocktail shrimp

1. Cook artichokes Seraphina's Way, but drain after they have cooked 45 minutes. Keep warm.

2. While they are cooking, simmer the cream and wine separately to reduce each a little. Add 1 teaspoon of the lemon juice to the wine. Combine wine and cream, stir, and keep hot.

3. Melt the butter, stir in the flour. Add the wine and cream, blend quickly until smooth. Simmer until sauce is like a thick mayonnaise.

4. Drain shrimp. Very, very gently push aside three lower rings of leaves on each artichoke. Pluck out the rest of the leaves. Scoop out the hairy choke with a rounded teaspoon. Scrape the largest of the plucked-out leaves with a sharp knife and mash the scrapings, then stir this into the cream sauce.

5. Set artichokes on dinner plates. Fill cavities with shrimp. Spoon cream sauce over them. Press outer leaves in around filling, dribble a bit of lemon juice into each artichoke, and serve.

Serves four.

PUREE OF ARTICHOKES AU BEURRE NOIRE

6 large fresh artichokes	1 tablespoon sweet butter
3 tablespoons butter	2 tablespoons salt butter
1 cup mashed potatoes, puréed	

1. Cook artichokes Seraphina's Way, but remove from heat after

30 minutes. Cool briefly, then cut away all but the hearts. Remove the leaves.*

2. Simmer hearts in 3 tablespoons butter until they are tender. Rub them through a fine sieve (or purée in an electric blender), then beat this purée into the purée of mashed potatoes, which should be quite liquid. Beat in the sweet butter. Melt the salt butter in a saucepan until it begins to brown. Pour over the purée.

Serves six to eight.

*Serve the leaves at another time with Vinaigrette Sauce as a first course.

FRANCESCA MORRIS'S MARINADE

In the South, where the artichoke crop can be tremendous, freezing yields some fine winter dishes. Serve this as a cocktail appetizer with food picks or as a first course.

12 to 18 frozen artichoke hearts	1 clove garlic, minced
2 cups fresh mushrooms	1 teaspoon salt
1/2 cup olive oil	2 teaspoons fresh, or 1 teaspoon
3 tablespoons lemon juice	dried, tarragon
3 tablespoons wine vinegar	Freshly ground black pepper

1. Thaw hearts and dry. Stem mushrooms, rub clean under water, and dry. Place artichokes and mushrooms in a small salad bowl.

2. Combine other ingredients and beat for 2 minutes, or blend for 1 minute at low speed in an electric blender.

3. Pour the mixture over the mushrooms and artichokes. Marinate at room temperature for at least 3 hours. Then chill.

Serves six.

ASPARAGUS AU NATUREL

The French cook most often prepares vegetables in large amounts of boiling water. At family meals in France we prop our plates on overturned forks, pick the asparagus up in our fingers, and dip it into sauce poured into the bottom of the tilted plates.

33 fat asparagus spears
1 teaspoon salt
4 quarts boiling water

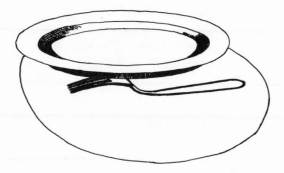

1. Trim cut ends from fresh-picked asparagus. Rub away loose scales, wash in cold water. Make bundles of eight, tying below tips and above ends. (The thirty-third spear is for testing!)

2. Lay bundles of asparagus in rapidly boiling salted water. Bring water back to a boil, reduce heat, and cook uncovered 8 to 12 minutes. Eat the extra spear to test for tenderness, and cook a little longer if you wish. The spear should bend, but never be cooked limp. Drain. Return to pan and shake slightly over heat to dry.

3. Untie and serve with Lemon Butter Sauce or Hollandaise Sauce on hot dinner plates—and always as a separate course; no other taste should blur the asparagus flavor.

Serves four to six.

ASPARAGUS TIPS IN CREAM

This is an elegant way to handle the really skinny spears that your garden produces.

32 to 48 skinny asparagus spears
1/2 cup light cream
2 tablespoons butter

1. Trim cut ends from asparagus, rub away loose scales, and break off bottom at point where spears snap easily. (Set lower pieces aside to use for soup.) Cut tips 2 inches from tops and tie into bundles of six. Cut remaining stalks into 1-inch lengths.

2. Drop these pieces into lots of boiling water. Bring water back to boiling and cook 5 minutes. Add bundles of tips, cook gently 3 to 5 minutes, or until tender. Drain quickly. Dry by shaking gently over heat.

3. In a small saucepan, bring cream to a boil. Simmer until it has thickened a little. Add butter and heat until it melts. Place asparagus pieces in small bowls with the untied tips on top. Pour hot cream over them and serve with toast.

Serves four to six.

ASPARAGUS BRUXELLES

| 1/2 cup parsley, minced | 32 asparagus spears |
| 1/4 pound melted butter | 4 to 6 eggs |

1. Put parsley in a small decorative dish that is one of a pair.
2. Melt the butter. Pour into a matching dish and keep hot.
3. Prepare Asparagus Au Naturel, and drain. Return to pan and shake dry over heat. Arrange spears in the center of a long platter and keep hot.
4. While asparagus is cooking, boil the eggs until they are hard enough to shell but soft enough for the yolks to be runny. It takes me about 5 minutes. Shell the eggs under cold running water.
5. Arrange the shelled eggs around the asparagus. Set the parsley and butter dishes at either end of the platter. Serve each person 6 or 8 spears and one egg. We crush the egg over the asparagus with a fork and mix parsley and hot melted butter into it, with salt and pepper to taste.

Serves four to six.

CREAM OF ASPARAGUS SOUP

1 tablespoon butter	6 cups hot milk
2 tablespoons minced onion	Salt, pepper, paprika
3 cups stem ends of asparagus	2 tablespoons sweet butter

1. Melt the butter in the top of a double boiler and simmer the onion in it until golden. Add asparagus pieces, cover with milk, and simmer 40 to 45 minutes, or until asparagus is tender.
2. Ladle asparagus into blender and whip until smooth. (You will have to do this a little at a time to avoid spattering the kitchen!) Or rub the cooked asparagus through a sieve. Return to the hot milk, add the seasonings, and simmer another few minutes.
3. Ladle into soup bowls, dot with sweet butter, and serve with Butter Biscuits for a delicious easy luncheon.

Serves six to eight.

HAM AND ASPARAGUS ROLLS

24 paper-thin slices cooked ham
24 cooked asparagus spears
14 ounces Gruyère cheese
4 tablespoons butter

8 small or 4 medium tomatoes,
  peeled
1 tablespoon minced parsley

1. Heat oven to 425 degrees.

2. Roll up the asparagus spears in the ham with the tips showing. Place in a large, shallow greased baking dish, and top each roll with a strip of cheese. Bake until cheese melts and bubbles a little.

3. Arrange rolls on a heated serving dish, surrounded by the tomatoes, lightly salted, and garnished with parsley. Serve with hot Butter Biscuits and your favorite wine, chilled.

Serves four to six.

STIR-FRIED ASPARAGUS

16 to 20 asparagus spears
3 tablespoons vegetable oil
Salt to taste

1. Break off tough bottom of asparagus, rub away any loose scales, wash, and drain. With a very sharp knife cut off half an inch of the asparagus at a very long diagonal; roll the spear halfway over, and cut. Repeat, until the spear is finished. This is called the "rolling" cut, and is designed to expose a long area across the grain of the asparagus so that it will cook more quickly and more readily absorb seasonings and juices. Rolling the asparagus as you cut it also gives pieces different shapes and keeps them from sticking together as they cook.

2. In a wok, a heavy skillet, or an electric frying pan, heat the oil until it is very hot but not smoking. Add the asparagus all at once, and toss in the oil and stir for about 2 minutes, or until the asparagus has turned bright green. Remove from the heat, and add salt to taste. Return to the heat, sauté for another minute, then remove from the fire and let it continue to cook in its own heat for 1 minute more. Serve hot as a side dish for an Oriental meal, or with rice and broiled or baked veal, chicken, or steak.

Serves four.

DILLED GREEN BEANS

4 to 6 cups green beans
2 large sprigs fresh dill, or
  1/2 teaspoon dried seed

4 tablespoons sweet butter
Salt and pepper
Sprig of fresh dill

1. Swish just-picked beans in cold water and snip off ends. To make all beans the same thickness, slice the larger ones lengthwise down the flat side.

2. Drop beans by the handful into 3 quarts of rapidly boiling, lightly salted water. Bring water back to a boil before adding another handful of beans. Place dill sprigs on top or stir in the dried dill seed. Boil rapidly 6 to 8 minutes, uncovered. Test for tenderness. Cook longer if you like. When beans are almost tender, drain, and return to the kettle. Shake over heat to dry. Add the sweet butter and lightly salt and pepper. Turn off the heat, partially cover the kettle, and let the beans finish cooking in their own heat while you prepare to serve the rest of the meal. (If you cover the pan completely, the beans will overcook and the butter will be watery.)

3. Serve on a hot platter with a garnish of fresh dill. For a company meal you might garnish with sautéed sliced mushrooms. If you don't like dill, substitute summer savory, sweet marjoram, or sage.

Serves only four to six—when the beans are fresh from your garden!

GREEN BEAN SALAD

4 to 6 cups large green beans
Oil-and-Vinegar Dressing
Coarse salt
1 shallot, minced
1 lettuce heart

1 tablespoon olive oil
2 tablespoons butter
1 garlic clove, crushed
2 slices stale French bread
2 sprigs fresh dill

1. Wash beans, snip off ends. French-cut them down the middle, and cook as for Dilled Green Beans. Drain and shake over heat to dry. Grind a little salt over them.

2. Prepare Oil-and-Vinegar Dressing. Add the shallot and mix well. Pour over the hot beans. Cook, uncovered, 2 to 4 minutes, then chill, covered, in the refrigerator, in a glass salad bowl.

3. Break the lettuce into bits and crisp them.

4. Before serving the salad, heat the oil and butter in a skillet.

Brown the garlic in it, then remove it with a slotted spoon. Fry the stale bread slices until golden, flipping often so both sides absorb the butter.

5. Toss lettuce bits into the chilled beans. Crumble the fried bread and add. Toss briefly and serve at once, garnished with the dill.

Serves six to eight.

If it is a warm day, the glass will "frost," which adds to the appeal of the salad. An excellent salad with mild fried chicken, hot Butter Biscuits, and a Mateus wine, chilled.

KENTUCKY WONDER APPETIZER

4 cups Kentucky Wonder beans or
  flat Italian green beans
1/2 teaspoon salt
1 cup sour cream

1/4 cup mayonnaise
1 tablespoon lime juice, strained
1 tablespoon curry powder
Salt

1. Snip stem ends off beans but leave pointed tips on. Drop into 3 quarts of furiously boiling water just a few at a time. Boil rapidly, uncovered, until beans are tender but still quite crisp. Drain and shake dry over heat. Salt lightly and chill.

2. Beat all other ingredients together to make a sauce, adding curry powder (I hope yours comes from an Indian specialty shop) and a pinch of salt. Chill.

3. Arrange beans, pointed tips outward, on a plate with a bowl of sauce in the center, and serve with cocktails. This is a great appetizer for people who are tired of potato chips.

GREEN BEANS FUKIEN

2 tablespoons vegetable oil
1 clove garlic, minced
1 pound ground pork
2 tablespoons soy sauce
1/4 teaspoon salt
6 slivered water chestnuts, or
  1/2 cup minced celery

2-1/2 to 3 cups diagonally sliced
  green beans (see "Stir-Frying")
1-1/2 cups boiling water
1 tablespoon cornstarch
1/4 cup cold water
1/2 head lettuce, shredded

1. Heat the oil almost to smoking in a wok, an electric fry pan or heavy skillet. Add the garlic clove and swish it around quickly

with a wooden spoon. Add the pork and brown it well. Add soy sauce, salt, water chestnuts or celery, and cook rapidly for 2 minutes, stirring.

3. Stir in the beans, and add the water in a thin stream. Mix well. Cover, bring mixture to boiling, turn the heat down, and simmer 4 minutes, stirring.

4. Mix the cornstarch with the cold water, and a minute or two before beans are done, stir cornstarch into the beans. Taste them for tenderness and cook a minute or two longer if necessary.

5. Serve on shredded lettuce on a warm shallow plate. Boiled rice and a nice sake are good with this.

Serves two to three.

WAX BEANS IN CREAM

4 to 6 cups wax beans
2/3 cup light cream
Salt and pepper

Freshly ground nutmeg, or paprika
2 tablespoons butter

1. Wash beans, snip off ends, and drop into a 3 quarts of rapidly boiling water, a few at a time. Cover and cook until *almost* tender, about 5 minutes. Drain and shake dry over heat.

2. Pour cream over the beans, and simmer, uncovered, until beans are tender. Drain, reserving the cream, and season beans lightly. Serve the beans in individual bowls, pour the cream in each, add a grating of fresh nutmeg or a sprinkling of paprika, and dot with butter.

To vary, add a garnish of minced parsley or chives. When the wax beans are young and have just come from the garden, they are almost as good as fresh corn.

Serves six to eight.

LIMA BEANS WITH LAMB AND ENDIVE—FOR GARLIC LOVERS

2 pounds fresh lima beans
1 head curly endive
1 or 2 garlic cloves, peeled
6-pound leg of lamb

Salt, pepper, curry powder
1 cup beef stock or bouillon
Garlic Dressing

1. Preheat oven to 425 degrees.
2. Shell the lima beans, using a sharp knife to open tough pods.

3. Pare out the core of the endive. Discard the darkest outer leaves. Wash well and crisp.

4. Insert slivers of garlic, a few or many according to your taste, into slits in the meat. Rub the roast with salt, pepper, and a bit of curry powder, and place in the oven. (I put roasts in a huge iron skillet; it seems to me the gravy is better, perhaps because the stock I add to the pan reduces more rapidly on the skillet's flat heavy base.) Sear the roast for 20 minutes, then reduce heat to 350 degrees and add half the stock or bouillon. It will require an hour more for the lamb to be medium rare, which is the way my family likes it, or 1-1/4 to 1-1/2 hours more to be well done. About half an hour before it is finished, baste with the drippings, and add the remaining stock.

5. Cook the lima beans in 2 cups of rapidly boiling water, covered, until almost tender, about 15 minutes. Drain and shake dry over heat.

6. When the lamb has cooked the allotted time, *turn off the heat.* Toss the beans into the drippings in the roasting pan. Set the oven door ajar and leave for 20 minutes more. Most of the juices will be absorbed but what remains will be a fine "gravy" requiring no thickening.

7. Dry the curly endive, break into pieces in the salad bowl, and toss in Garlic Dressing.

8. Serve the lamb on a large heated platter. Arrange the endive around the outer rim and the lima beans between the salad and the meat. Serve with French bread, sweet butter, and a light Bordeaux rouge. This is heavenly food, but for garlic lovers only.

Serves six to eight.

Very young lima beans can be cooked in the pod: Drop into lots of boiling water, cook until tender, or 20 to 25 minutes, plunge into cold water, and shell.

Traditionally, this recipe is made not with lima beans, but with dried white shell beans, *flageolets.* (My aunt's favorite use of dried shell beans is as a vegetable casserole; the beans are covered with cold water, and cooked for 2 to 4 hours at a low simmer with 3 or 4 1-inch pieces of salt pork and 4 to 6 cloves of garlic, peeled.)

BEETS MOTHER'S WAY

My children prefer baby beets this way to any other vegetable.

8 medium or 12 small beets   Coarse salt
3 tablespoons sweet butter   Freshly ground pepper

1. Cut off beet tops, leaving an inch of stem. Do not remove root tips or skins. In a large kettle, cover with cold water and bring to a boil, covered. Turn down heat and cook until tender—20 minutes to an hour, depending on the size and age of the beets. When a fork pierces them easily, drain, and slip skins off under cold running water.

2. Slice or dice larger beets, but leave baby beets whole. Shake dry over heat. Melt sweet butter over them, stirring. Turn into warmed serving plate and season with freshly ground pepper and coarse salt. Serve hot, with or without Lemon Butter Sauce. Serves four to six.

GABRIELLE'S BEET RELISH

6 to 8 large beets   2 tablespoons good vinegar
2 large garlic cloves, minced   1 tablespoon lemon juice
2 tablespoons olive oil   Salt
1 tablespoon vegetable oil   1/2 cup minced parsley

1. Cook beets Mother's Way and dice into a mixing bowl.

2. Add the garlic, oils, vinegar, lemon juice, and salt to taste. Toss until garlic is evenly distributed. Add parsley and toss, taking care not to bruise the parsley. It is important that both parsley and garlic be minced really fine. Refrigerate, covered, 1 to 2 hours to let flavors blend. Toss before serving. We serve this on lettuce leaves as a first course with crusty French bread and butter, or with cold meat for lunch. And it is always a success.

Serves six to eight.

PAINLESS BORSCHT

6 large beets   1 teaspoon sugar
8 cups beef stock or bouillon   1 tablespoon vinegar
1 tablespoon butter   6 tablespoons sour cream
Salt

1. Remove beet tops and root ends, wash, and peel. Shred into a heavy kettle with about 3 cups of the stock. Cook, covered, for 15 minutes; add the rest of the stock, and cook until beets are soft.

2. Add butter, salt to taste, sugar, and vinegar, and simmer 20 minutes. Add more stock to thin, if necessary.

3. Serve in deep soup bowls, topped with at least 1 tablespoon of thick sour cream. (Canned beets make a good borscht, too, but use a little less stock.)

Serves six.

BEET AND APPLE PUREE FOR PORK

4 medium beets	4 cooking apples
3 tablespoons butter	Salt and nutmeg
1 onion, minced	2 tablespoons sweet butter

1. Cook beets Mother's Way. Peel and slice thin. Keep warm.

2. Melt butter in a heavy skillet. Add onion and simmer until transparent. Peel, core, mince the cooking apples, and add to the onion. Season with salt and nutmeg to taste. Mix in sliced beets and simmer until apples have blended with beets, about 15 minutes.

3. Turn into a warm serving bowl, dot with sweet butter, and serve with grilled pork or a pork roast (in lieu of that same old blob of applesauce).

Serves six.

BEET GREENS

Greens fresh from the garden are my family's favorite "spinach." Served with a poached egg on top, beet thinnings make a fine light supper.

12 cups beet greens and thinnings	3 tablespoons soft butter
1/2 cup water	Salt

1. Wash greens in several changes of water, leaving tiny beets attached to the stems. Snip off root strings. Pack into half a cup of boiling water in the bottom of a heavy kettle, cover, and cook rapidly until tender—6 to 15 minutes depending on the size of the tiny beet and the stalks. Don't overcook! Beets much larger than the stalk should be treated as beets rather than as greens.

2. Drain and shake dry over heat. Chop soft butter into the greens, salt lightly.

Late in the season the greens will have a stronger flavor and you may then prefer to serve them chilled with a Sauce Vinaigrette. Serves six.

LILY'S POLISH BEETS

3 large beets
2 strips fat bacon, cut up
3 tablespoons flour

1/2 cup vinegar
Salt

1. Cook beets Mother's Way, cool, and grate.
2. Fry bacon until crisp in a medium saucepan. Stir in the flour, simmer 1 minute, add the beets, then the vinegar, a little at a time, stirring. Add salt to taste. Simmer another 30 minutes to smooth the flavor, stirring occasionally. The beets "spit" while simmering. Lily does beets this way to serve with game and beef. Serves four to six.

BEET SALAD ESCOFFIER

6 large beets
2/3 cup light cream
2 tablespoons strained lemon juice

2 tablespoons Maille or Dijon
   mustard
Salt and pepper

1. Cook beets Mother's Way, skin, and cut into thin strips. Chill.
2. Mix cream with lemon juice, mustard, salt and pepper to taste, and pour over beets just before serving. Toss well at the table. Serves six to eight.

BROCCOLI À L'ITALIENNE
This is wonderful as a first course with crisp French bread and butter, or as a side dish with an Italian meal.

2 to 3 broccoli heads, medium
2 tablespoons olive oil

2 tablespoons tarragon vinegar or
   lemon juice
Salt and pepper

1. Soak broccoli in cold water for 10 minutes and cut away tough outer skin from the stalks. Cook with the florets above water

in rapidly boiling water until stems are tender. Drain, shake dry over heat, and arrange on a warm serving platter.

2. Blend olive oil, vinegar or lemon juice, a little salt and pepper, and pour over hot broccoli. Marinate at room temperature for 1 hour and chill. The broccoli can be marinated in a Vinaigrette Sauce if you prefer a stronger flavor. Or simply chill the cooked broccoli and serve with mayonnaise.

Serves six.

BROCCOLI AU GRATIN

4 to 6 broccoli heads
3 tablespoons butter
1 tablespoon onion, minced
2 tablespoons flour
1 cup water broccoli cooked in, or
    light cream

1/4 cup grated Swiss or Parmesan
    cheese
1/4 cup grated Parmesan
3 tablespoons bread crumbs
1 tablespoon butter

1. Prepare and cook broccoli as for Broccoli à l'Italienne. Keep warm, reserve cooking liquid.

2. Melt butter in small saucepan. Stir in minced onion, and cook until translucent. Stir in the flour, stir in the warm broccoli cooking water, and simmer, stirring, until smooth, or about 5 minutes. Stir in 1/4 cup Swiss or Parmesan cheese, grated.

3. Butter a baking dish, pour a little cream sauce into the bottom, lay the broccoli on it, pour remaining sauce over it, sprinkle with crumbs, dot with butter, and sprinkle over it the 1/4 cup grated Parmesan. Place under a medium-hot broiler until it browns, and serve at once. I sometimes turn this into a mock Chicken Divan by warming sliced white chicken meat in the cream sauce, then burying it in the broccoli before putting it under the broiler.

Serves about six or eight.

BROCCOLI WITH CHESTNUTS

4 to 8 broccoli heads
1 tablespoon olive oil
1 tablespoon butter
1 clove garlic, whole
1 onion, chopped coarsely

12 boiled chestnuts
1 teaspoon salt
2 tablespoons lemon juice
1 cup water
2 tablespoons butter

1. Soak broccoli in cold water 10 minutes, pare away tough portion of the stalks, and cut in thin spears with a few florets attached.

2. Grease small saucepan with olive oil, stir in the butter, add garlic clove and onion and brown lightly. Add broccoli, chestnuts, salt, lemon juice, and water. Cover and simmer 15 to 20 minutes, or until broccoli is tender. Drain.

3. Turn into a buttered heated serving dish, dot with butter, brown briefly under the broiler, and serve at once.

Serves about six.

SAVORY BRUSSELS SPROUTS

4 cups Brussels sprouts
1/2 cup salt
3 tablespoons butter
1/3 cup slivered onion

1/4 cup sliced mushrooms
1/3 cup beef bouillon or stock
Salt

1. Soak the sprouts for 10 minutes in cold water to which the salt has been added. Drain. Cut away the thick base where leaves are sparse. Drop a few sprouts at a time into 2 quarts of rapidly boiling water; cook uncovered for about 5 minutes. Test, and if necessary, cover and cook another 2 to 3 minutes until almost tender. Drain. Shake dry over heat.

2. While sprouts are cooking, melt the butter in a saucepan. Stir in the onion and mushrooms, and cook rapidly for 6 minutes or until onions begin to color.

3. Add the bouillon or stock and the sprouts. Coat the sprouts with the sauce and simmer until the liquid has been absorbed and the sprouts are completely tender, 5 to 10 minutes.

4. Salt lightly to taste. Serve with a pork roast, broiled fowl, or frothy omelet.

Serves six.

BRUSSELS SPROUTS IN CREAM

6 cups Brussels sprouts
2 tablespoons butter
Salt

3/4 cup heavy cream
Minced parsley

1. Cook sprouts as for Savory Brussels Sprouts. Chop coarsely.
2. Melt butter in a heavy saucepan. Add sprouts and stir to coat. Cook, stirring, over high heat to dry out remaining moisture. Season with salt.
3. Return to kettle, pour in heavy cream, and cook at moderate heat until cream has been absorbed. Sprinkle with parsley and serve with roast pork, turkey, or duck.

Serves eight.

BRUSSELS SPROUTS MILANAISE

4 cups Brussels sprouts
1-1/2 tablespoons soft butter
Salt and pepper
4 tablespoons melted butter

1/2 cup grated Swiss cheese
1/2 cup grated Parmesan cheese
2 tablespoons melted butter

1. Preheat oven to 350 degrees.
2. Cook sprouts as for Savory Brussels Sprouts. Shake dry over heat.
3. Coat a baking dish with the soft butter. Arrange sprouts head up in the dish, add salt and pepper. Sprinkle the 4 tablespoons of melted butter over all and put in the oven for 5 minutes.
4. Remove from the oven, and turn heat up to 425 degrees. Empty sprouts into a bowl. Mix the cheeses and sprinkle over the bottom of the baking dish. Return sprouts to the dish, a layer at a time, sprinkling each layer with cheese and butter. Top with rest of the cheese, and the 2 tablespoons of melted butter. Return to the oven till cheese has browned, about 10 minutes. Sprouts baked this way are wonderful with grilled tomatoes and red meats. Serve with a young Beaujolais.

Serves six.

CREAM OF BRUSSELS SPROUTS SOUP

2 cups sprouts
3 tablespoons butter
2 cups veal, chicken stock, or
  bouillon

2 medium potatoes
Milk
1 tablespoon butter
2 tablespoons croutons

1. Prepare as for Savory Brussels Sprouts, then simmer in butter in a soup kettle for 3 or 4 minutes. Add stock, turn up heat.

2. Peel and slice the potatoes (old ones are better for thickening soups). Gently boil potatoes and sprouts together, uncovered, until sprouts are tender but retain their fresh color. Turn vegetables into the electric blender with enough stock to keep the mixture from binding. Whip at low speed until smooth, or rub through a sieve. Return to kettle and simmer a few minutes more.

3. Melt butter and sauté croutons in it, making sure all the butter is absorbed. Sprinkle the croutons on each bowl of soup.

Serves four to six.

CABBAGE PIE

The Vendée is famous for having resisted Napoleon, and also for its cabbages. In fact, Vendéens are called *Chouans,* an embroidery on the word for cabbage, *choux.* We even make a pie of it! Serve this as a main dish with slices of Bratwurst and Weisswurst, or any good sausage, fried, and with iced Danish beer.

Pastry for 2-crust, 8-inch pie
3 tablespoons butter
1 medium cabbage, shredded

2 hard-cooked eggs, chopped
Salt and pepper

1. Preheat oven to 425 degrees. Line glass pie plate with rolled-out pastry.

2. Melt butter in a heavy skillet and sauté cabbage until all moisture is absorbed and cabbage is tender.

3. Spread cabbage evenly in pie shell. Top with eggs, cover with pastry, and bake until done, 30 to 40 minutes.

Serves six.

CABBAGE SOUP L'ENARDIÈRE

2 tablespoons butter	1 stalk celery, diced
1 small onion, minced	1 small cabbage, shredded
2 large potatoes, diced	Salt
1 carrot, diced	Parsley, minced

1. Melt butter in a large soup kettle, add the onion and simmer until translucent.

2. Add 2 quarts of water, bring to a boil. Toss in potatoes, carrot, and celery. Simmer until mixture begins to thicken, about 30 minutes.

3. Add shredded cabbage and simmer 20 to 30 minutes more. Salt to taste just before serving, and add the parsley. We like to grind black pepper onto our cabbage soup at the table and add a dab of butter.

Serves six to ten.

CABBAGE SOUP WITH POTATO DUMPLINGS

A good winter meal for tired skiers. I serve this with popovers dripping butter and big mugs of cold German beer.

4 tablespoons butter	2 quarts chicken stock or bouillon
4 cups shredded cabbage	2 teaspoons salt
2 tablespoons dark brown sugar	8 potato dumplings

1. Melt butter in a large skillet, add cabbage and sauté, stirring, until it begins to turn brown. Add sugar and cook long enough to melt sugar, stirring occasionally. Add chicken stock or bouillon, and salt; cover and simmer for 45 minutes.

2. Add the hearty potato dumplings, cover, cook 15 minutes, and serve very hot. Do not remove the cover until you are ready to serve, or dumplings will be heavy.

Serves six to eight.

POTATO DUMPLINGS

These can be made before the soup, stored in the refrigerator, and brought to room temperature before cooking.

4 tablespoons butter
2 onions, chopped
3/4 pound cooked ham, diced
2 egg yolks, beaten

6 boiled potatoes, peeled
1-1/2 teaspoons salt
3/4 cup sifted flour

1. Melt butter in saucepan, sauté onions until translucent. Add the ham, sauté 5 minutes. Set aside.

2. Beat egg yolks until lemon colored. Put the potatoes through a ricer. Beat egg yolks, salt, and flour into the potatoes. Knead into a dough and shape into a roll about 1 inch across. Take off pieces of dough about 2 inches long, flatten gently, and cover with a tablespoon of the ham mixture. Gather edges of dough up around the ham and shape into a dumpling, sealing edges carefully so ham won't fall out.

STUFFED CABBAGE

1 medium head cabbage
1 pound (2 cups) chopped cooked
    beef, veal, or pork
1/4 cup uncooked rice
1 egg, slightly beaten
1 onion

1 carrot
1 teaspoon salt
1/4 cup vinegar
1/2 cup brown sugar
1 cup canned tomato sauce
Butter

1. Soak cabbage head in water, cut away core and discolored leaves. Drop whole into boiling salted water and cook until outer leaves come off easily—4 to 8 minutes. Drain. Remove 12 largest leaves and chop the rest of the cabbage.

2. Combine meat, uncooked rice, and lightly beaten egg. Grate onion and carrot into the mixture, and add salt. Spread a little of the mixture over each cabbage leaf and roll up lengthwise, leaving a generous flap at either end. Then tuck the flaps under.

3. Place the stuffed cabbage in a skillet, add vinegar, brown sugar, tomato sauce, and water to cover. Cover tightly and cook over moderate heat 30 minutes.

4. Butter a baking dish. Spread the chopped cabbage over the bottom and arrange the stuffed leaves on top. Clean out the skillet with a little water, scraping up the juices, and pour over the stuffed

leaves. Bake 20 minutes. Add a little water if the dish dries out. Serve with creamy mashed potatoes and good beer.

Serves four to six.

CHINESE CABBAGE WITH CRABMEAT SAUCE

1 head Chinese cabbage	Pinch of pepper
2 tablespoons vegetable oil	Boiled rice
1/2 teaspoon salt	Crabmeat Sauce

1. Clean the cabbage, quarter, and core. Plunge into boiling water for 1 minute. Drain and shake dry over heat.

2. Heat the oil in a heavy skillet until almost smoking. Add the cabbage and sauté until soft. Season with salt and pepper. Place on a platter and pour hot Crabmeat Sauce over it. Serve at once with boiled rice.

Serves two.

CRABMEAT SAUCE

2 tablespoons vegetable oil	1/2 teaspoon salt
1/2 pound fresh crabmeat, cut into	1/2 teaspoon pepper
small strips	1/2 cup water
1 tablespoon sherry	1 tablespoon cornstarch
1 cup chicken stock	

1. In the skillet in which the cabbage cooked, heat the oil and sauté the crabmeat for 1 minute. Add the sherry and chicken stock and season with salt and pepper. (You may want less pepper.)

2. Stir the water into the cornstarch, add to the crabmeat, and stir until the sauce thickens, in 1 or 2 minutes.

HOMEMADE SAUERKRAUT

1. Wash and shred firm heads of cabbage, omitting as much core as possible.

2. In a large container, mix the cabbage thoroughly with salt, using 1/2 cup of salt for every 10 pounds of cabbage. Place cabbage loosely in a clean stone crock. Cover with a clean cloth. Weight the cabbage and protect from the air by placing over it a large

plastic bag which has been filled with water, placed within a second large plastic bag, and sealed. While the cabbage is curing—this takes between 5 and 6 weeks—remove the scum which forms at the top of the crock each day. (The best way to remember to do it is to do it first thing every morning.) Keep the cloth clean. The cabbage works best at a temperature of 68 to 72 degrees. When the scum stops forming, the cabbage is cured.

3. Place sauerkraut in a large preserving kettle, and heat to simmering, 185 to 210 degrees. Do not boil. Pack into clean jars and cover with strained juice from the crock. If there is not enough juice, add hot brine prepared by adding 2 tablespoons of salt to 1 quart of boiling water. Cap, leaving 1/2-inch headroom, place in boiling water, and process 20 minutes. Cool on rack.

Makes about 3 quarts.

SAUERKRAUT DINNER CHIMNEY HILL

5 cups sauerkraut
2 to 4 pounds corned beef
2 carrots, cut in rounds
1 stalk celery
1/2 teaspoon marjoram
1/2 teaspoon thyme
1 onion, stuck with 3 cloves
1/2 teaspoon chervil or parsley
1 crumbled bay leaf
2 Polish sausages

6 large potatoes, peeled and
  halved
2 tablespoons butter
3 tablespoons flour
2 cups stock from the cooked
  meats
1 cup very dry white wine,
  optional
Salt and pepper
1 cup heavy cream
1 teaspoon caraway seeds, optional

1. Drain the kraut, soak in cold water for half an hour, changing the water 3 times.

2. Put the corned beef in a large soup kettle, cover with cold water, add carrots, celery, marjoram, thyme, onion with cloves, chervil or parsley, and bay leaf. Cover, and simmer for 3 hours. Add more water to cover the beef, if necessary, and the sausages. Simmer 1 hour more. Bury potatoes in the stock. Bring to a boil and turn off the heat.

3. Melt the butter in a large saucepan, stir in the flour, stir in 1 cup of stock and the wine (or substitute 1/4 cup mild vinegar and 3/4 cup of stock). Simmer 5 minutes, add salt and pepper to taste, and stir in cream. Add the drained sauerkraut. Remove the

potatoes, bury in the sauerkraut, and simmer until potatoes are tender, 20 to 30 minutes. Add caraway seeds.

4. Arrange the beef and sausages on a large platter, surrounded with potatoes and sauerkraut, and serve with a light German beer or a Riesling wine.

Serves six to eight.

CARROTS IN CREAM

1-1/2 pounds (about 5 cups) carrots
1-1/2 cups water
1-1/2 tablespoons butter
1/2 teaspoon salt

1 cup heavy cream
2 tablespoons softened butter
Freshly ground black pepper
Herbs, optional

1. If you are using carrot thinnings or baby carrots, cut off tops and tips, wash, brush clean, and cook whole. Fresh young carrots should be scraped and halved. Stored winter carrots should be peeled and quartered.

2. Lay carrots on the bottom of a wide saucepan that has a tight lid. Add water, butter, salt, and bring to a boil. Cover, and cook slowly until liquid has evaporated and carrots are almost tender, about 20 minutes.

3. Bring cream to a boil in a small saucepan, and pour over the carrots. Simmer slowly, uncovered, until cream has been almost absorbed by the carrots or until the carrots are tender. Do not overcook.

4. Just before serving, add the softened butter, pepper, and, if you like, 1 tablespoon of mixed minced parsley, chervil, and chives; or half a tablespoon of summer savory or minced basil, or a pinch of minced fresh, or dried, thyme. Toss lightly until butter has melted and serve.

Serves six to eight.

GLAZED CARROTS AU CITRON

5 cups carrots
1-1/2 cups beef stock or bouillon
2 tablespoons sugar
6 tablespoons butter

2 teaspoons strained lemon juice
Salt and pepper
2 tablespoons minced parsley

1. Cook carrots as for Carrots in Cream. Then simmer in stock or bouillon with sugar, butter, and lemon juice until they are completely tender and the liquid has reduced to a syrup.

2. Add salt and pepper to taste, roll carrots gently in the syrup until glazed on all sides, and serve sprinkled with parsley.

Serves six to eight.

DIDI'S CARROT AND RAISIN SALAD

2/3 cup seedless raisins
2 cups coarsely grated raw carrots
Mayonnaise

1 small onion
1 teaspoon lemon juice
Salt

1. Plump raisins in hot water for 5 minutes. Drain and dry.

2. Moisten carrots with mayonnaise to taste. Using fine side of grater, grate the onion over the carrots. Stir in raisins and lemon juice, and toss well. Salt to taste. Chill two hours before serving. Children and most adults will eat this by the pound!

Serves six.

MRS. BARTLETT'S CARROT MARMALADE

2 cups thinly sliced lemon
Rind of 1 orange, cut up
2 cups raw carrots, shredded
4 cups water

4 cups sugar
1/4 cup maraschino cherries,
  halved

1. Combine lemon, orange rind, carrots, and water in a glass bowl; let stand overnight. After breakfast bring the mixture to a boil and cook, covered, for about 20 minutes.

2. Add the sugar, stir until it melts, then cook, stirring quite rapidly until the syrup sheets on a spoon. Stir in cherries. Pour into hot sterilized jars, leaving 1/8-inch headroom. Seal with hot paraffin.

Makes four to five 8-ounce jars.

CARROT COOKIES

My children love to make these, but you should see the kitchen afterward!

1/8 teaspoon baking soda
1/2 cup honey
1/2 cup butter
1 egg, slightly beaten
1 cup sifted flour
1 teaspoon baking powder

1/8 teaspoon salt
1 cup quick-cooking oatmeal
1/2 cup chopped nuts
1/2 cup seedless raisins
1/2 cup grated raw carrot
1 teaspoon vanilla

1. Preheat oven to 250 degrees.
2. Stir baking soda into the honey. Cream the butter, beat the egg into it. Add the honey mixture.
3. Sift flour, baking powder, and salt into the honey-and-butter mixture, and mix well. Fold oatmeal, nuts, raisins, and grated carrots into the mixture, and add the vanilla.
4. Drop by the teaspoon onto a greased cookie sheet. Bake for 12 minutes, or until golden brown.
Makes about 50 cookies.

GRATINÉE OF CAULIFLOWER WITH WATERCRESS

1 medium cauliflower
2 cups milk
2 tablespoons butter
3 tablespoons flour
1/2 cup mixed grated Parmesan
and Swiss cheese

Salt and pepper
Paprika or nutmeg
4 tablespoons bread crumbs
2 tablespoons melted butter
2 cups crisped tips of young
watercress

1. Soak cauliflower, head down, in cold water for 5 minutes. Break into small florets of fairly uniform size. Cut out any really thick stem parts.
2. Bring milk to a boil in a heavy kettle, toss in florets and simmer about 5 minutes, or until they are almost tender. Drain, reserving milk. Keep cauliflower warm.
3. Preheat oven to 375 degrees.
4. Melt butter in an enameled saucepan, stir in flour, and the cauliflower milk, plus enough more milk to make 2 cups. Simmer, stirring for 5 minutes. Remove from heat and beat in grated cheese, salt, pepper, and paprika or nutmeg to taste.
5. Butter a baking dish, spread one-third of the sauce over the

bottom of the dish, and stand the florets up in it. Pour over them the rest of the cream sauce, sprinkle with the crumbs, and dribble on the melted butter. Cook in the lowest third of the oven long enough to brown the crumbs lightly, 15 to 20 minutes. Set the baking dish on a plate and serve wreath of watercress around it.
Serves six.

CAULIFLOWER SALAD

1 medium-sized fresh cauliflower
Oil-and-Vinegar Dressing
1 teaspoon fresh chervil, minced

1. Prepare cauliflower as for Gratinée of Cauliflower but cook in water and drain and dry while florets are still quite firm. Shake dry over heat. Arrange in a salad bowl.

2. Pour Oil-and-Vinegar Dressing, or your own favorite oil-and-vinegar combination, over the warm cauliflower and sprinkle with the chervil. Marinate at room temperature until cool, then chill, covered, in refrigerator until time to serve.
Serves four to six.

CAULIFLOWER AND SHRIMP SALAD

1 pound fresh or frozen shrimp
2 cups boiling water
1 tablespoon salt
1 bay leaf
1 pinch thyme

1 slice onion
1 medium cauliflower
1/2 cup Oil-and-Vinegar Dressing
1/2 cup hot melted butter or
 olive oil

1. Drop shrimp into the boiling water with the salt, bay leaf, thyme, and onion, and poach until tender, about 5 minutes.

2. Prepare florets as for Gratinée of Cauliflower, and in the last few minutes of cooking, set a few tiny tender cauliflower leaves on top of the florets to steam. Drain. Pick off cauliflower leaves and set aside. Shake florets dry over heat.

3. Pour Oil-and-Vinegar Dressing into salad bowl, and toss drained, still warm shrimp in it. Add florets and toss again. Garnish with the leaves and pour the melted butter or olive oil over all. Serve with Butter Biscuits and a chilled Graves wine.
Serves four.

BEEF, CAULIFLOWER, AND SNOW PEAS

Edible pea pods, called snow peas in the Orient, are a delicious home-garden crop.

2 tablespoons vegetable oil
1 clove garlic
1 pound beef, sliced thin and cut
  into strips
4 tablespoons chopped onion
2 teaspoons salt
Pepper

1 cup chicken stock or bouillon
1 cup cauliflower florets
1 cup edible pea pods, stemmed
1 tablespoon cornstarch
2 tablespoons soy sauce
1/4 cup water

1. Heat oil in a wok, an electric fry pan, or a large heavy skillet until quite hot. Brown garlic in it, then discard the clove. Add the beef, toss quickly, and sauté 20 seconds. Add the onion, salt and pepper, and sauté another 10 seconds, tossing.

2. Heat the chicken stock or bouillon, pour into the skillet, and bring quickly to a boil. Add cauliflower florets a few at a time, so the water will not stop boiling. Add peas and cook, stirring, for another 5 minutes or until florets are tender *but not limp.*

3. Mix soy sauce and water with cornstarch, add to the skillet, and stir until the sauce thickens. Then turn meat and vegetables into a shallow bowl and serve immediately with boiled rice on the side. With cauliflower fresh from the garden, this dish is marvelous.

Serves four.

CELERIAC À LA FRANÇAISE

3 medium celeriac
1 teaspoon lemon juice
3 medium potatoes
1/2 cup hot milk

3 tablespoons butter
Salt
Minced parsley

1. Wash and peel celeriac and cut into slices 1/8 inch thick. Soak 5 minutes in cold water and lemon juice. Cover with boiling water and cook until partly tender.

2. Pare and slice potatoes in 1/4-inch rounds, add to the celeriac and cook until both vegetables are tender. Drain and shake over heat to dry.

3. Mash vegetables until fluffy, beat in hot milk, beat in half of the butter, and salt to taste. Place in heated serving dish and garnish with dabs of remaining butter and a little parsley.

Serves six.

AUNT ANDRÉE'S CELERIAC HORS D'OEUVRE

2 medium celeriac
2 tablespoons strained lemon juice
Salt
3 to 4 tablespoons Maille or
　Dijon mustard
2 tablespoons boiling water

1/3 cup olive oil
2 tablespoons white wine vinegar
6 hard-cooked eggs
1/2 cup mayonnaise
Minced chervil or parsley

1.　Peel the celeriac and cut into thin strips. Toss in a bowl with the lemon juice and a little salt, and marinate.

2.　Set a mixing bowl that narrows at the bottom over a kettle half-filled with boiling water. Put the mustard into the bottom of the bowl and whip in the boiling water, a little at a time. Beat in the oil, drop by drop, then the vinegar. Season to taste.

3.　Rinse the celeriac in cold water, drain, and shake dry over heat, but don't cook. Toss in the mustard sauce, until the celeriac is well-coated, cover, and marinate for several hours.

4.　Shell the eggs and slice into rounds.

5.　On each hors d'oeuvre plate arrange a bed of sliced eggs, pile marinated celeriac on top, and decorate with a spoonful of firm mayonnaise and a sprinkling of chervil or parsley.
Serves six.

CELERIAC CASSEROLE, MADAME MALRAUX

2 small celery roots
1 cooking apple
1 teaspoon lemon juice
6 to 8 medium potatoes
1/2 pound grated Parmesan or
　Swiss cheese

12 Weisswurst or Bratwurst
　sausages
2/3 cup butter
1/2 cup beef stock or bouillon
Salt

1.　Preheat oven to 350 degrees.

2.　Peel roots, core and peel apple. Soak both in cold water with the lemon juice for 5 to 10 minutes. Peel potatoes. Slice potatoes, celery roots, and apple into thin slices of the same size, but keep separate.

3.　Butter a large baking dish. First put in a layer of potatoes. Then layers of cheese, celeriac, apple, and sausages. Repeat layers, ending with a top layer of potatoes and a sprinkling of cheese. Dot with butter, and moisten with stock or bouillon, lightly salted.

4. Bake for about 1 hour, or until a fork easily pierces through the layers. Serve with chilled, sparkling cider and Dilled Green Beans.

Serves six.

GREEN CELERIAC SOUP

1 celeriac root	1 slice of onion
1 large potato	2 cups large green peas
1 teaspoon lemon juice	2 tablespoons butter
2 cups milk	Salt
2 cups cold water	Paprika

1. Wash and peel celeriac and potato. Cut into 1/4-inch strips and soak in cold water with lemon juice for 5 minutes.

2. Heat milk to simmering, add the drained celeriac and potato, and simmer 13 to 15 minutes, or until tender; then mash together.

3. Bring water to a boil, drop in the onion and peas and simmer, uncovered, until peas are quite tender, about 10 minutes.

4. Put the peas with their cooking liquid into a blender and purée until smooth. Beat the purée into the celeriac and potato. Add butter; salt to taste. Serve with a sprinkle of paprika.

Serves six to eight.

CELERY GUACAMOLE
A delicious hors-d'oeuvre

8 to 12 celery stalks	Paprika
1 ripe avocado	1 tablespoon minced celery leaves
1 teaspoon crushed onion	1/3 cup mayonnaise
1/2 small garlic clove, crushed	Salt
1 dash Tabasco sauce, optional	

1. Pare strings from large celery stalks and cut off tops, but save a few of the smaller leaves. Wash in cold water, roll firmly into a damp towel, chill.

2. Prepare the avocado mixture earlier, if you like, so that you have only to put ingredients together just before guests arrive. Quarter the avocado, scoop out the meat, mash with a fork, add the onion, garlic, Tabasco, paprika, minced celery leaves, and salt.

Beat all this together and turn into a small bowl. Spread over it a thin layer of about half the mayonnaise, which should be very stiff. This prevents air from darkening the avocado. Cut celery stalks in halves or thirds and refrigerate all until ready to use.

3. Mix the layer of mayonnaise in the Guacamole, and stuff the celery stalks. Cover the filling with the remaining mayonnaise to keep it from discoloring. Serve immediately.

Makes 16 to 30 pieces.

LAZY-DAY CELERY SOUP
A subtle soup, easy to prepare

2 cups 1-inch pieces celery
1 tablespoon butter
1 teaspoon minced shallot or
  onion

3 cups hot milk
Salt and pepper
1 tablespoon butter

1. Chill the celery.
2. Melt butter in the top of a double boiler, add shallot or onion, and simmer. Add milk and celery, and simmer until celery is tender, about 1 hour.
3. Put celery and some of the milk into the blender, and whip at low speed until creamed. Return to the double boiler to heat, add salt and pepper, and stir. Pour into soup bowls and dot with butter.

Serves four to six.

GOOD BRAISED CELERY
An excellent vegetable with a roast of beef

16 celery stalks
2 tablespoons bacon drippings or
  butter
1/4 cup sliced onion
1/4 cup carrot rounds

3 cups beef stock or bouillon
1 bay leaf
2 whole cloves
8 peppercorns
Salt

1. Preheat oven to 375 degrees.
2. Wash celery, trim off tops, cut into 3-inch pieces.
3. Heat drippings or butter in a 2-quart baking dish. Add the onion, carrots, and celery. Toss to coat, and simmer 5 minutes. Add stock or bouillon, bay leaf, cloves, peppercorns, and salt to taste. Bring to a boil, then put into the oven and bake, covered,

until tender, about 40 minutes. (I sometimes toss in a little leftover dry Vermouth just to empty a bottle.)

4. Remove vegetables from the baking dish, boil to reduce liquid until there is just enough to coat the celery. Serve in a heated dish.

Serves six to eight.

CELERY À LA CHINOISE

A fine way to cook celery at the last moment for a company meal. But try it for your family first.

1 small bunch celery	2 tablespoons soy sauce
1/4 cup fresh mushrooms	1 teaspoon salt
2 tablespoons vegetable oil	1 teaspoon sugar

1. Wash celery, pare off any strings, and cut stalks into half-inch strips.

2. Heat oil in a wok, an electric fry pan, or heavy skillet until almost smoking. Toss in mushrooms, coat quickly with oil, then add the soy sauce, salt, and sugar. Mix well with mushrooms, stir a few seconds, then add the celery. Cook, stirring continuously, 2 to 4 minutes. Serve very hot.

Serves two to six.

STUFFED CHARD RIBS PAYSANNE

14 to 16 chard ribs	1/4 teaspoon salt
1-1/2 pounds ground lamb	1/8 teaspoon pepper
shoulder	5 tablespoons olive oil
3 eggs	6 tablespoons lemon juice
3/4 cup sifted flour	

1. Wash the chard and cut off the leafy part. You can save it to cook later the same way as spinach. Trim off and discard the toughest parts of the stalks, clean the ribs, and cut into 4-inch lengths.

2. Mix the lamb, 2 eggs, 2 teaspoons of the flour, and salt and pepper. Stuff the ribs with this mixture.

3. Beat the remaining egg. Dip the filled side of each rib into the egg, then into the remaining flour.

4. Heat 3 tablespoons of olive oil in a skillet and brown the filled side of the ribs over medium-high heat. As you finish them, lay them in layers in a casserole. When all are browned, pour re-

maining oil over the ribs, sprinkle with lemon juice, and add water to cover. Simmer, covered, over very low heat for about 2 hours. Serves four.

CORN ON THE COB, THE RIGHT WAY

2 to 4 ears corn per person
4 quarts water
1 tablespoon salt

1 small square stale bread per person
1 large pat fresh butter or more per person

1. Set hot water to boil in a large kettle. Add salt and turn heat high.
2. Go out to the corn patch. Pick the ripe corn, then run back to the kitchen. Remove husks, rub silk off gently with a stiff-bristled brush, and break off empty tips and long stumps so ears are of uniform size and fit the kettle easily.
3. Place the corn in rapidly boiling water. Bring water back to a boil, cover. Young corn should be cooked in a scant 8 to 10 minutes, perhaps less. More mature corn may take a minute or two longer. Remember that the corn keeps on cooking as it sits piled on the serving platter for at least a minute or two. So don't overcook in the kettle.
4. Serve at once. For family meals we give each person a small square of stale white bread holding a big lump of butter; a comfortable and economical way to butter the ears. (The butter can already be salted and peppered so the corn is ready to eat in one easy operation.)

EASY CORN FRITTERS

4 or 5 ears uncooked corn
2 eggs
1 teaspoon minced green pepper
1/4 teaspoon salt

Freshly ground black pepper
4 to 6 tablespoons Clarified Butter
Salt

1. Score the rows of kernels with a paring knife, then squeeze out pulp by pressing the blunt side of the knife down on the rows.
2. Beat eggs until thick and lemon colored, and don't skimp on the beating. Add the green pepper, salt, and pepper. (I use quite a lot of pepper for this recipe.) Whip the beaten egg mixture into the corn.

3. Heat the Clarified Butter in a heavy skillet, drop the corn mixture into it by tablespoons, and sauté until golden brown on both sides. Serve very hot with broiled chicken, a mixed green salad, and a bottle of chilled Liebfraumilch.

Serves four.

CORN PUDDING
Wonderful for a buffet meal featuring glazed ham

2 cups fresh corn kernels
4 egg yolks
Salt and freshly ground pepper
1 teaspoon sugar
1 small green pepper, minced
Paprika

Nutmeg
2 tablespoons sifted flour
1 teaspoon baking powder
2 tablespoons butter, melted
2 cups milk, scalded
4 egg whites

1. Preheat oven to 325 degrees. Score corn as for Easy Corn Fritters, and press out pulp until you have 2 cups of it.

2. Beat egg yolks until thick and lemon colored, add to the corn, beating it in with salt and pepper, sugar, minced green pepper, paprika, and nutmeg. Mix with flour, baking powder, and melted butter; then whip in the milk.

3. Beat egg whites until stiff but not dry, and fold into the corn mixture. Turn into a 2-quart buttered baking dish, set in hot water in the bottom third of the oven, and bake until a knife inserted in the middle comes out clean, about 45 minutes.

Serves six to eight.

CRACKERJACK POPCORN

1/2 cup dried corn kernels
2 tablespoons vegetable oil
1/2 teaspoon salt
2/3 cup molasses
1-1/2 cups sugar

1 teaspoon vinegar
1/2 cup water
1/2 teaspoon salt
3 tablespoons butter
3 cups roasted peanuts

1. Put on a pair of clean garden gloves, then rub the kernels from dried corn by twisting ears back and forth as though you were wringing a dishcloth. Measure out half a cup.

2. In a heavy kettle—I use my pressure cooker with the lid set loosely on top—heat oil until almost smoking. Drop in kernels, shake to coat with the oil, and cover loosely. Turn heat high and

cook, shaking kettle continually until you hear the kernels begin to bounce against the lid. Reduce heat a little and continue cooking, shaking all the while, until popping sounds stop. Turn off heat and remove lid at once. Toss the popped corn with salt and turn into buttered glass bowl.

3. In a heavy saucepan, combine molasses, sugar, vinegar, water, and salt. Stir over low heat until mixture begins to boil. Cook without stirring until heat reaches 270 degrees, or the hard-ball stage on your candy thermometer. Remove from heat, stir in the butter, mix well with a wooden spoon, and pour over popped corn, taking care to coat all kernels. Throw in the peanuts. Toss all together until nuts are fairly evenly distributed through the corn. Now break into chunks and let cool.

Makes 8 cups.

CUCUMBER AND VEAL SCALLOPS

1 large cucumber
1 cup boiling water
1 tablespoon vegetable oil
2 tablespoons butter

4 thin veal scallops
1 tablespoon strained lemon juice
1/2 pint heavy cream
Salt and paprika

1. Peel the cucumber and cut into 8 sticks. Place in 1 cup of rapidly boiling water, simmer uncovered about 4 minutes, or until tender. Drain, shake dry over heat, keep warm.

2. Spread oil over the bottom of a heavy skillet, melt the butter, heat to frothing, and then lower the heat and add the scallops. ("Scallops" are slices of meat 3/8 of an inch thick which have been pounded to a 1/4 inch thickness.) Cook scallops over a moderately fast heat for about 4 minutes on each side. Sprinkle with lemon juice, then place in a warmed serving platter.

3. Turn heat very low, add cream, mix with juices in bottom of the pan, season with salt and paprika. Add cucumbers, baste quickly with cream, place on the serving platter, and pour the cream sauce over all. Serve very hot with buttered wild rice, a peppery watercress salad, and a chilled rosé wine.

Serves four.

CUCUMBER SOUP
A fine soup for a hot day

1/3 pound butter	Fresh grated pepper
1 small onion, minced	2 egg yolks
4 cucumbers, peeled and sliced thin	1 tablespoon cooking sherry
3 tablespoons flour	1 cup heavy cream
6 cups hot chicken or veal stock	Salt
	3 tablespoons minced parsley

1. Melt butter in an enameled saucepan, add onion and cucumbers, and stir with a wooden spoon until just tender but not browned. Sprinkle with flour and mix well. Add the stock, a little at a time. Bring to a boil, grind pepper over the mixture, turn heat low, and simmer 10 minutes.

2. Purée in a blender, or mash through a sieve.

3. Beat egg yolks in a large bowl until thick and lemon colored. Add sherry, then cream, and mix. Beat the cucumbers into the eggs. Reheat. Add salt to taste, sprinkle parsley in soup bowls, and pour in hot soup, or serve it chilled.

Serves six to eight.

ICY SUMMER SALAD
A delicious cold salad to serve with charcoal-broiled steak on a hot August day

3 to 4 cucumbers	2 tablespoons tarragon vinegar or lemon juice
Salt	Salt and paprika
1/2 cup sour cream, chilled	Dill, optional

1. Peel cucumbers and cut into thin slices. Arrange in layers in a bowl, lightly salting each layer. Cover with plastic, put a weight on top, and set in the refrigerator for 3 to 6 hours. During this time drain off the cucumber water once or twice. The cucumbers should be dry before using.

2. Toss in a chilled bowl with the sour cream and the chilled tarragon vinegar. Check the flavoring and add a little salt and paprika, if you like, but usually none is needed. I snip quite a lot of dill over the cucumbers.

Serves six to eight.

BREAD-AND-BUTTER PICKLES

6 quarts cucumber slices (24 to 30
   small cucumbers)
6 medium onions, sliced thin
3/4 cup salt
2 cups water

1 quart white vinegar
4 cups sugar
3 tablespoons celery seed
3 tablespoons mustard seed

1. Wash cucumbers, cut into quarter-inch slices but do not peel,
and measure to 6 quarts. Arrange slices in layers with the onions
in an earthenware crock or bowl. Sprinkle each layer with salt.
Cover and let stand 3 hours. Drain off juice as it accumulates.

2. Combine water, vinegar, sugar, celery, and mustard seeds.
Set over moderate heat, stirring until sugar dissolves. Boil for 3 minutes. Add cucumbers to liquid, bring back to boiling, but do not
boil.

3. Pack at once into hot sterilized jars and cap. Process in boiling water for 5 minutes. Cool on racks.

Makes about 4 quarts.

KOSHER DILL PICKLES

50 3-inch cucumbers
3 quarts water
3 cups salt

For each quart jar:

2 bay leaves, crumbled
1/4 teaspoon celery seed
1/2 teaspoon whole mixed spices
1 tablespoon cider vinegar

2 cloves garlic
Bunch dried dill
2 grape leaves

1. Wash and drain cucumbers, and pack into sterilized quart
jars. To each jar, add the bay leaves, celery seed, spices, vinegar, and
garlic.

2. Bring water and salt to a boil, and fill the packed jars. Top
each jar with a cluster of dill, and cover with grape leaves. These
help to preserve the green cucumber color. Seal and process in
boiling water for 15 minutes. Cool on racks.

Makes 5 to 6 quarts.

MESS OF GREENS

12 cups dandelion greens	Butter
1/2 pound salt pork or thick-sliced bacon	Salt and pepper

1. Wash, crisp, and drain the greens.
2. Cut salt pork or bacon into small pieces, and throw into a heated wok, electric fry pan, or heavy skillet. When half cooked, add the wet greens, stirring quickly to coat with bacon fat and to wilt. Simmer about 20 minutes more, or until tender. Keep warm in a heated serving bowl. Chop in butter, and salt and pepper to taste. Serve hot.

I sometimes top this with a poached egg and serve with French bread and butter as a main luncheon course.

Serves six to eight.

DANDELION FLOWER OMELET

1-1/2 cups fresh dandelion flowers	8 eggs
1 cup dandelion greens	1/2 teaspoon dry mustard
2 tablespoons olive oil	4 tablespoons flat beer, or water
1 tablespoon fresh chervil	2 tablespoons butter
Salt	2 tablespoons melted butter
Paprika	Salt

1. Pick just-opened flowers and yellow inside leaves of plants. Wash and dry, and slice all the stems from the flowers.
2. Simmer the flowers in olive oil in an omelet pan; when they are almost tender, add chervil, salt, and paprika. Lift from the pan with a slotted spoon and keep warm.
3. Break the eggs into a large bowl, two at a time, beat to a froth with mustard and 1 tablespoon of the beer or water. Heat the pan almost to smoking. Add a bit of butter; when it stops frothing, pour in the eggs. Stir until omelet is almost dry, add one-fourth of the dandelion flowers, fold omelet, cook a minute more, and slide onto a heated platter. Make 3 more omelets this way. Then top each with a bit of butter and chervil, and serve on the greens, which have been dredged in the 2 tablespoons of melted butter and salted.

Serves four.

DANDELION AND LETTUCE SALAD

4 cups lettuce thinnings
4 cups dandelion greens, packed
4 small onions
1/2 green pepper
1/3 pound Swiss cheese

Salt and black pepper
3 tablespoons olive oil
4 tablespoons vinegar
2 medium tomatoes
2 hard-cooked eggs

Wash and crisp lettuce and greens; cut into small pieces with onions, green peppers, and cheese. Add salt and black pepper, mix well. Add olive oil and vinegar. Mix again, then add peeled and quartered tomatoes and the eggs, sliced. Toss gently, so tomatoes and eggs stay intact, and serve.
Serves six to eight.

OLD-FASHIONED DANDELION WINE

Dandelion wine is quite sweet, and makes a delightful before-dinner apéritif served over ice cubes and cut with 1/3 sparkling soda.

2-1/2 gallons dandelion blossoms
6 oranges

10 pounds sugar
4 to 4-1/2 gallons lukewarm water

1. Pick only newly opened perfect dandelion blossoms, and avoid including any of the stem. I find a large brown paper grocery bag holds about 2 gallons of blossoms.
2. In the bottom of a 5-gallon crock layer the blossoms, 1 unpeeled orange sliced into thin rings, and sugar. Repeat 6 times and top with any remaining sugar. The crock should be half full. Fill the crock with water, cover with a clean cloth, and keep at room temperature until the liquid stops bubbling, or "working." Two or three weeks later, when it becomes absolutely still, strain through 2 thicknesses of cheesecloth, bottle, and cap.
Makes about 16 to 18 quarts.

DUTCH DANDELION SALAD

10 cups tender dandelion greens
4 slices bacon
1/4 cup butter
1/2 cup cream
2 eggs

1 tablespoon sugar
4 tablespoons vinegar
1 teaspoon salt
Paprika

1. Wash, crisp, and dry the greens, and arrange in a large salad bowl; place in the warming oven.
2. Cut bacon into cubes, fry quickly, and drop over the dandelions.
3. Melt butter in an enameled saucepan, add cream, and heat a little. Beat eggs until light. Add sugar, vinegar, salt, and paprika. Beat a little of the hot cream mixture into the eggs, then pour eggs back into the cream and cook, stirring very gently, until the mixture begins to look like custard. Don't overheat and make scrambled eggs!
4. Pour at once over the dandelion greens, toss well, and serve with hot Butter Biscuits.

Serves six to eight.

EGGPLANT CASSEROLE

2 small eggplants
Salt
1/4 cup butter
4 tablespoons flour
1 cup cream, heated

2 7-ounce cans of minced clams
Salt and pepper
1/4 cup bread crumbs
2 tablespoons butter

1. Preheat oven to 325 degrees.
2. Peel eggplant, cut into chunks, and cook in lightly salted water until tender. Drain, shake dry over heat, and mash.
3. Melt butter in an enameled saucepan, stir in flour, add the cream, and beat with a whisk until smooth. Add clam juice and clams, and simmer, stirring until thick and smooth. Very gently fold in the eggplant, and add salt and pepper.
4. Pour into a 2-quart buttered baking dish, sprinkle with bread crumbs, dot with butter, and bake 45 minutes.

Serves four to six.

GAY'S EGGPLANT SALAD

1 medium eggplant	1 sprig dill, snipped
1/2 cup diced celery	1/4 teaspoon oregano
1/3 cup canned pimiento strips	1/3 cup olive oil
1 clove garlic, minced	1/3 cup wine vinegar
2 tablespoons chopped capers	1/2 teaspoon salt
2 tablespoons minced parsley	1/8 teaspoon pepper

Wash and stem the eggplant, drop into boiling water, and cook from 12 to 20 minutes, until tender. Cool, peel, cut into 1-inch cubes. Turn into a large salad bowl with all the other ingredients; toss to mix well, cover, and refrigerate for a day if possible before serving. Gay serves this with a shish kebab, rice pilaf, and Bardolino.
Serves six to eight.

TURKISH "CAVIAR"

1 medium eggplant	Olive oil
1 tablespoon grated onion	Strained lemon juice
1 garlic clove, crushed	Salt and pepper
2 tomatoes	

1. Preheat oven to 350 degrees.
2. Wash eggplant and place unpeeled on foil on a cookie sheet. Bake until cooked through, an hour or more. Split, scoop out the center, and mash through a stainless-steel strainer. Add grated onion and crushed garlic.
3. Peel tomatoes, slice, let the juice drain off. Add to the eggplant mixture, and chop to a fine pulp. Beat in the salad oil and lemon juice; salt and pepper to taste. Serve as spread for cocktail crackers, or on cups of lettuce as a first course.

QUICHE AUX ENDIVES

4 cups chopped and sliced Belgian
  endives
1-1/2 tablespoons butter
1/4 teaspoon salt
1/8 cup water
1 teaspoon lemon juice
3 eggs

1-1/2 cups heavy cream
1/8 teaspoon mace
Pepper
8-inch unbaked pastry shell
1/4 cup grated Swiss cheese
1 tablespoon butter

1. Preheat oven to 325 degrees.

2. Layer sliced endives in a 2-quart heavily buttered baking dish. Add the salt to the water, stir in lemon juice, and pour over the endives. Make a round of brown paper, butter it, and place it over the endives. Cover the dish and bake in the oven for 20 to 30 minutes, or until just tender.

3. While the endives are baking, beat the eggs until thick and lemon colored, and beat in cream, mace, and pepper.

4. Remove endives from oven and drain. Raise oven temperature to 375 degrees. Fold endives into egg mixture, pour into the pastry shell, sprinkle with cheese, and dot with butter. Bake in the upper part of the oven for 25 to 30 minutes. I consider a quiche too filling for an appetizer and prefer to serve it as a luncheon dish.

Serves four to six.

SUMMER PORCH SUPPER

4 cups shredded leaf lettuce or
  escarole
6 large Belgian endives
Oil-and-Vinegar Dressing
3 pounds veal, cut very thin
Salt
1 tablespoon lemon juice

1 cup light dry white wine
1/2 teaspoon thyme
1/3 cup vegetable oil
1/3 cup olive oil
1/3 cup butter
Hollandaise Sauce

1. Crisp the lettuce and turn into a salad bowl. Break off the ends of endives, separate leaves, and wipe each with a damp paper towel. Add to the salad bowl. Pour Oil-and-Vinegar Dressing over all. Chill.

2. Cut veal into strips about 2 inches long. Salt lightly. Combine the lemon juice, wine, and thyme, and marinate the meat in the mixture for at least 2 hours.

3. Heat the oils and butter in a small saucepan, adding a little of the marinade.

4. At serving time, pour the oil, butter, and wine mixture into a fondue dish, light the candle under it, and take it to the dinner table with the veal strips and the salad. Give everyone an individual bowl of Hollandaise and a fondue fork. Let each one cook his own meat in the fondue dish, fishing it out with his fork, and adding Hollandaise Sauce to taste. Serve hot Butter Biscuits or crisped French bread and a nice Orvieto wine with this supper.

Serves five to eight.

FINE GARLIC SOUP

2 large heads of garlic	4 sprigs parsley
2 quarts cold water	3 tablespoons olive oil
2 tablespoons salt	3 egg yolks
Freshly ground black pepper	4 tablespoons melted butter
2 whole cloves	6 to 8 pieces of stale French bread,
1/4 teaspoon sage	buttered
1/4 teaspoon thyme	1/2 cup grated Swiss cheese

1. Separate the garlic cloves, scald, and slip off the skins.

2. Pour cold water into a soup kettle and add garlic, salt, pepper, cloves, sage, thyme, parsley, and oil. Bring to a boil and simmer 30 minutes.

3. Beat egg yolks until thick and lemon colored. Beat in the melted butter, drop by drop. Strain the soup a little at a time into the egg yolks, beating after each addition.

4. Place a piece of buttered French bread in the bottom of each soup bowl with a little grated cheese. Pour the soup and serve hot. This doesn't really taste like garlic, and it tastes very good. But I have never found a good description of its flavor. You try.

Serves six to eight.

AIOLI

The recipe for this garlic mayonnaise is given in the Sauce section, page 193.

GARLIC DRESSING

This also is given under Sauces, page 194.

GARLIC SOUP PAYSANNE

4 cups beef stock or bouillon
3 tablespoons butter
1 small clove garlic, minced

4 thick slices stale French bread
4 teaspoons minced parsley

1. Heat stock or bouillon (which can be made by dissolving 6 beef bouillon cubes to 4 cups of water).

2. Melt the butter in heavy skillet, stir in the garlic, and lightly sauté the bread on both sides. Place a piece in each heated soup bowl with a teaspoon of parsley on top.

3. Pour hot stock or bouillon over the bread, and let stand a minute or two while the bread absorbs the liquid and is softened, but don't let it stand too long or the bread gets soggy. This soup *does* taste like garlic.

Serves six.

PICKLED HORSERADISH

2 cups grated horseradish root
Salt and pepper

White vinegar to cover
1/4 teaspoon dry mustard

1. Wash roots, scrape away most of the skin, and cut out any discolored spots.

2. Grate roots on a fine grater, sprinkle with salt and pepper, and pack lightly into a sterilized jar. Fill with the vinegar, mix in the mustard, seal, and store in a cool place.

Makes 1 pint.

HOT HORSERADISH SAUCE

1/2 cup grated horseradish
1 teaspoon flour
Salt
Paprika

3/4 cup heavy cream
1 tablespoon butter
1 egg yolk

1. In a small ceramic cooking dish, combine horseradish, flour, salt, and paprika. Add cream and butter and cook very, very slowly, stirring constantly, until the mixture thickens. Remove from heat.

2. Beat egg yolk a little, stir in a *little* of the hot sauce, beat quickly, then blend the egg mixture into horseradish. Cook half a minute more and serve. This is a marvelous sauce with a roast or boiled beef.

Makes about 1-1/2 cups.

ICED HORSERADISH

1 cup heavy cream
1/2 teaspoon salt
I teaspoon paprika

2 tablespoons grated fresh
  horseradish
1 tablespoon lemon juice

1. Fill a large bowl with cracked ice. Set a smaller bowl in it and whip the cream in this. Then stir in the salt, paprika, horseradish, and lemon juice. Serve immediately.

Makes about 1 cup.

JERUSALEM ARTICHOKES BÉCHAMEL

6 to 8 Jerusalem artichokes
2 tablespoons lemon juice
1 quart boiling water
1/4 cup light cream

1 cup Sauce Béchamel
Salt and pepper
Minced parsley

1. Wash and peel artichokes, and cut into the shape of large olives. Add lemon juice to the water, and cook artichokes until just tender. Drain, shake dry over heat, and keep warm in a serving dish.

2. Thin the Sauce Béchamel with cream, heat, and stir in the artichokes. Then return artichokes and sauce to the serving dish. Garnish with parsley.

Serves four to six.

STIR-FRIED KALE

8 cups fresh kale
3 to 4 tablespoons vegetable oil
Salt and pepper

1. Wash the kale, tear off the green part of leaves, discard the stalks, and drain.

2. Heat the oil in a wok, an electric fry pan, or a heavy skillet. The oil should be almost smoking. Throw in the kale, keep tossing and stirring until it wilts completely. Stir-cook another 5 minutes. This is an excellent vegetable side dish for an Oriental menu; it is also a tangy accompaniment for any creamed casserole.

Serves four.

CREAMED KALE CASSEROLE

6 to 8 cups kale
Salt
1 old potato
3/4 cup Sauce Béchamel
1/4 cup milk

1 onion, slivered
2 tablespoons butter
1/2 cup grated Parmesan cheese
1/2 cup dry bread crumbs
2 hard-cooked eggs

1. Preheat oven to 375 degrees.
2. Wash kale, tear off green part of leaves, and discard stalks. Chop the leaves and then cook 10 minutes in a little boiling water. Drain and shake dry over heat. Salt to taste.
2. Peel the potato, pare off very thin slices with a potato-peeler, and set in cold water.
3. Thin the Sauce Béchamel with milk.
4. Sauté onion in butter until light brown. This can be done right in the baking dish. Stir in the kale, then lift out half of it. Over the kale remaining in the dish, spread a layer of potatoes. Pour half the sauce over potatoes. Turn in the rest of the kale and top with remaining sauce. Sprinkle cheese and breadcrumbs over the sauce, and bake, uncovered, for 15 minutes. Serve garnished with the eggs pressed through a ricer.
Serves four to six.

KALE BOHEMIAN STYLE
Nice with pickled beets topped with sour cream

2 pounds brisket of beef
4 cups kale
1/2 cup uncooked rice

2 medium potatoes
2 onions
1 teaspoon salt

1. Cut the meat into 6 portions and refrigerate.
2. Wash the kale quickly, tear off the green part of leaves, discard stalks, drain and chop coarsely. Chill. Peel potatoes and cut into pieces, as for French frying. Sliver the onions.
3. Turn all ingredients into a large heavy kettle, toss so they are well mixed, and simmer, covered, for 1-1/2 hours. The juice from the kale will probably provide enough moisture; if it doesn't, add a little water. The dish is ready when the rice is cooked.
Serves six.

KOHLRABI IN CREAM

8 small kohlrabi   1 tablespoon butter
1/2 cup water   4 tablespoons heavy cream
1/2 teaspoon salt

1. Wash kohlrabi, cut off tops, remove discolored leaves and tough parts of stems. Chop the greens, and peel and dice the bulbs.

2. Bring water to a boil, drop in the diced kohlrabi. Stir, then cover and simmer for 5 to 8 minutes, or until almost tender. Add salt, then the chopped greens, and cook, uncovered, until the greens are wilted. If some water remains, boil down or drain off.

3. Stir in the butter, stir in the cream, toss the greens and diced kohlrabi well in the sauce. This dish is particularly good with turkey or chicken.

Serves four to six.

KOHLRABI L'ENARDIÈRE

4 kohlrabi   1/2 teaspoon lemon juice
2 large potatoes   Salt
2 large carrots   Freshly ground black pepper
3 tablespoons butter

Peel and dice the three vegetables. Cover with boiling water, cover, and cook until almost tender, 10 to 15 minutes. Drain and shake dry over heat. Turn off heat and add butter, lemon juice, and salt. Toss to mix. Allow to "rest" partly covered until the meal is ready. Serve with poultry, pork roasts, or grilled meats.

Serves six to eight.

GREEN LEEK SOUP

This is the way leek soup is made in the Vendée, and I prefer it to the dressed-up refined version, which is *Gauloise*.

2 tablespoons butter	3 cups diced old potatoes
1 small onion, slivered	Salt
4 large or 6 small leeks	1 tablespoon butter
2 quarts water	1/2 cup heavy cream

1. Melt butter in a soup kettle, add onion and simmer until translucent.

2. Cut away root tops and toughest green parts of leeks, and slice lengthwise down the center. Separate the stalks, wash carefully, and cut lengthwise into strips.

3. Add the water to the onion, add potatoes, bring to a boil, and boil rapidly until potatoes are tender. Add leeks, boil rapidly, uncovered, until potatoes begin to thicken the soup. Don't overcook or this will taste like warmed-over mashed potatoes. In all, it should cook about 40 to 60 minutes.

4. Lower the heat, mash the vegetables with a potato masher until they have disintegrated and the leeks are stringy. Salt to taste. Stir in butter and cream and serve hot.

Serves six to eight.

SOUPE GAULOISE

2 tablespoons butter	2 quarts chicken stock or bouillon
1 very small onion, slivered	Salt
5 large or 8 small leeks	1 cup heavy cream
3 cups diced old potatoes	2 tablespoons chopped chives

Prepare and cook onion, leeks, and potatoes as for Green Leek Soup, but cut away *all* the green portion of the leeks. Put through the blender, 2 cups at a time, at low speed. Or mash through a sieve. Salt to taste and chill for several hours. You now have a leek and potato soup base. To make this Soupe Gauloise, add all the cream and garnish with chopped chives.

Serves six to eight.

POT-AU-FEU AUNT ANDRÉE

8 large leeks
1 tablespoon bacon drippings
1-1/2 pounds flank of beef
4 quarts cold water
4 chicken giblets
1 tablespoon salt
3 veal bones
2 pounds top round of beef

1 small onion
4 mushrooms
1/4 teaspoon each thyme, chervil,
   marjoram, peppercorns
1 crushed bay leaf
1 carrot
1 stalk celery

1. Remove root tip and toughest green parts of leek stalks. Wash carefully but do not separate stalks.
2. Melt bacon drippings in a heavy skillet and sear beef flank on both sides until dark brown. Place in a very large soup kettle. Swish some of the water around in the skillet, scraping up juices, and pour, with the remaining water, into soup kettle. Add giblets, salt, and bones, and bring to a boil. Skim surface repeatedly until scum stops forming. Then add all other ingredients, placing leeks last, neatly, on the top round. Simmer 2 hours, or until top round is tender.
3. At Aunt Andrée's table the meat and leeks and soup are ladled into very large soup bowls and eaten with forks and soup spoons. She serves it with French bread (but no butter), a dark green salad, and a nice red Bordeaux.
   Serves six to eight.

EARLY SPRING SALAD

1 head romaine lettuce
Equal amount of lettuce thinnings
1/4 cup wine vinegar

3/4 cup light cream, chilled
Salt and pepper

1. Wash romaine, tear into bits, and toss into salad bowl. Remove roots from lettuce thinnings, wash carefully, dry, and add to romaine. Place bowl in refrigerator to chill. Chill the vinegar.
2. Just before you serve dinner, mix the cream with vinegar and salt and pepper to taste.
3. Drain off any water that has accumulated in the salad bowl. Pour dressing over lettuce, serve, and toss at the table.
   Serves six to eight.

JAN'S SPRING LETTUCE SOUP

2 cups lettuce thinnings
6 cups canned beef consommé
1 tablespoon butter

1. Remove roots from tiny lettuce thinnings, wash in several changes of water, and dry.
2. Bring consommé to a boil. Toss in lettuce thinnings, turn off heat. Add butter and serve immediately.
Serves six.

LETTUCE À LA NORMANDE

8 cups garden lettuce or thinnings
1/2 teaspoon each of chopped
fresh chives, parsley, tarragon,
and chervil
5/8 cup heavy cream
1/8 cup strained lemon juice
Salt

1. Wash and crisp lettuce, or lettuce thinnings, from your garden. Place in a salad bowl, sprinkle with chopped fresh herbs, and chill.
2. Just before serving combine cream, lemon juice, and salt to taste. Pour over the lettuce, and toss at the table.
Serves six to eight.

ROSY LETTUCE SOUP

4 cups leaf lettuce
2 tablespoons butter
1 cup peeled and chopped
tomatoes
Salt and pepper
4 cups chicken stock or bouillon
1 teaspoon minced parsley or
chervil

1. Wash lettuce, dry, and shred. Heat the butter in a heavy kettle and throw in the lettuce. Cook at very low heat for about 5 minutes, stirring.
2. Add tomatoes to lettuce, and cook 5 minutes more. Season with salt and pepper.
3. Heat the stock or bouillon, pour over lettuce and tomatoes. Bring to a boil and simmer for 20 minutes. Serve hot garnished with parsley or chervil.
Serves six.

LETTUCE MELBOURNE

4 heads lettuce or 4 cups leaf
  lettuce
1 cup Sauce Béchamel
1/4 cup heavy cream
1 teaspoon salt

1/4 teaspoon curry powder
1/2 cup bread crumbs
1/2 cup chopped walnuts or
  filberts
2 tablespoons butter

1. Heat oven to 425 degrees.
2. Discard outer leaves of lettuce, quarter heads, and wash thoroughly. Turn into a colander and pour boiling water over the greens. Drain, and place in a kettle full of boiling water. Simmer until tender, about 5 minutes. Drain and shake dry over heat. Keep warm.
3. Thin the Sauce Béchamel with the cream and season with salt and curry powder. Heat gently until mixture boils, then simmer for 5 minutes.
4. Dry the lettuce again by shaking over heat, and place in a buttered baking dish. Pour the cream sauce over it, sprinkle with crumbs and nuts, dot with butter, and bake 15 minutes, uncovered, or until it browns.
Serves six to eight.

SOUR CREAM LETTUCE

1 head lettuce, or equivalent of
  leaf lettuce
1 teaspoon salt
2 hard-cooked egg yolks
1 teaspoon sugar
1/4 teaspoon salt

Pepper
1 tablespoon vinegar
1/2 cup sour cream
1 teaspoon chopped fennel
1/4 cup diced, unpeeled
  cucumber

1. Wash and crisp lettuce. Dry, sprinkle with salt, and chill for half an hour.
2. Put the remaining ingredients into a blender—except the fennel and cucumber—and beat until yolks have disappeared. Chill until ready to serve salad.
3. Arrange lettuce in a salad bowl, pour dressing over it, add the fennel and cucumber, and toss.
Serves six.

WATERMELON DESSERT COCKTAIL

4 cups watermelon balls
1/4 cup B&B or Cointreau
2 tablespoons strained lemon juice

1 tablespoon confectioner's sugar
2 cups heavy cream, whipped

1. Put the watermelon balls in a small bowl. Mix the B&B with the lemon juice. (If you use Cointreau, omit the lemon juice.) Pour over the melon balls and toss gently. Cover and chill well.

2. Serve in tall glass compotes with a sprinkling of half the sugar, and a dollop of whipped cream to which the rest of the sugar has been added.

Serves six.

PICKLED WATERMELON RIND

1 large watermelon
1/2 cup salt
3 quarts cold water
1 lemon, peeled
1-1/2 quarts boiling water
3 cups cider vinegar

6 cups sugar
3 tablespoons allspice
3 tablespoons whole cloves
1 tablespoon powdered mace
1 tablespoon whole mustard seeds
5 cinnamon sticks

1. Remove all pink meat from the watermelon and peel off the green rind. The melon should be slightly underripe. Cut into 1-inch squares, and measure. There should be 4 quarts.

2. Prepare a brine of the salt and 3 quarts of cold water. Put the rind in a crock and pour the brine over it. Cover and let stand overnight. Drain and rinse with fresh water.

3. Place in a deep kettle, cover with 3 quarts of cold water, and bring to a boil. Simmer until tender, about 10 minutes. Drain.

4. Bring 1-1/2 quarts water to a boil and add the lemon and all remaining ingredients. Bring to a boil. Add the watermelon rind and simmer until the rind becomes transparent, about 45 minutes.

5. Pour immediately into hot sterilized jars and seal at once.

MELON AND FRUIT COMBINATIONS

To serve with ice cream, preferably vanilla, or alone in tall chilled compotes, the edges rimmed with sugar as for champagne cocktails, combine:

1. strawberries, halved, with raspberries, red currants, slices of ripe peaches, and melon balls—all sprinkled with sugar

2. diced pineapple, stemmed-and-pitted black cherries, peeled seedless green grapes, and melon balls, topped with a mint leaf

3. mixed cantaloupe and honeydew melon balls marinated in 1 tablespoon lime juice, with a sprinkling of sugar.

To make melon balls, scoop out the meat with a rounded teaspoon or melon scoop.

To make melon baskets, first pencil a circle crosswise around the melon. With a thin, sharp, pointed knife mark a sawtooth pattern with the penciled circle as the center. Then pull the halves apart gently. To make handles for the baskets, cut a second melon in half crosswise, scoop out the seeds, and slice a 1-1/2-inch round from an open end of a half. Cut in half through the middle, this will make a handle for your sawtoothed halves.

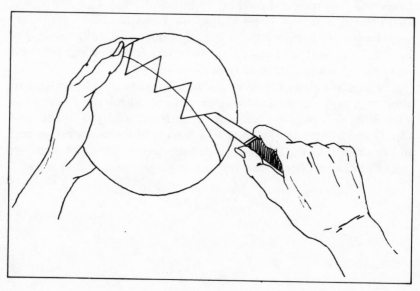

To make decorative cantaloupe halves

BEURRE SABLAIS

A fine mushroom garnish for meats or vegetables

1/2 pound (1 cup) mushrooms	3 tablespoons minced parsley
1/4 pound (1 stick) butter	1/4 pound (1 stick) butter,
2 tablespoons minced shallots or	softened
scallions	Salt and pepper
1 clove garlic, minced	

1. Wash and coarsely chop mushrooms; simmer in 1/4 pound of butter in a heavy skillet. Add the shallots or scallions, garlic, parsley, and salt and pepper to taste.

2. Put the softened butter in a blender or mixer. Add mushroom mixture and pan juices, and beat for 20 seconds, or until just creamed and blended.

3. Turn out onto waxed paper, roll as the bank does pennies, turn in ends, and refrigerate or freeze. I slice off rounds of this garnish onto broiled steak and it melts on its way to the table.

ELEGANT MUSHROOM SOUP

4 tablespoons chicken fat or butter	3 cups chicken stock
1 clove garlic, minced	2 cups mushrooms
6 to 8 scallions	1/2 cup cream
4 tablespoons flour	Pinch chopped tarragon

1. Melt the fat or butter in a soup kettle and sauté the garlic. Slice scallions, discard white parts, and add green part to the kettle. Simmer until mushy but without browning. Stir in the flour, add the stock, bring to a boil, and cook a few minutes. Pour into a blender.

2. Peel, stem, and slice the mushrooms, add to the blender, and run at low speed. Reheat in the pan, add cream and tarragon. Heat, but do not boil, and serve.

Serves six to eight.

BAKED MUSHROOMS
Serve these with Special Hamburgers

16 large mushroom caps
3 to 4 tablespoons butter
Salt

1. Preheat oven to 375 degrees.
2. Stem mushrooms, wash under running water, and dry carefully. Butter a large baking dish, arrange mushrooms upside down on it, and drop bits of butter and salt into the caps. Bake until tender, about 10 to 20 minutes. Mushrooms will have a dry wrinkled look when they are done and be filled with browning butter.

I serve these with Special Hamburgers made of ground sirloin (yes, sirloin) to which I add a quarter cup of heavy cream per pound. To vary, I add grilled tomato slices. This is simple fare, but very good and deserves to be served with a fine Chateauneuf-du-Pape or a red Bourgogne.

Serves four.

RISOTTO CON FUNGHI
(Rice with Mushrooms)

4 tablespoons butter
4 tablespoons beef marrow,
  optional
1 onion, chopped
2 cups sliced mushrooms
2 cups rice, short-grained
3/4 cup dry white wine

Several filaments of saffron
6 to 8 cups hot chicken stock or
  bouillon
Salt and pepper
4 tablespoons butter
4 tablespoons grated Parmesan
  cheese

1. Melt butter and beef marrow in a large heavy kettle. In it sauté the onion until it begins to brown. Add the mushrooms and sauté 5 minutes more. Add the rice and stir well to coat with the butter. Stir in the wine. Let this cook until the wine is almost absorbed.
2. Meanwhile, crush the saffron filaments to a powder and soak in 1/4 cup of the stock.
3. Add 6 cups of stock to rice, and salt and pepper. When stock boils, reduce heat, and simmer gently for 20 to 30 minutes, stirring from time to time, until the rice is cooked. About 5 minutes before

the rice is done, add the stock with the saffron in it, and add more stock if needed.

4. Stir in the 4 tablespoons of butter and 2 tablespoons of the cheese. When these have melted, serve with the remaining Parmesan on the side. My friend Maria usually serves this with sautéed chicken livers in wine and a chilled Moselle.

Serves six.

OKRA AND SHRIMP VINAIGRETTE

6 very small okra
4-ounce can tiny shrimp

Vinaigrette Sauce
1 cup lettuce thinnings

1. Wash the okra, break off the stems. Cover with boiling water for 1 minute, drain, and dry. Slice into chunks, turn into a salad bowl, and chill.

2. Drain the shrimp. Make the Vinaigrette Sauce with lemon or lime juice instead of vinegar, and pour over the shrimp. Add the shrimp and sauce to the okra.

3. Wash just-picked lettuce thinnings, remove roots, dry, and add to the salad. Toss well and serve. This goes well with omelet and a cold Riesling.

Serves four to six.

OKRA-STUFFED PEPPERS

3 strips thick-sliced bacon
6 mushrooms
4 cups diced okra
1 clove garlic, minced

3 tomatoes, peeled
4 large green peppers
2 tablespoons butter

1. Sauté the bacon in a heavy skillet until it is crisp; lift, drain, and set aside.

2. Chop the mushrooms, and simmer in the bacon fat until partly cooked. Lift out with a slotted spoon and set aside.

3. Stem the okra, cover with boiling water for 1 minute, drain, and dice. Place in the skillet with the garlic and cook quickly until seared but not burned. Cut the tomatoes into thin strips, add to the okra, and cook briskly about 30 minutes. Remove from the heat, add the mushrooms and bacon, mix gently.

4. Preheat oven to 350 degrees.

5. Wash the green peppers, drop into boiling water for 5 minutes, cut out stem ends and seeds. Stuff with the okra-and-tomato mixture. Place in a buttered baking dish and bake for 10 minutes. Serve with dabs of butter melting on top. I like this with meats cooked à l'Italienne and à la Provençale. Good, too, with Mexican food.

Serves four.

NEW ORLEANS FRESH CRAB GUMBO

12 small or 3 medium crabs
3 tablespoons butter
6 tomatoes, peeled
1 onion, chopped
1/8 teaspoon thyme
1 teaspoon minced parsley

1 bay leaf
2 cups (1 pound) okra, sliced in
　rounds
2 quarts boiling water
Salt and pepper

1. Wash, scald, and clean crabs. Cut off the claws, crack, remove the body from the shell, and cut into quarters.

2. Heat butter in a large skillet and sauté the crab quickly till slightly colored. Add tomatoes, onion, thyme, parsley, and bay leaf. When the onion begins to brown slightly, add the okra, and cover with boiling water. Season with salt and pepper. Simmer for 1 hour.

3. Give each person a portion of the claws as well as the crab meat. If you are using large crabs, remove meat from claws just before serving as it is hard to do this graciously in a soup plate! Serve the gumbo with boiled rice, a crisp salad, and chilled white wine.

Serves six.

CHICKEN BRUNSWICK STEW WITH OKRA

1 large stewing chicken	2 onions, grated
1 teaspoon salt	2 cups okra rounds
1 pinch thyme	4 to 6 tomatoes
1 tiny bay leaf	2 cups fresh lima beans
1 sprig parsley	Salt and paprika
4 cups fresh grated corn	4 tablespoons butter

1.   Put the chicken into a deep kettle, cover with cold water, and add salt, thyme, bay leaf, and parsley. Bring to a boil, then simmer until tender, about 1 hour. Remove chicken from the kettle, cool, bone, and cut into 2-inch cubes. Reserve the broth. (I save the remains of the chicken for my stock pot.)

2.   While the chicken simmers, stem the okra and cover with boiling water for 1 minute. Drain, dry, and slice into rounds. Peel and slice the tomatoes. Chop the lima beans. Add all the vegetables and the cubed chicken to the chicken stock. Boil quickly, uncovered, until the liquid reduces and thickens. You can add a few bread crumbs for thickening if you like. Serve this stew with a mixed green salad and French bread. A light Chianti goes well with it.

Serves eight to ten.

ONIONS, SOUTHERN STYLE

4 cups chopped onions	6 eggs
1 clove garlic	1/4 cup heavy cream
Milk	Salt and pepper to taste
1/4 cup butter	

1.   Cover onions and garlic with milk and simmer until tender. Drain, discard milk, and keep onions warm.

2.   Melt butter in a medium-sized saucepan and add the onion.

3.   Beat the eggs until thick and lemon colored. Beat the onions into the eggs, then pour back into the saucepan. Add the cream, salt and pepper, and stir over very low heat until the beaten eggs have a creamy texture and are not quite dry.

I also do shallots this way, omitting the garlic, but they take a long time to peel even when you blanch them first in boiling water. Eggs cooked this way can be poured into a baked pastry shell, reheated briefly, and served as a luncheon pie.

Serves four to six.

ONION SOUP LES HALLES

As students, we used to go to the big Paris market for fresh seafood and onion soup at midnight, when the farmers began to arrive with produce for the next day's market. If we lingered long enough over soup and conversation, the flower stalls would be set up before we left, and they were something to see in the early dawn light, blocks and blocks of flowers.

6 medium onions, thinly sliced	Salt and pepper
3 tablespoons butter	2 ounces slivered Swiss cheese
6 cups strong beef bouillon	6 small slices stale French bread
1/4 cup dry white wine, optional	Grated Swiss cheese

1. Simmer onions in butter very slowly until slightly browned.
2. Preheat the oven to 325 degrees.
3. Stir in the bouillon and the wine, and simmer for about 30 minutes. Season with salt and pepper.
4. Pour the bouillon, dividing the onions evenly, into individual soup pots. Stir in the slivered cheese, break the bread into 1-inch chunks, and place two or three in each serving. When the bread floats to the surface, sprinkle with the grated Swiss cheese. Bake in the oven about 20 minutes, then set briefly under the broiler to brown the top. This soup is only as good as the bouillon that goes into it. It makes an appreciated after-ski snack.

Serves six.

QUICK BERMUDA ONION RINGS

Fritter Batter	Milk
2 to 4 large Bermuda onions	Fat for deep frying

1. Prepare the Fritter Batter and chill.
2. Peel the onions and cut into half-inch slices. Separate the rings, cover with milk, and soak 1 hour.
3. Heat the fat for deep frying to 300 degrees. Drain and thoroughly dry onion rings. Coat well with batter and fry a few at a time, until golden. Drain on paper toweling and keep hot until all are fried.

Onion rings prepared this way bear no resemblance to the frozen product. We enjoy them as a side dish with juicy hamburgers, a crisp green salad, and popovers.

Serves four.

SIZZLED PARSLEY GARNISH

1 cupful parsley sprigs
1/3 cup olive oil or Clarified Butter

1. If you can, pick parsley that is so clean it won't have to be washed; otherwise wash it, drain, and let dry for several hours on a paper towel. Cut away most of the stems, leaving only the thinnest strands attached to the leaves. The parsley should be in quite small bunches.

2. Pour the oil into a saucepan small enough so that there is some depth to the oil, and let it get very hot—but not smoking—over a low flame. With a slotted spoon, lower one parsley tuft into the oil, and lift it out before it darkens. That is, at once. Practice a few times to acquire a sense of timing, and then cook the parsley a tablespoon at a time. Drain well on paper toweling and set aside until dinner is ready.

Parsley fried properly stays bright green, is crisp enough to crumble at a touch, and makes a delicious garnish for veal, lamb, and chicken roasts or for creamed vegetable dishes. This is simple to prepare, but does require practice.

GREEN PARSLEY SOUP

6 cups of Soupe Gauloise
1/2 to 1 cup minced parsley
2 tablespoons sweet butter

1. Prepare Soupe Gauloise, omitting cream and chives. Heat to boiling and add the parsley. Turn off the heat. Leave the soup uncovered.

2. Get out the soup plates and put a dab of sweet butter in the bottom of each. Serve the soup so the parsley is distributed evenly.

Parsley will stay bright green and impart an excellent flavor to the soup if it is served at once. If it stays in the soup too long or if the kettle is covered, it will taste rather like grass.

Serves six.

OMELETTE LES SABLES
(Stuffed Omelet)

4 tablespoons butter
1/4 cup minced onion
1 clove garlic, minced
1 cup mushrooms, minced
1 cup chopped parsley
1/2 teapsoon dried tarragon

2 tablespoons bread crumbs
1 egg, slightly beaten
Salt and pepper
8 eggs
2 tablespoons butter

Stuffing: Melt butter in a large heavy skillet, add onion, and simmer until it is translucent. Add garlic and mushrooms, and simmer until they are limp. Add parsley, tarragon, and bread crumbs. Stir to mix. Add the one egg and stir until it is cooked, about 2 minutes. Remove from the heat. Season to taste with salt and pepper and keep the mixture warm.

Omelet: Make 4 omelets following the procedure for Dandelion Flower Omelet, but wait to add the parsley stuffing until the omelet is done. Fold the omelet after it is filled. Serve as a first course or for luncheon, with Boston lettuce in Oil-and-Vinegar Dressing and a chilled white Graves wine.
Serves four.

SADIE AGNES'S PARSNIP CAKES

8 to 10 fresh parsnips
2 tablespoons butter
Pinch of salt

1/2 cup flour
4 tablespoons Clarified Butter

1. Wash the parsnips, cover with unsalted boiling water, and cook rapidly until tender, 20 to 30 minutes. Drain and slip off skins under running water. Drain again, and shake dry over heat. Mash and season with butter and salt. Shape into thin 2-inch cakes and dredge with flour.

2. Heat Clarified Butter in a heavy skillet and sauté the parsnip cakes until golden. Drain on paper toweling. Serve on a hot platter. Sizzled Parsley makes a pretty garnish for this.
Serves four to eight.

PARSNIPS À L'ORANGE

6 to 8 fresh parsnips
2 cups boiling water
2 teaspoons grated orange rind
1/2 cup orange juice

1/3 cup brown sugar
1 teaspoon salt
1/2 cup butter

1. Preheat oven to 375 degrees.

2. Wash, scrape, and quarter parsnips. Drop into boiling water, and cook 5 to 10 minutes, or until almost tender. Drain and shake dry over heat.

3. Mix orange rind and juice. Arrange parsnips in layers in a buttered baking dish and sprinkle each layer with sugar, orange juice, and a little salt. Dot with butter. Bake for 20 to 30 minutes. Excellent with fried chicken if you like slightly sweet vegetables.

Serves six.

BOILED BEEF AND PARSNIPS

3 pounds boneless brisket
2 quarts boiling water
2 carrots
2 leeks
1 bay leaf
6 peppercorns

1 onion stuck with 3 cloves
1 stalk parsley or chervil
1 pinch marjoram
1 tablespoon salt
6 to 8 fresh parsnips

1. Place brisket in boiling water. Bring back to boiling and cook for about 10 mintues, skimming scum from sides of kettle. When scum stops forming, add carrots. leeks, bay leaf, peppercorns, and the onion with the 3 cloves, the parsley or chervil, marjoram, and salt. Simmer gently for 1-1/2 hours.

2. Half an hour before the meat is cooked, bring 2 cups of water to boiling in another kettle. Wash, scrape, and quarter the parsnips, and cook in the rapidly boiling water for about 5 minutes. Drain and shake dry over heat. Keep warm.

3. When the meat is cooked, carve it and arrange slices on a large platter with the parsnips as a garnish. Moisten with some of the stock. Serve with boiled potatoes and a Vinaigrette Sauce. This is a good simple meal when you are tired of rich food. A Médoc wine is nice with it.

Serves six to eight.

PAPA'S PETITS POIS

4 cups shelled peas
2 heads garden lettuce
1 tablespoon water
12 tiny pearl onions

1 teaspoon sugar
1/4 teaspoon salt
1/8 teaspoon pepper
4 tablespoons butter

1. Shell the peas and wash the lettuce.
2. Put the water in the bottom of a heavy kettle, add the peas, pearl onions, sugar, salt, pepper, and butter. Place the lettuce on top of the peas so as to hold in the steam. Set over high heat, but turn the heat down when water begins to boil. Simmer, covered, for about 20 minutes, or until the peas are tender and the liquid reduced. Remove the lettuce, shred it, mix with the peas and the onions, turn onto a hot serving dish, and dribble on the remaining moisture from the kettle.

Serves six to eight.

PEA SOUP À L'ANGLAISE

4 cups tiny peas, unshelled
1 quart boiling water
2 tablespoons butter
1 teaspoon sugar

1 sprig fresh mint
1/2 cup light cream
Salt and pepper

1. Wash pods and shell peas, reserving all unblemished pods. Bring the water to a boil, put in pea pods and cook, uncovered, 30 minutes. Strain the liquid into another kettle and discard pods. Boil this liquid until it has reduced to 2 cups.
2. Melt butter in a heavy kettle, add shelled peas and simmer about 5 minutes. Don't let them brown and don't mash them out of shape. Pour in the pea-pod stock, add sugar and mint. Simmer until peas are tender, about 10 minutes. Reserve a quarter cup of the peas, put the rest of the soup into a blender, or mash through a sieve. Return to the kettle, add the cream, and salt and pepper to taste. Just before serving, add the reserved peas to the soup as a garnish.

Serves six.

PISELLI AL PROSCIUTTO

2-inch cube salt pork
3 tablespoons beef stock or
  bouillon

2 medium-thick slices cooked ham
2 cups fresh peas, shelled
Salt and pepper

1. Mince salt pork, simmer in a heavy kettle until most of the fat is rendered. Remove dried bits of pork with a slotted spoon. Add stock to the kettle.

2. Cut ham into very thin strips. Add to the stock. Stir quickly, then add peas, salt and pepper to taste, and mix. Cover kettle tightly and simmer peas until they are tender. This is a good Sunday supper dish with some noodles or a little rice on the side, and a tomato salad.

Serves four.

GORGEOUS SOUFFLÉ OF PEAS

1 cup fresh shelled peas
1 cup mushrooms
1 teaspoon minced scallions
2 tablespoons sweet butter
2 tablespoons flour

1 cup light cream
5 eggs, separated
1/4 teaspoon salt
1/8 teaspoon pepper
Paprika

1. Drop the peas by the handful into 2 cups of rapidly boiling water, adding more peas only after water has returned to boiling. Cover, and cook peas quite rapidly until tender, about 5 to 7 minutes. Then drain.

2. Preheat oven to 350 degrees.

3. Chop about three-fourths of the mushrooms and sauté with the scallions in sweet butter. Stir in flour and cream and cook until thickened. Cool.

4. Beat egg yolks until thick and lemon colored. Beat egg whites until stiff but not dry. Add the peas, creamed mushrooms, and seasonings to egg yolks; then fold in the stiffly beaten egg whites.

5. Pour into a buttered soufflé dish, top with the rest of the mushrooms. Set in a pan of boiling water and place in the lower third of the oven. Bake until set, about 45 minutes.

Serves six.

PAN-FRIED PEPPERS

8 green peppers   1 small clove garlic
2 cups water   Salt and pepper
4 tablespoons olive oil

1. Wash and seed peppers, cut into eighths. Bring the water to a boil and cook the peppers in it for 4 minutes. Drain and shake dry over heat.

2. In a wok, an electric fry pan, or a heavy skillet, heat olive oil and brown the garlic clove in it; then remove the garlic. Put in the peppers, stir quickly to coat with oil, and cook rapidly, stirring, until all sides are browned and peppers are tender. Drain on paper toweling and serve hot. This is a wonderful side dish with veal or broiled steaks.

Serves six to eight.

STUFFED PEPPERS PROVENÇALE

8 large green peppers   1 small bay leaf
2 tablespoons olive oil   1/4 teaspoon thyme
2 onions, slivered   2 cups cooked rice
3/4 pound ground veal or lamb   1 cup good tomato sauce
2 tomatoes, peeled and chopped   2 tablespoons butter
1 clove garlic, minced   Pinch of minced fresh basil
Salt and pepper

1. Wash the peppers and cut off the tops, reserving these. Seed the peppers, remove the white pulp, and boil rapidly for 5 minutes in water to cover. Drain well.

2. Preheat oven to 350 degrees.

3. Heat oil in a large skillet and sauté the onions in it until browned. Add the meat, mix with onions, and brown a little, stirring constantly. Stir in tomatoes, garlic, salt, pepper, bay leaf, and thyme. Cook until the tomatoes are pulpy but not dry. Add the cooked rice, and mix well.

4. Stuff peppers with the rice-and-meat mixture, replace the caps loosely, and put in an oiled baking dish. Bake about 10 minutes, longer if the peppers are very thick. During the last few minutes of cooking time, heat the tomato sauce, melt butter into it, season with fresh basil, and pour over the peppers. I like the peppers without the tomato sauce, too.

Serves six to eight.

PAT'S GORGEOUS PEPPERS WITH KIDNEYS

3 pounds lamb kidneys
2 large Bermuda onions
2 green peppers
1/4 pound (1 stick) butter
Salt and pepper

1/2 teaspoon garlic powder
1 teaspoon oregano
1 can tomato purée
1/2 cup heavy cream
1/2 cup brandy

1. Halve kidneys and remove fat. Wash in cold water. Soak in cold water in refrigerator for 3 hours. Chop onions and seeded peppers.
2. Melt butter in a large heavy skillet and brown onions and peppers. Add kidneys and tomato purée (not paste), salt and pepper, garlic powder, and oregano. Cook 10 minutes at medium heat.
3. Turn off heat; add the brandy. Stir in the cream. Return to heat just long enough to warm through. Stir well and serve at once with plain boiled rice, a mixed salad, and a rosé wine.
Serves six.

MEXICAN CHILI

For pickling, select small hot peppers, cut from the vine and dried in the sun. You can also break them into bits to drop into chowders, soups, or stews. Or serve this Mexican dish with meat and beans.

1/4 cup vegetable oil
3/4 cup chopped onions
1/2 cup chopped green pepper
2 cloves garlic, minced
2 cups cooked or canned kidney
  beans

1 pound ground meat or 2 cups
  diced cooked beef
12 chili peppers
2 cups tomato sauce
2 teaspoons minced fresh or
  1/2 teaspoon dried oregano
Salt

1. Heat the oil in a soup kettle, and sauté the onions, green peppers, and garlic, until the onion becomes transparent.
2. Stir in the kidney beans, and simmer while you seed and chop the chili peppers: 12 peppers make this quite hot, and you might start with 3 and work your way up to the true Mexican flavor. Add the ground meat, chili peppers, tomato sauce, oregano, and salt to taste. Mash the beans into the liquid to thicken it. When the meat is cooked, turn off the heat, and let the dish stand for an hour to draw out the chili flavor.
Serves six.

GREEN PEPPER RELISH

8 large onions   1 cup sugar
5 medium green peppers   1 quart vinegar
5 sweet red peppers   4 teaspoons salt

1. Run onions and peppers through a grinder, using the fine blade. Place in a preserving kettle with sugar, vinegar, and salt. Bring to a boil. Cook until slightly thickened, about half an hour, stirring occasionally.

2. Pack the relish in hot sterilized jars. Seal, leaving about half an inch of headroom. Process in boiling water for 5 minutes. Cool on racks.

Makes 5 to 6 pints.

MIXED MUSTARD PICKLES

3 green peppers   1-1/2 cups salt
3 sweet red peppers   3/4 cup flour
1 large head cauliflower   1/3 cup dry mustard
2 quarts green tomatoes   4 cups brown sugar
2 cups celery   2 teaspoons turmeric
2 cups pearl onions   1 quart vinegar
1 quart gherkins   2 teaspoons celery seeds
3 quarts water   1 tablespoon mustard seeds

1. Wash the vegetables. Seed the peppers and cut into 1-inch cubes. Break cauliflower into florets; cut tomatoes into quarters or eighths depending on size; cut celery into half-inch pieces; peel the onions.

2. Combine all the vegetables, including gherkins, in a deep kettle. Make a brine of 2 quarts of the water and the salt. Pour it over the vegetables and let stand overnight. Heat to boiling point but do not boil. Drain.

3. Combine flour, dry mustard, sugar, and turmeric. Add a little of the water and stir to a smooth paste; stir in remaining water. Add vinegar, celery, and the celery and mustard seeds. Bring to a boil and boil for 5 minutes. Add the vegetables and bring to a boil again.

4. Pack the vegetables into hot sterilized jars, fill with the liquid, and seal. Process for 5 minutes in boiling water. Cool on racks.

Makes 4 quarts.

FRAN'S FINE NEW POTATO SALAD

16 to 20 new potatoes
1/2 cup Oil-and-Vinegar Dressing
Coarse salt
2 cloves garlic, minced

2 scallions or shallots, minced
1/2 cup mayonnaise
Carrot shreds and parsley sprigs for
garnish, optional

1. Wash tiny new potatoes and drop, unpeeled, into a kettle of boiling water to cover. Cook rapidly until potatoes pierce easily with a fork. They should be just done, not overdone. Drain and allow to cool slightly.

2. While still warm, cut into halves or quarters, depending on the size, and put them in a bowl. Pour Oil-and-Vinegar Dressing over them. Sprinkle with the salt and toss with the garlic and scallions or shallots. Let marinate, but not in a refrigerator, until potatoes cool completely; toss occasionally so they absorb all the dressing.

3. Add the mayonnaise, and toss the potatoes to coat them. Garnish with shreds of carrot and sprigs of parsley if you wish. Cover and refrigerate until ready to serve.

Serves four to six.

NEW POTATOES IN CREAM

16 to 20 tiny new potatoes
3 egg yolks
1 tablespoon Maille or Dijon
mustard

1 cup beef or veal stock or
consommé
Salt and pepper

1. Wash the potatoes, boil, unpeeled, about 10 minutes. Drain and peel under cold water. Shake dry over heat.

2. Beat the egg yolks until light. Turn into the top of a double boiler, add mustard, stir in the stock or consommé, and stir over hot, not boiling, water, until the mixture begins to thicken. Add the potatoes, and let simmer a few minutes. Then salt and pepper to taste and serve. A sprinkling of Sizzled Parsley dresses this up for company meals.

Serves four.

POTATO NESTS

8 large old potatoes
Fat for deep frying
Salt

1. Heat fat for deep frying to 360 degrees.
2. Peel potatoes, cut into long thin strips. Soak in cold water. Drain and dry on paper toweling.
3. Line the bottom of a fine-mesh strainer 4 inches in diameter with potato strips, and press into shape with a smaller strainer that fits loosely inside the 4-inch strainer. Lower these into deep fat and cook until the potatoes are well browned. Use a wooden spoon to keep the small strainer in place during the frying. When potatoes have browned, drain carefully, turn out of the strainer, and salt lightly.

At the Tour d'Argent restaurant in Paris exquisite little puff potatoes are served in Potato Nests. Sadie Agnes used them as edible containers for tiny fried smelts.

Serves six.

ALICE SCHRIER'S POTATO LATKES
(Potato Pancakes)

6 medium preferably old potatoes   **1 teaspoon salt**
1 onion   **3 tablespoons vegetable oil**
2 eggs   **2 tablespoons butter or bacon**
1/2 cup flour   **   drippings**

1. Pare potatoes, grate into a mixing bowl, press out the potato juice. Grate the onion into the potatoes. Beat the eggs until thick and lemon colored. Stir into the potato mixture with the flour and salt.
2. Heat a large heavy skillet, coat with vegetable oil, and melt the butter or drippings in it. When this is quite hot, drop the batter by the tablespoon into the shortening, press flat into a pancake shape, and fry over moderate heat until quite brown and crisp. Drain and keep hot until all are fried.

Alice cooked these as a midnight snack, served with beer, when we were all young and gay, and I shall never forget them. She never could keep up with the demand.

Makes 12 to 14 pancakes.

JANSSON'S TEMPTATION

3 medium onions	12 anchovies
3 tablespoons butter	2 tablespoons bread crumbs
8 medium potatoes	1 cup heavy cream

1. Preheat oven to 425 degrees.

2. Peel and mince the onions, and simmer a little in the butter.

3. Peel potatoes and cut into long thin strips. Butter a glass baking dish. Arrange a layer of potatoes, scatter a few anchovies over them, next add a layer of onions, and sprinkle with bread crumbs. Repeat the layers until all the ingredients are used. End with bread crumbs on top.

3. Bake in the oven for 20 minutes. Remove, pour the cream over all and cook 20 to 35 minutes, or until potatoes are soft and liquid is absorbed.

This is usually part of a hot buffet in Sweden—Småvarmt—and once you have tasted it, you will understand Jansson's weakness.

Serves six to eight.

POMMES DE TERRE SAUTÉES
(Fried Potatoes)

24 2-inch-long new potatoes	Salt
4 tablespoons Clarified Butter	Clove of garlic

1. Scrape the skin from the potatoes. Larger potatoes cut to the 2-inch size will do if new potatoes are not available; just peel the potatoes and pare to the shape of a gigantic ripe olive. Use parings to make soup, or boil and make into mashed potatoes.

2. Set a very large skillet, preferably cast iron, to heat at medium temperature, and film it with the clarified butter. When the butter is very hot, slip potatoes into the skillet and cook on one side for 2 minutes. Shake the skillet until all the potatoes are coated with butter and have turned over, then cook 2 minutes more. Repeat until the potatoes are golden all over, about 4 or 5 minutes more. Sprinkle with salt to taste, lower the heat, cover the skillet, and cook 15 minutes, shaking every 3 to 4 minutes enough to flip the potatoes over. They are done when a fork pierces them easily.

My niece Sylvie Gremillion serves these in a large wooden salad bowl in which she has rubbed a garlic clove. It is her favorite accompaniment for steaks.

Serves four.

SOUTHERN SWEET POTATO BALLS

Fat for deep frying
2 cups cooked and riced sweet
  potatoes
3 tablespoons butter

1/2 teaspoon salt
Black pepper
1 egg
Flour

1. Heat fat for deep frying to 360 degrees.
2. To the riced sweet potatoes, add butter, salt and pepper. Beat egg until thick and fold into the potato mixture, a little at a time. Shape mixture into 2-inch balls. Roll in flour and fry in the deep fat until crisp. Drain on paper toweling and serve at once. An "extra" for holidays or to dress up a tired cold turkey.

Serves four.

NEW ORLEANS "PAIN PATATE"

(Potato Bread)

5 sweet potatoes
3 eggs, separated
2 cups sugar

2 tablespoons melted butter
1 cup light cream
Salt

1. Preheat oven to 350 degrees.
2. Bake potatoes for 20 to 30 minutes or until tender. Scoop out the shells and put the potatoes through a ricer.
3. Beat the egg yolks until thick and lemon colored. Add sugar, melted butter, and cream. Beat this mixture into the riced potatoes. Beat the egg whites until stiff but not dry. Fold into the potato mixture, which should be quite liquid. Pour into a buttered pie plate and bake until well browned, about 1 hour. This is a dessert in New Orleans, and I usually serve it with stewed rhubarb.

Serves six to eight.

SHERRIED SWEET POTATOES
Excellent with turkey, chicken, or glazed ham

4 small round sweet potatoes	1/4 cup fine sherry
3 tablespoons sweet butter	1/4 cup heavy cream
1 teaspoon salt	1/2 cup heavy cream, whipped,
Freshly ground black pepper	optional
Cinnamon	

1. Preheat oven to 350 degrees.
2. Bake potatoes 20 to 30 minutes, or until tender. Cut the top off each potato, scoop out the meat with a spoon, and rice it into a mixing bowl. Reserve the skins.
3. Add butter, salt, pepper, and as much cinnamon as you care for. Whip until fluffy. Now add the sherry a few drops at a time; it should be of good quality. Take care not to add more sherry than the potatoes can absorb. Beat the potato mixture again thoroughly and return to the skins. Brown under the broiler for a minute and serve with a dollop of unsweetened, stiffly whipped cream.

Serves four.

PUMPKIN SOUP
An unusual delicacy

6 cups pumpkin	1 teaspoon sugar
1 large tomato, peeled and halved	Salt and pepper
1 small onion	2 egg yolks
2 cups light cream	2 tablespoons sweet butter

1. Split and seed the pumpkins, and scoop out the meat. Or make this soup as I do from the insides of jack-o'-lanterns. Cut the meat into chunks. Put the pumpkin, tomato, and onion into a heavy soup kettle with a tight lid. Turn the heat low until they render their juices, then simmer for 1 hour. Put in a blender or mash through a sieve. Pour the purée into a saucepan, dilute with the cream. Season with sugar, salt, and pepper, and keep warm.
2. Beat egg yolks until thick. Add a *little* hot purée to the eggs, then beat the eggs into the purée a little at a time. Stir over very low heat for 2 minutes, then serve in soup bowls with a dab of sweet butter in each. The soup has a delicate flavor, and besides, it uses up the jack-o'-lanterns.

Serves six to eight.

PUMPKIN WEDGES

1 small to medium pumpkin	Mace
Vegetable oil	Salt
1/4 cup brown sugar	3 tablespoons butter

1. Preheat oven to 350 degrees.
2. Wash the pumpkin, cut it into as many wedges as you have diners, seed and scrape away all the stringy part.
3. Place in a glass baking dish. Brush with a little vegetable oil, sprinkle with sugar, mace, and salt. Add more sugar if you like things sweet. Bake for 45 minutes. Turn off oven, dot the wedges with butter, and let cool until the meal is ready. A nice vegetable to go with hamburgers and chops.

Serves six to ten.

MY FAVORITE PUMPKIN PIE

3 eggs	1/4 teaspoon nutmeg
3/4 cup light brown sugar	1/2 teaspoon ground ginger
1 cup heavy cream	1/2 teaspoon salt
1-1/2 cups steamed pumpkin, strained	8-inch unbaked pastry shell
	1/2 cup heavy cream, sweetened
1 teaspoon cinnamon	and flavored with brandy

1. Preheat oven to 450 degrees.
2. Beat eggs until thick and lemon colored. Beat in the sugar. Stir in the cream, pumpkin, cinnamon, nutmeg, ginger, and salt. Pour into pastry shell, and bake at 450 degrees for 15 minutes. Reduce the heat to 300 degrees and bake 45 minutes longer, or until a knife inserted in the center comes out clean. Serve with chilled brandy-flavored whipped cream.

Serves six.

PUMPKIN NUT BREAD

3 cups all-purpose flour
1 teaspoon salt
1 teaspoon baking soda
1 teaspoon baking powder
1/2 teaspoon cinnamon
1/2 teaspoon ginger

1/2 teaspoon nutmeg
4 eggs
2 cups sugar
2 cups steamed pumpkin, strained
1-1/4 cups melted butter
1 cup chopped nuts

1. Preheat oven to 350 degrees.
2. Sift flour, salt, baking soda, baking powder, cinnamon, ginger, and nutmeg together three times.
3. Beat the eggs until thick, adding sugar gradually as you beat. Whip in the pumpkin, then the melted butter. Beat in the dry ingredients and mix well. Fold in the nuts. Pour into two buttered and floured bread pans. Bake for 1 hour, or until a food pick inserted in the center comes out clean.

Makes 2 loaves.

RADISHES AU BEURRE

At home in France, tiny new radishes with butter and good fresh bread are served as a first course—and consumed by the quart.

36 radishes
Butter

1. Snip off the leaves about half an inch from the top of the radishes, and cut off the rootlets. Wash well. Make 6 slits from the root end of each radish to the top, and with a thin sharp knife, cut under the skin sections so these stand away like petals. The petals have to be very thin to curl nicely. Put the radishes in cold water, toss in 2 trays of ice cubes, and leave until petals curl back.
2. Drain and dry the radishes, and insert a bit of butter between each petal and the radish core. You can serve these radishes as appetizers skewered to a tiny piece of French bread with a food pick.

Serves six.

DILLED RADISHES

3 dozen large radishes
1 tablespoon butter
2 tablespoons flour
1 cup light cream

Salt
Paprika
I large piece of dill

1. Snip off root ends and stems from the radishes, and peel them. Simmer in slightly salted water until just tender. Drain and shake dry over heat.

2. Melt butter in a small enameled saucepan, and stir in the flour. Add cream and simmer another 5 to 10 minutes, stirring. Add salt and paprika to taste (you should be able to taste the paprika). Pour over the hot radishes. Snip the dill over the sauce to color and flavor it. Serve these radishes with broiled steaks.

Serves four to six.

RADISH GREENS WITH SOUR CREAM

Tops from 3 dozen radishes
2 cups spinach leaves
2 tablespoons vegetable oil

1 cup sour cream
Pinch of salt

1. Wash the radish greens, discard discolored pieces, and cut off any large stem ends. Wash the spinach thoroughly and shred both greens. Heat the oil in a wok, an electric fry pan, or a heavy skillet. Add the greens and toss quickly with a pancake turner until wilted. Reduce heat and simmer, covered, for 5 to 8 minutes.

2. Arrange the greens on a hot serving plate, pour the sour cream into the cooking utensil, without heat under it, and stir until warmed. Pour over the greens, and add a pinch of salt.

Serves four to six.

CHINESE BEEF WITH RADISHES

1/2 pound beef thinly sliced
  (bottom round)
12 large radishes
2 tablespoons soy sauce
3 tablespoons cornstarch

2 tablespoons vegetable oil
2 tablespoons vinegar
6 tablespoons water
4 tablespoons sugar

1. Cut beef into 1/4-inch-wide strips. Cut radishes into thin strips.
2. Mix soy sauce with 2 tablespoons of cornstarch, and marinate the beef in this for about 8 minutes.
3. Mix the oil with the vinegar, water, sugar, and remaining cornstarch. Heat in a wok, an electric fry pan, or a heavy skillet. When the mixture is hot, toss in the beef, stir quickly to coat on all sides, and cook for 2 minutes, stirring constantly. Add the radishes, and when they have become hot but not limp, turn off the heat. Serve immediately.

This is a nice quick dish for two served with plain boiled rice and stir-fried greens. Or it can be one of the main dishes of a Chinese meal.

Serves two.

BARBRO'S COLD RHUBARB SOUP

2 cups 2-inch pieces rhubarb
1 quart water
1/4 cup sugar
1 tablespoon potato starch or
  cornstarch

2 tablespoons cold water
2 egg yolks
1/2 cup heavy cream, whipped

1. Put rhubarb into a kettle with the water and bring to a boil. Cover and cook until soft, about 20 minutes. Whip briefly in a blender or force through a sieve.
2. Return to the kettle and add sugar. Dissolve potato starch or cornstarch in the cold water, stir into the soup, and simmer until clear, stirring constantly.
3. Beat egg yolks in a small bowl. Then beat a little of the hot soup into the eggs. Pour the eggs slowly back into the kettle, stirring constantly. Continue to heat for a minute or two. Then chill.
4. Just before you serve it, place a dollop of whipped cream in the bottom of each soup bowl. Then pour the soup over the cream.

A good way to begin a summer meal.

Serves six.

RHUBARB MOTHER'S WAY

4 cups 2-inch pieces rhubarb
1/2 to 2/3 cup sugar
2 tablespoons butter

1/2 teaspoon vanilla
Sweetened whipped cream,
optional

1. Select the tender pink or red stalks of rhubarb fresh from the garden. Place the cut pieces in a deep heavy kettle. Cover and heat slowly until the juice is rendered. Uncover, and cook more rapidly until rhubarb is almost tender. Stir in sugar and simmer until tender, about 30 minutes in all.

2. Turn off the heat, add butter and vanilla and mix well, but gently. Serve cold with sweetened whipped cream, or hot as a sauce for ice cream.
Serves eight to twelve.

HASTY-TASTY RHUBARB MOUSSE

2 cups diced young rhubarb
1/2 cup sugar
1 tablespoon gelatine
1/4 cup cold water

2 teaspoons lemon juice
2/3 cup heavy cream, whipped
Extra whipped cream

1. Place rhubarb in a heavy kettle, cover, and heat slowly until the juice is rendered. Uncover, add sugar, and cook rapidly until tender.

2. Soften gelatine in the cold water. Beat it into the hot rhubarb and stir until the gelatine is dissolved and well mixed. Add lemon juice. Chill until mixture begins to thicken.

3. Fold the cream into the thickened rhubarb and chill until firm. Serve with additional whipped cream, sweetened.
Serves six.

GAY'S RHUBARB JAM

4 cups 1-inch pieces of rhubarb   4 cups strawberries
6 cups sugar   1 cup blanched almonds, slivered

1. Cover rhubarb with half the sugar and let stand for several hours.
2. Hull strawberries, crush, and put into a deep kettle. Pour the rest of the sugar over them and add the sweetened rhubarb. Cook over low heat, stirring until sugar is dissolved. Then cook more rapidly for about 15 minutes. Add almonds. Cook another 15 minutes or until the syrup "sheets" from a clean spoon.
3. Pour into hot sterilized 8-ounce jars and seal.
Makes six to eight 8-ounce jars.

MRS. WETMORE'S RHUBARB MARMALADE

2 lemons   1/2 cup walnuts or almonds
4 cups inch-long rhubarb pieces   1/2 cup white raisins
4 cups sugar

1. Squeeze lemons and reserve the juice. Simmer the skins until soft, and with a spoon scoop out and discard the pulp. Cut the peel into very fine strips. Mrs. Wetmore uses a razor blade. Pour the lemon juice over the rhubarb. Add lemon peel and sugar. Let stand overnight.
2. Transfer to a preserving kettle, simmer until sugar dissolves, then boil until the jam is thick.
3. Add nuts and raisins and boil 5 minutes more. Pour into hot sterilized jars and cover with hot paraffin.
Makes four or five 8-ounce jars.

UNCLE MARC'S SALSIFY OMELET

6 eggs
1/4 teaspoon dry mustard
2 tablespoons stale beer or water
1-1/2 cups salsify buds with bits of
   stem

2 tablespoons Clarified Butter or
   vegetable oil
1 tablespoon butter
Salt
Pepper
Paprika

1. Beat eggs until frothy. Add dry mustard and beat again. Beat in the stale beer or water.

2. Very gently rinse salsify buds under cold water. Drain and dry with paper toweling. Heat Clarified Butter in a medium omelet pan or a skillet. Stir buds in carefully and simmer 4 to 5 minutes.

3. Pour the eggs over the buds and simmer, stirring with a wooden spoon until the egg mixture is almost dry. Remove to the side of the stove to set for a minute or two, then distribute the butter over the surface of the omelet. Sprinkle with salt, pepper, and paprika, fold the omelet in two, and serve at once. We like crisp French bread with this, a green salad, and beer.

Serves four.

MOCK OYSTER SOUP

4 to 6 salsify
1 teaspoon lemon juice
1 tablespoon butter
1 small leek or onion, minced
3 cups milk

1 teaspoon salt
5 peppercorns
1/3 cup diced celery
1 teaspoon butter
1/4 cup small oyster crackers

1. Wash, scrape, and quarter the salsify, and soak in cold water with lemon juice.

2. Melt butter in a soup kettle, add minced leek or onion, and simmer until tender. Add milk, salt, peppercorns, and celery and stir until the mixture comes to a boil. Simmer until the salsify is tender. Ladle the salsify into a blender and mix at low speed until smooth. Or mash through a sieve. Reheat briefly and serve with a bit of butter and a few oyster crackers in each bowl.

Serves six.

MILD SALSIFY SALAD

1 medium cucumber	3/4 cup Boiled Dressing
Salt	2 ripe tomatoes, peeled
1 pound salsify	Dill
2 tablespoons lemon juice	

1. Wash cucumber, peel, and slice thinly into a bowl, salting lightly between layers. Chill.

2. Wash and scrape salsify quickly. Soak in cold water with 1 tablespoon of the lemon juice. Bring 2 cups of water to a boil, quarter salsify, and turn into boiling water. Cook until tender, about 30 minutes. Drain and shake dry over heat. Put in a salad bowl and sprinkle with the remaining lemon juice. Cover with Boiled Dressing.

3. Cut tomatoes into rather thin slices and arrange on a platter. Drain and dry the cucumbers, mix with the salsify and Boiled Dressing, and heap over the tomato slices. Chop a little dill over the vegetables as a garnish.

Serves six.

MRS. FRIEDLANDER'S SPINACH MOLD

2 tablespoons butter	1/2 cup bread crumbs
2 tablespoons chopped onions	Salt and pepper
2 cans cream of mushroom soup	Nutmeg
3 cups chopped cooked spinach	2 eggs, separated

1. Melt butter and simmer onions in it until tender.

2. Heat the undiluted soup, stirring smooth, and stir in the butter and onions, the spinach, bread crumbs, salt, pepper, and nutmeg to taste.

3. Preheat the oven to 375 degrees.

4. Beat egg yolks until lemon colored and thick. Stir a little of the spinach mixture into the yolks, then stir the yolks back into the spinach mixture, and set at the side of the stove. Beat egg whites until stiff but not dry. Fold into the spinach mixture and pour into a buttered ring mold. Set the mold in a pan of hot water and bake for 45 minutes, or until set. Unmold and serve hot. Very good with fried chicken.

Serves six.

GREEN BORSCHT

4 cups spinach, packed
6 cups beef stock or bouillon
1 tablespoon butter
Salt and pepper

1 tablespoon sugar
1 tablespoon vinegar
6 tablespoons sour cream

1.   Wash the spinach in several changes of water. Dry and shred.
2.   In a kettle bring to a boil 1/3 cup of the stock or bouillon. Add spinach and cook until tender, 2 to 3 minutes, at a rapid boil. Add the rest of the stock and cook a minute or two more. Add butter, salt and pepper to taste, sugar, and vinegar. Simmer 5 to 10 minutes.
3.   Serve in deep soup bowls, each topped with a dollop of sour cream.
Serves six to eight.

OTTO'S SPINACH AND CHEESE RAVIOLI
Pasta

3 cups flour
1/2 teaspoon salt
2 eggs, slightly beaten
3/4 to 1 cup water, warmed

Spinach Filling
3 quarts water
1 tablespoon olive oil
Salsa Bianca

1.   Sift flour and salt into your largest bowl. Make a depression in the center of the flour; pour the eggs into the depression and add about 1/4 cup of the warm water. With your fingers, stir the water until it has picked up a lot of the flour and has thickened. Now add 1/4 cup more of water, and repeat. Add 1/4 cup more of water and work the dough with your fingers until it has picked up all the flour in the bowl. Add water if necessary. Knead the dough on a floured board until it is quite elastic and doesn't stick to the board or your fingers any more. This will happen between 5 and 10 minutes after you have started to work the dough. Cover with a damp cloth, and let sit for 15 minutes.
2.   Flour the counter and your rolling pin. Roll the dough until quite thin. The dough is elastic and this may take a little doing. Cut the dough into 3-inch circles with a glass or a cookie cutter. Spoon a dab of Spinach Filling into the center. Fold over into half-circles, and with a wet fork crimp around the edges on both sides to seal. Ravioli can be made in advance, but don't heap them together to store, or they will become an inseparable mass.

3. Bring to a boil 3 quarts of water to which you have added olive oil. Put the ravioli into this all at once. Stir around with a spoon to keep them from sticking. Cook 10 to 15 minutes. Before draining, eat one to make sure they are done. Serve with Salsa Bianca or with your favorite Italian meat sauce. Otto also serves with this dish a white Chianti, slightly chilled.

Serves eight.

Spinach Filling

4 cups spinach
1 egg, slightly beaten
1/4 cup grated Parmesan cheese
1/4 cup diced Mozzarella cheese
1/4 cup ricotta or cottage cheese

1 small clove garlic, crushed
1 teaspoon minced parsley
1/2 teaspoon minced basil
1/8 teaspoon oregano
Salt and pepper to taste

Wash the spinach in several changes of water. Turn it into a large kettle, cover tightly, and turn heat to medium. Simmer until spinach is cooked, 3 to 6 minutes. Drain, toss a little in the colander to get rid of all water, and return to the kettle. Shake over the heat to dry a little more. Turn off the heat and beat all the other ingredients into the spinach. Refrigerate to stiffen until you are ready to use.

Salsa Bianca

1 tablespoon olive oil
1/2 cup (1 stick) butter
1/4 cup grated Parmesan cheese

1/8 teaspoon minced basil
1 tablespoon minced parsley

Heat oil in a small saucepan. Stir in the butter. Add cheese, basil, and parsley, one at a time, the parsley last. Remove from the heat almost at once. Serve hot over the ravioli.

JANE YAMAMOTO'S SUMMER SQUASH

8 straightneck summer squash,   Salt
  4 to 6 inches long   Freshly ground black pepper
1/2 cup light cream or milk   2 tablespoons butter

1. Pick the squash and immediately wash, dry, cut off the green necks (but don't peel), and slice into rounds 1/2-inch thick. Put into a heavy kettle and turn heat to medium low. When squash juice begins to bubble, cover and cook rapidly for 5 to 6 minutes, or until squash begins to look clear and the liquid is gone. Turn heat high to dry out any liquid in the bottom of the kettle.

2. Add cream or milk, boil rapidly a minute or two, and season to taste with salt and pepper. Stir in the butter and serve. It should not take more than 7 or 8 minutes in all to be ready. Excellent with steaks and grilled hamburgers. Young zucchini can be cooked this way, too. Add chopped dill to either as a variation.

Serves six to eight.

SWEET ACORN SQUASH

4 young acorn squash   1 teaspoon salt
4 teaspoons sugar   1 package cream cheese
2 teaspoons lime juice   1/4 cup melted butter

1. Preheat oven to 375 degrees.

2. Wash the squash and slice in half lengthwise. Scrape out the seeds and the stringy part. Sprinkle the inside with sugar, lime juice, and salt. Set in a baking dish and bake until partly tender, about half an hour.

3. Remove from the oven. Spread cream cheese inside the squash halves and over the top. Pour melted butter into each half and bake until tender, about 30 minutes more. If the cheese begins to burn, turn the heat down a little.

Serves eight.

SADIE AGNES'S BUTTERNUT SQUASH PIE

3 eggs
1 cup sugar
4 tablespoons brandy
1 cup heavy cream
1 cup steamed and strained
  butternut squash
1 teaspoon cinnamon

1 teaspoon nutmeg
3/4 teaspoon ginger
1/4 teaspoon mace
1/2 teaspoon salt
9-inch unbaked pie shell
1 cup heavy cream, whipped

1. Preheat oven to 450 degrees.
2. Beat eggs until thick and lemon colored. Add sugar. Stir but do not beat in the brandy, cream, squash, spices, and salt. Mix well, pour into the unbaked pie shell, and bake 15 minutes at 450 degrees. Reduce heat to 300 degrees and bake 45 minutes more, or until a knife inserted in the center of the custard comes out clean. If the shell tends to burn, cover the edges with foil. Serve with chilled whipped cream.

Serves six to eight.

TOO-MANY-TOMATOES SOUP

10 very ripe tomatoes
2 cups water
1/4 cup chopped parsley
1 small onion
1 bay leaf
1 teaspoon peppercorns
4 cloves

1/2 teaspoon Worcestershire sauce
2 slices lemon
2 teaspoons salt
1/2 cup grated carrot
1/2 cup chopped green pepper
1/2 cup grated celery
Sour cream

1. Wash and quarter the tomatoes and put them into a soup kettle with water, parsley, onion, bay leaf, peppercorns, cloves, Worcestershire sauce, lemon, and salt. Crush the tomatoes a little with a potato masher, and simmer until soft, about 20 minutes. Put in a blender until smooth, or mash through a sieve.
2. Strain out the herbs and add the grated vegetables. Serve warm with dollops of sour cream, or chill and serve with sour cream and 1 tablespoon minced fresh basil.

Serves eight.

DAVID'S TOMATO BREAKFAST

6 thick strips of bacon
6 large, ripe tomatoes
1 large clove garlic

2 tablespoons olive oil
6 eggs

1. In a heavy skillet, sauté the bacon until it is quite crisp. Drain and reserve. Don't wash the skillet.
2. Wash tomatoes, stem them, and cut in half. Crush garlic clove and insert bits of it in the tomato halves.
3. In the same skillet, heat oil until not quite smoking, then turn down the heat. Place tomatoes, cut side down, in the oil and cook 5 minutes. Don't let the skin burn. Turn them over and cook 2 minutes more. Then break the eggs carefully into the pan and cover. When the eggs are cooked, ease the tomatoes and eggs onto a serving plate. Garnish with the bacon and serve with French bread and butter.
    Serves six.

TOMATO RAREBIT ON TOAST

2 tablespoons butter
2 tablespoons flour
3/4 cup light cream
3/4 cup stewed and strained
   tomatoes
1/3 teaspoon baking soda

2 cups diced American white
   cheese
2 eggs, slightly beaten
1/4 teaspoon mustard
Salt and freshly ground black
   pepper
4 to 6 slices whole wheat bread

Melt the butter in a chafing dish and stir in the flour. Add the cream and stir until mixture thickens. Add tomatoes, mixed with the soda. Stir until smooth. Add cheese, eggs, mustard, and seasonings to taste. Don't forget the mustard. As soon as the cheese melts, serve on the buttered, toasted bread, with a mild salad. Follow with a pastry dessert.
   Serves four to six.

GREEN OR YELLOW TOMATO PRESERVES

4 quarts small green or yellow
  tomatoes
Sugar

1 lemon, sliced thin
4 pieces whole ginger

Scald and skin the tomatoes, and then weigh them. Add an equal amount of sugar by weight, and the lemon. Crush and add the ginger. Cook in a preserving kettle until sugar melts, stirring occasionally. Raise the heat and cook until tomatoes are transparent. Spoon the tomatoes into hot sterilized jars, fill with the liquid, and seal at once. Process in boiling water for 5 minutes. Cool on rack.

Makes five to six 8-ounce jars.

HOT GREEN TOMATO RELISH

24 green tomatoes, chopped
6 large green peppers, chopped
3 large red peppers, chopped
6 large onions, chopped
4 cups cider vinegar

1/2 cup brown sugar
2 sticks cinnamon, broken
2 teaspoons allspice
4 teaspoons salt

1. In a food chopper, using the medium blade, grind separately the tomatoes, green peppers, red peppers, and onions. Boil 30 minutes with all other ingredients, except the salt. Salt after the mixture boils.

2. Seal in hot, sterilized jars and process in boiling water for 5 minutes. Cool on rack.

Makes about 8 pints.

TOMATO CHUTNEY

3 quarts pared and chopped
tomatoes
3 quarts pared and chopped
apples
2 cups seedless white raisins
2 cups chopped onions

2 pounds brown sugar
1 quart white vinegar
4 teaspoons salt
1 teaspoon ground ginger
1/4 cup whole pickling spices

1. Combine all ingredients except the pickling spices, and bring to a boil in a preserving kettle. Tie the spices into a small cheesecloth bag, and add to the boiling mixture. Cook slowly, stirring frequently until mixture thickens, about 1 hour. Remove the spice bag.

2. Pack into sterilized pint jars, leaving 1/2 inch of headroom. Seal and process in boiling water for 5 minutes. Cool on rack.

Makes about 7 pints.

PICCALILLI

5 pounds green tomatoes
1 sweet red pepper
2 green peppers
2 pounds chopped onions
1/2 cup salt
1 quart cider vinegar

2 cups sugar
1 tablespoon prepared horseradish
1 tablespoon celery seeds
2 tablespoons mustard seeds
1 teaspoon whole cloves

1. Grind the tomatoes, or chop coarsely with the red and green peppers and the onions. Season with the salt, mix, cover, and let stand overnight. Drain.

2. Combine vinegar, sugar, and horseradish. Add the seeds and cloves, tied in a little cheesecloth bag. Bring to a boil, and add the drained vegetables. Heat again to boiling, but do not boil. Pack in hot sterilized jars and seal immediately. Process in boiling water for 5 minutes. Cool on rack.

Makes 4 pints.

TOMATO SALAD MADAME BERTRAND

4 very ripe red tomatoes
1/2 green pepper
1/2 Bermuda onion
1 small Boston lettuce,
   or leaf lettuce
1 cucumber
1 small garlic clove

1/2 teaspoon salt
4 tablespoons olive oil
1 tablespoon mild vinegar
Salt
2 tablespoons minced basil
10 ripe black olives, pitted

1.   Peel the tomatoes and cut into wedges. Mince green pepper and onion. Wash, drain, and dry the lettuce. Peel cucumber and cut into small chunks. Chill everything but the tomatoes.

2.   In a wooden salad bowl, crush the garlic into the salt with a pestle. Add olive oil, vinegar, and salt to taste, and mix.

3.   Put the tomatoes in the dressing, sprinkle basil over them, and marinate while you prepare the rest of the meal. Just before serving, add the remaining ingredients. Toss briefly in the dressing.

Serves four to six.

TURNIP AND CARROT MÉLANGE

2 cups peeled and diced white
   turnips
2 cups scraped and diced carrots

3 tablespoons melted butter
1/4 teaspoon salt
1 teaspoon lemon juice

Cover turnips and carrots with boiling water and cook until just tender, about 20 minutes. Drain and shake dry over heat. Add butter and salt, sprinkle on the lemon juice, and turn off the heat. Let the vegetables "rest" partly covered for a few minutes.

This is a delicately flavored dish to be entrusted only to a delicately flavored main course, such as veal or chicken.

Serves four to six.

CREAMED TURNIP CUPS

6 small white turnips
1-1/2 cups Sauce Béchamel
Cream
1 cup tiny Dilled Green Beans
   (or canned peas)

Salt and pepper
1/2 cup crumbs
2 tablespoons butter

1. Peel the turnips, cover with boiling water, and cook until tender, 20 to 30 minutes. Drain and shake dry over heat. Scoop out and discard some of the inside of the turnips. Set the turnip cups in a buttered baking dish.
2. Thin the Sauce Béchamel with a little cream; stir in the beans or peas and season to taste.
3. Fill turnip cups with the creamed vegetable, top with bread crumbs, dot with butter, and run under the broiler to reheat and brown.
Serves six.

CANARD AUX NAVETS
(Duck with Turnips)

5- to 6-pound duck
Salt and pepper
1/8 teaspoon curry powder
3 tablespoons Clarified Butter

1/8 teaspoon thyme
12 to 16 small fresh turnips
2 tablespoons minced parsley

1. Preheat oven to 325 degrees.
2. If the duck is frozen, thaw it completely and dry. Prick it all over with a fork. Rub with salt, pepper, and curry powder. Heat the Clarified Butter in a good-sized casserole that has a lid. Brown the duck in it on all sides, turning frequently. Sprinkle thyme inside the duck. Cover the casserole and put it in the oven. The duck should roast very slowly for about 1-1/2 hours.
3. About an hour before it is done, peel the turnips. Cut into chunks about 1-inch thick and drop into boiling salted water. Cook 5 minutes. Drain. Skim off fat from the casserole and, about 40 minutes before the duck is finished, add the blanched turnips.
4. To serve, place the turnips around the duck on a platter. Remove the fat from the duck juices and serve in a gravy boat with a sprinkling of parsley.
I much prefer this to pressed duck or duck with orange.
Serves six.

WALTER'S CHINESE BEEF WITH TURNIPS

2 pounds beef
1-1/2 cups water
4 tablespoons soy sauce
2 tablespoons sherry

1 teaspoon salt
6 medium white turnips
1 teaspoon sugar

1. Cut the meat into 1-inch strips and place, with the water, in a wok, electric fry pan, or heavy skillet. Bring to a boil and add soy sauce, sherry, and salt. Lower the heat and simmer 1 hour.

2. Peel the turnips and cut into strips 1-inch thick. Add to the meat and continue to simmer for half an hour. Add sugar and cook gently another half hour. Serve with a leafy green that has been stir-fried.

Serves four to six.

MADAME PAQUET'S TURNIPS AND PORK

9 small white turnips
3 tablespoons butter
9 half-inch-thick pork chops

3 tablespoons dry white wine
   or chicken stock
Salt, pepper, and curry powder
Watercress

1. Wash, peel, and quarter turnips.

2. Melt butter in two heavy skillets so that chops will not be crowded. Lightly brown chops on each side. Add turnips and wine or stock, and season with salt, pepper, and curry to taste. Cover the skillets, reduce the heat and cook, shaking the pans occasionally, until turnips are tender and browned on all sides, about 40 minutes.

3. Serve very hot, garnished with the crisp watercress.

Serves six to eight.

WALTER'S CHINESE WATERCRESS SOUP

2 cups tightly packed watercress	1 teaspoon salt
1/2 pound lean beef	3 cups stock or bouillon
1 tablespoon soy sauce	3 cups water
1 tablespoon oil	1/4 teaspoon butter

1. Soak, drain, and dry watercress. Cut off heavy stem pieces.

2. Cut beef into 1/4-inch strips and mix well in a bowl with the soy sauce, oil, and salt. Marinate about 20 minutes.

3. Mix the stock or bouillon and water in a kettle, and bring to a boil. Drop in the meat. Bring the water back to a boil, stirring, and add the watercress and butter. Return to the boil once more. Stir thoroughly and serve at once.

Serves five.

WATERCRESS AND AVOCADO SALAD

4 cups fresh watercress	3 tablespoons vegetable oil
2 ripe avocados	2 tablespoons lemon or lime
1 small garlic clove	juice
1 teaspoon salt	2 ounces Danish blue cheese

1. Soak the watercress to rid it of any little crawly things. Drain and crisp.

2. Quarter the avocados and scoop out teaspoon-sized chunks. Cut off a thin layer of the darkest green outer part.

3. Use a pestle to mash garlic clove with salt in the bottom of a large wooden bowl. Mash in the dark green avocado meat and add the oil and the lemon or lime juice.

4. Crumble the blue cheese. Mash any really tiny bits into the salad dressing to make it creamy. Then add the crumbles.

5. Turn the avocado chunks into the dressing and toss well. Add watercress just before you serve, and toss again.

Serves six to eight.

HOT WATERCRESS AND MUSHROOMS

4 cups watercress tips	1 cup light cream
2 tablespoons butter	2 tablespoons sherry
1 tablespoon flour	1/2 cup sliced mushrooms

1. Soak, drain and dry the watercress. Cut off heavier stem parts and break into 1/2-inch pieces.
2. Melt butter in an enameled saucepan and stir in the flour, then the cream and sherry. Simmer until somewhat thickened. Add mushrooms and simmer for 5 minutes. Add watercress, coating it well with the hot sauce, and simmer 3 minutes. Taste and simmer a little longer if necessary.

Serves six.

JOHN MORRIS'S ZUCCHINI SALAD

4 small zucchini	1 tablespoon vinegar
2 tablespoons olive oil	5 tablespoons olive oil
2 heads of romaine	1 teaspoon minced fresh tarragon
1/2 cup mushrooms	Salt and pepper

1. Wash zucchini, remove stems, quarter, and sauté briefly in olive oil. Simmer over very low heat until just tender.
2. Wash and crisp the salad greens. Wash and quarter the mushrooms.
3. Mix the vinegar with the tarragon, salt, and pepper in an electric blender or in the salad bowl.
4. Put the mushrooms and zucchini, which should be fairly dry, into a small bowl. Add the dressing and marinate until mealtime.
5. Break small pieces of lettuce into the salad bowl, discarding any tough stems. Top with the mushrooms and zucchini. Toss at the table.

Serves six to eight.

GIANT ZUCCHINI

At the end of summer you occasionally will come across a zucchini which was not picked when tiny and tender and which has become a seedy, tough-skinned but handsome giant about 18 inches long. These are delicious stuffed, baked, and served with breaded veal scallops with lemon wedges, and a salad of sliced ripe tomatoes in a light Garlic Dressing sprinkled with 3 tablespoons of minced fresh basil and 1 tablespoon of minced chives. A dry rosé, or a young, light red Bourgogne are good choices with this meal.

1 zucchini about 18 inches long
2 tablespoons olive oil
1 small onion, minced
1 clove garlic, minced
1 cup sliced mushrooms
1/2 teaspoon saffron

1/2 teaspoon fresh, minced
    rosemary, or 1/4 teaspoon,
    dried
2 cups cooked rice
Salt and pepper
8 strips thin bacon

1. Heat oven to 350 degrees.

2. Wash zucchini, remove stem end, cut in half lengthwise, and scoop out the seeds.

3. Heat olive oil in a medium-sized skillet, and simmer onion and garlic in it until onion is transparent. Stir in the mushrooms, turn heat to medium high, and cook mushrooms until barely tender, 3 to 4 minutes. Stir in saffron, rosemary, and rice, which has been cooked to barely tender, turn off the heat, and keep stirring and tossing rice until mushroom slices are mixed evenly through it and it has been completely colored by the saffron. Salt and pepper generously to taste.

4. Place zucchini halves on foil on a cookie sheet, stuff with the rice mixture, top with strips of bacon, and bake until tender, about 45 minutes.

Serves six to eight.

ZUCCHINI WITH MEAT SAUCE

6 to 8 4- to 6-inch zucchini
4 tablespoons olive oil
Salt

4 cups canned Italian meat sauce
6 slices French bread
1 garlic clove, minced

1. Wash the zucchini, cut off the stem ends, and slice into long strips, unpeeled, half an inch thick. Place in a kettle with 1 tablespoon oil over medium-low heat and, when squash juice begins to bubble, cover. Cook quickly until tender, 3 or 4 minutes, or until liquid is absorbed. Salt lightly, remove from the heat, and keep warm.

2. Heat canned meat sauce (or make your own), and while it warms, heat 3 tablespoons oil and garlic in a skillet. Fry in it French bread from which the crusts have been trimmed. You may prefer butter to oil.

3. Place 1 bread slice on each dinner plate, heap a mound of zucchini strips beside it, and cover both with hot meat sauce. Serve grated Parmesan separately and a green salad. Bardolino would be a good wine to accompany this.

Serves four to six.

ZUCCHINI APPETIZER

Zucchini is as good raw as it is cooked. Try it cut into fingers with mayonnaise to which 1 tablespoon of curry has been added. This is one of Helen Van Pelt Wilson's elegant canapés.

COMBINED VEGETABLES

There comes a moment in every summer when our garden produce overwhelms us. Perhaps we have a choice of half a dozen crops at peak quality for the evening meal. At this point the pure joy of gardening can turn to pure frustration as I try to decide which one, or which two, or which three. . . . It is then that I prepare one of these vegetable medleys. If you don't have at hand the vegetables called for in these recipes, use what you have. For example, in the Boiled Dinner recipe, parsnips can replace carrots, rutabaga can replace turnips, and Brussels sprouts or broccoli, added in the last 20 minutes of cooking, can replace cabbage or cauliflower.

You will find that the last recipe in this chapter, Ratatouille Pastry, is a most unusual hors d'oeuvre. The appreciation of your guests will always compensate you for the extra effort involved.

SUMMER VEGETABLE SOUP

3 pints beef stock or bouillon
1/4 pound salt pork
1 cup kidney, lima, or shell beans
4 cups spinach or other greens
1 cup peas
2 stalks celery, cut up
1 small cabbage, chopped,
   optional

4 young carrots, cut up
3 medium tomatoes
1 small onion
1/2 cup rice
1/8 teaspoon sage
1 teaspoon chopped parsley
2 cloves garlic
4 tablespoons grated Parmesan
   cheese

Put the stock in a large kettle and boil 1 minute. Add the pork, cut into 1-inch pieces, and the kidney beans, soaked overnight, or the fresh lima or shell beans. Add all other ingredients except the cheese. Simmer until most of the liquid is gone. Stir in the cheese. Serve with French bread and a green salad as the main course.

Serves eight to ten.

WINTER VEGETABLE SOUP

1 cup kidney, lima, or shell beans,
  dried
1 cabbage
3 to 4 large potatoes
2 large winter carrots
1 rutabaga or turnip

2 leeks, cut up
2 large onions
1 clove garlic
1/4 teaspoon thyme
Salt and pepper to taste
1 pound salt pork

1. Soak the kidney beans overnight.
2. Clean the cabbage, cut away the toughest part of the stalk, quarter it, and throw into boiling water for 4 minutes.
3. Put it into a large soup kettle with the kidney beans; potatoes, peeled and halved; carrots, scraped and thickly sliced; rutabaga or turnip, peeled and diced; the leeks, onions, garlic, and thyme. Season with salt and pepper. Simmer gently for 1-1/2 hours. Add the salt pork, and simmer another hour, or until the pork is thoroughly cooked.

This soup is usually served in large soup plates in which a thick slice of rather stale French bread, which has been fried in a little butter, has been placed. Pork is cut up and served in the plate, too. This makes a complete meal.

Serves eight to ten.

DI'S GAZPACHO

4 large dead-ripe tomatoes
1 large cucumber
1 medium onion
1 green pepper

1 cup tomato juice
1 tablespoon wine vinegar
1 clove garlic, minced
Salt and pepper to taste

1. Peel and chop the tomatoes and cucumber. Peel and shred the onion. Remove seeds and shred the green pepper.
2. Combine the vegetables, add tomato juice, vinegar, garlic, and salt and pepper. Chill overnight. Serve as a first course with crisp fresh bread and butter curls, or with Di's Biscuits.

Serves four to six.

SUCCOTASH

2 tablespoons butter
1 onion slice, minced
1 tablespoon minced celery
2 cups cooked fresh corn, cut
  from the cob

2 cups cooked lima beans
1/2 teaspoon salt
1/2 cup light cream
Ground black pepper
2 teaspoons minced parsley

Melt the butter in a medium saucepan, and sauté the onion and celery in it for 5 minutes. Stir in corn, lima beans, salt, and cream. Simmer about 3 minutes, or until most of the cream has been absorbed. Grate pepper over the succotash just before serving, and garnish with parsley.

Serves six to eight.

VEGETABLE CHOP SUEY

2 tablespoons vegetable oil
1/4 cup sliced pork
1/4 cup sliced celery
1/2 cup shredded cabbage
1/4 cup sliced onion
1/2 cup canned bean sprouts

1/2 cup chicken stock
1/2 teaspoon salt
1/8 teaspoon pepper
1/2 teaspoon soy sauce
2 teaspoons cornstarch
4 tablespoons water

1. Heat the oil in a wok, electric fry pan, or slope-sided heavy skillet. Throw in the pork and toss well in the oil. Add vegetables. Toss well and sauté for 2 minutes. Add the stock, salt, and pepper. When the stock boils, cover, and turn down the heat. Simmer about 5 minutes.

2. Mix soy sauce, cornstarch, and water. Stir into the vegetables and keep stirring until the mixture thickens a little and becomes smooth. Turn out onto a shallow platter and serve at once. This should be one of two or three other dishes—perhaps a bowl of stir-fried greens and a large platter of plain boiled rice.

Serves two.

ANITA WESTSMITH'S SUKIYAKI

1-1/4 pounds beef fillet	1/2 cup green peppers
1 cup green onions	1/4 cup beef bouillon
1 cup large mushrooms	1/4 cup soy sauce
2 cups bamboo shoots	2 tablespoons sugar
1 cup celery	2 tablespoons butter

1. Have your butcher cut the meat into thin, flat pieces; cut these into strips about 2 by 4 inches. Cut onions, mushrooms, bamboo shoots, celery, and green pepper into strips of about the same size. Arrange the meat in a tidy heap in the center of a large serving platter, and place the vegetables around it in a decorative pattern. At a Japanese dinner two or three flowers decorate the platter, and the cooking is done at the dinner table.

2. Mix the bouillon, soy sauce, and sugar and put into a small decorative bowl.

3. Melt the butter in an electric skillet which you can bring to the table. (If you have a small Japanese stove and a wok, of course, use those.) Sauté the beef, tossing about 4 minutes. Add the blended stock and cook for 2 minutes.

4. Now add all the vegetables, but one at a time. Stir-fry, keeping the vegetables in separate piles in the skillet. Cover and simmer for about 15 minutes. Serve with steamed rice.

Serves four to six.

IRENE'S VEGETABLE CURRY

2 tablespoons butter	2 medium cucumbers
1 medium onion, minced	2 medium summer squash or
1 small clove garlic, minced	zucchini
1 tablespoon Indian curry	4 sliced tomatoes
2 pounds lamb shoulder, cut into	4 hard-cooked eggs, sliced
1- to 2-inch cubes	1 apple, minced
1 cup beef stock	1/2 cup fresh grated coconut
1 cauliflower	Chutney

1. Melt the butter in a wok, electric fry pan, or heavy skillet. Add the onion, sauté until translucent, and add the garlic. Stir in the curry, cook a minute or two, then add the meat. Coat on all sides and brown for several minutes. Add the beef stock.

2. Set vegetables on top of the meat and simmer, covered, until the lamb is tender and the vegetables steamed. Remove the lid if mixture seems to be too liquid. Serve with the eggs, apple, coconut, and chutney. Irene serves a white Almadén wine with this.
  Serves six to eight.

BOILED DINNER WITH A DIFFERENCE

2 Polish sausages	3 small white turnips
1/8 teaspoon each of sage,	1 small head cabbage or
thyme, and bay leaf	cauliflower
6 medium potatoes, peeled	2 tablespoons butter
4 winter carrots, scraped	

1. Place the sausages in a large heavy kettle. Fill the kettle about half full with cold water, add the herbs, and bring to a boil.
2. Add potatoes and carrots. Simmer for about 20 minutes, then add turnips, and cabbage or cauliflower cut in half. Simmer until the cabbage is cooked. Drain, reserving a little of the stock. Cut up the sausages.
3. Ladle some of each vegetable into each soup bowl and add a portion of sausage. Melt the butter with 4 tablespoons of the stock and pour over the vegetables. A mild French mustard is nice with this.
  Serves six.

RATATOUILLE PASTRY

Here is an hors d'oeuvre with a vegetable mélange to serve with cocktails or as an after-swim snack. Most recipes for Ratatouille include many more vegetables than those listed here; but this is the way it is made in southern France, and I prefer it to the others, which are always quite liquid. The trick is to get all the vegetables cooked in their own and the tomato juices without turning it into a mush.

1/3 cup olive oil	3 medium onions
3 large garlic cloves, minced	2 teaspoons salt
4 large ripe tomatoes	Dash of pepper
1 eggplant, peeled	1/2 teaspoon oregano
2 red or green peppers, seeded	1/2 teaspoon thyme
2 medium zucchini	Easy Short Pastry

1. Heat the oil in a heavy kettle, add garlic, and cook about 2 minutes.

2. Cut tomatoes into 2-inch chunks, toss into the hot oil. Cut eggplant, peppers, zucchini, unpeeled, and onions into 2-inch pieces. Add to the kettle when the tomatoes are soft. Add salt and pepper, oregano, and thyme. Mix gently and simmer uncovered until the mixture has become a purée. It should be quite dry, since it will be spread on pastry.

3. While the Ratatouille cooks, prepare the pastry. Roll it out to fit a cookie sheet, and bake. Set on top of oven to keep warm.

4. Just before serving, butter the cooked pastry shell to protect it from the moisture of the vegetables. Spread this mixture evenly over pastry. Set briefly under the broiler to warm the shell, and serve in squares.

Serves twelve or more.

7 Sauces and Pastries

Treasured by every great chef are his recipes for sauces. He carries these in his head and varies them to suit the main ingredient. If, admiring a delectable Hollandaise, you ask "How did you make it?" he will look pleased and tell you it was the little extra bit of something or other that made it so good. But ask Otto, for instance, "How much something or other?" and he cups his left hand, pretends he is lifting a pinch from it, and then looks helplessly at the ceiling. "A quarter teaspoon, don't you think?" I ask David's mother, and she opens her hazel eyes wide and says, "I don't know dear, it takes just enough. . . ."

Good cooks can't really tell you the exact proportions they have spent years perfecting. However, starting with a good basic formula for a sauce or a fine pastry, you can vary it to suit your own good taste until you too have developed a treasured incommunicable recipe.

COLD SAUCES AND DRESSINGS

Mayonnaise as the French make it is first in any collection of cold sauces for vegetables. It does more for cold vegetables and meats and salads than any other sauce I know. Vegetables marinated in Sauce Vinaigrette or Oil-and-Vinegar Dressing or a remoulade and served dolloped with mayonnaise are quite special. Mayonnaise is versatile, too. Add whipped cream or honey and serve it with fruit salads; add crushed garlic and it becomes Aioli to serve with hot fish; or add any of your favorite herbs in amounts to suit your taste. Used instead of the prepared, commercial product, Fresh

Mayonnaise will make old favorites, such as Russian Dressing, spectacular.

The other sauces in this group are familiar. I have included them to provide a choice for salad greens. Old-fashioned Boiled Dressing was Sadie Agnes's favorite.

FRESH MAYONNAISE

2 egg yolks
1/2 teaspoon salt
1/2 teaspoon dry mustard

1 tablespoon vinegar
1 cup vegetable oil, or more
2 to 3 tablespoons lemon juice

1. Drop egg yolks into a medium-sized bowl that narrows at the bottom. This keeps the yolks together and seems to work better. Beat the yolks with a whisk or fork until they are thick; beat in the salt, the mustard, and the vinegar. The vinegar thins out the yolks.

2. Now dribble in a little of the oil, beating hard as the oil goes in. Be sure the yolks have absorbed each dribble of oil before you add more. As the mayonnaise thickens it is hard to keep the bowl from skidding, so I place it inside a larger bowl, lined with wet crumpled paper towels, and set it in a corner of the sink. (It took me years to figure that out.)

3. Keep dribbling in oil until about half of it is gone and the mixture is quite stiff.

4. Now thin it by beating in the lemon juice. Then add oil in larger dribbles until the mayonnaise is as thick as you want it. It can be made stiff enough to stand up like soft butter. Any spices, herbs, or special flavorings you want should go in after the lemon juice. Taste often. It usually needs more salt, depending on what it is to be served with.

Makes about 1 cup.

Mayonnaise made with vinegar instead of lemon juice, tightly capped and stored in the refrigerator will keep at least two weeks.

These are variations:

Aioli. Mash up to 4 cloves of peeled garlic in the bottom of the bowl in which you will make the mayonnaise, and proceed with the Fresh Mayonnaise recipe.

Mayonnaise Chantilly. Fold 1/2 cup of whipped cream into the finished mayonnaise. For fruit salads.

Fruit Mayonnaise. Flavor the finished mayonnaise with honey to taste and 1/2 teaspoon celery seed.

Russian Dressing. Put 1/2 cup of mayonnaise into a blender or mixing bowl, and beat in 1/2 cup chili sauce, 2 tablespoons finely chopped onion, 2 tablespoons minced pimiento, 1 hard-cooked egg, riced, and 2 tablespoons lemon juice.

New York Green Goddess Dressing. Put 1 cup mayonnaise into a blender or mixing bowl and beat in 1 clove minced garlic, 3 teaspoons minced chives, 4 teaspoons lemon or lime juice, 1/2 cup minced parsley, and 1/2 cup heavy cream.

ALMOND MAYONNAISE

2 cups Mayonnaise Chantilly
1/4 cup chopped maraschino cherries
1/2 cup slivered almonds

Fold the cherries and the almonds into the mayonnaise and stir smooth. This is a delightful topping for a slightly sour fruit salad, such as one of grapefruit, sliced oranges, and peaches.
Makes 2-1/2 cups.

GARLIC DRESSING

1 large clove garlic
1 teaspoon salt
4 tablespoons olive oil

2 tablespoons vinegar or lemon or
  lime juice
1/2 teaspoon dry mustard
Salt and pepper

Slice the garlic clove into a wooden salad bowl. Sprinkle with the salt and mash garlic and salt together with a pestle. Stir in the oil, then the vinegar, lemon or lime juice. Add mustard, then salt and pepper. Taste and correct seasonings. If you wish, add for variety a little minced onion, chives, or other herb.

To prepare garlic dressing in advance, blend all ingredients, except the garlic, at high speed for a few seconds. Taste and correct seasonings. Mince the garlic into the dressing, and chill for at least 3 hours in a refrigerator in a well-capped bottle. Before using, strain out the garlic.
Makes 1/4 to 1/2 cup.

OIL-AND-VINEGAR DRESSING

4 tablespoons olive oil
1 tablespoon vinegar or lemon
  juice

1/8 teaspoon dry mustard
Salt and pepper to taste

Put all ingredients in a blender and mix at low speed, or mix with a fork in a salad bowl. Or pour the oil and vinegar over salad greens, stir in the seasonings, and toss well.

Makes about 1/4 cup.

OLD-FASHIONED BOILED DRESSING

2 egg yolks
1/4 cup water
3/4 cup vinegar
1 tablespoon butter
1/3 cup sugar

2 tablespoons flour
1 teaspoon dry mustard
1/2 teaspoon celery salt or
  1 teaspoon celery seed

1. Beat the yolks with the water.
2. In the top of a double boiler, heat the vinegar and butter. Mix sugar, flour, mustard, celery salt or seed with eggs and water and stir into the hot vinegar. Cook over boiling water until thickened, stirring constantly. Store in a covered jar in refrigerator until ready to use.

Makes 1-1/2 to 2 cups.

Fruit Dressing. Fold whipped cream into an equal amount of chilled Boiled Dressing. Add sugar to taste if you like.

ROQUEFORT DRESSING

1/3 cup Roquefort or Danish blue
  cheese
1/3 cup vegetable oil

3 to 5 tablespoons wine vinegar
Salt and pepper to taste
Minced garlic, optional

Crumble the cheese in a bowl with a fork. Then beat in the oil. Add the vinegar, a little at a time, until the mixture tastes right to you. Add salt and pepper, and minced garlic if you wish. This is excellent in avocado halves.

Makes a little less than 1/2 cup.

QUICK REMOULADE SAUCE

1-1/4 cups Fresh Mayonnaise
1 tablespoon capers
1/4 cup coarsely cut pickles
1 tablespoon Dijon or Maille
  mustard

1/2 tablespoon minced parsley
1/2 tablespoon chervil
1 teaspoon tarragon

Combine all the ingredients in a blender or beat in a bowl with a fork.
Makes about 1-1/2 cups.

SOUR CREAM DRESSING

1/2 cup sour cream
1 tablespoon lime juice
1/4 teaspoon salt
Freshly ground black pepper
1/4 teaspoon dry mustard

1/2 tablespoon minced parsley or
  chives
1 teaspoon finely chopped onion
1 tablespoon Worcestershire
  sauce

Combine ingredients in the order in which they are listed, beating after each addition. Keep refrigerated.
Makes a little over 1/2 cup.

FRESH MINT SAUCE

1/2 cup fresh mint leaves
1/8 cup sugar

1/2 cup white vinegar
4 tablespoons water

Wash and dry mint leaves and cut into tiny strips. Mix well with all other ingredients, and marinate at least 2 hours in the refrigerator. Try this instead of mint jelly with lamb.
Makes 1/2 to 3/4 cup.

SAUCE VINAIGRETTE

1 clove garlic
1 teaspoon salt
1/2 cup olive oil
1/2 teaspoon dry mustard
2 tablespoons white wine vinegar
2 tablespoons tarragon vinegar

1 tablespoon minced shallot or
  onion
1 tablespoon minced chives
1 tablespoon minced parsley
Salt and pepper to taste

Slice the garlic clove into a wooden salad bowl. Sprinkle with salt and mash with a pestle. Stir in the oil, then the mustard and the vinegars. Add remaining ingredients. Season with salt and pepper. Beat well before serving.

Makes about 3/4 cup.

HOT SAUCES

An easy way to dress a boiled vegetable is to serve it with a hot sauce. I can't think of a vegetable that Lemon Butter Sauce doesn't enhance; on the other hand, I can think of many vegetables that are made tasteless if smothered in a plain white sauce. At home in France, Sauce Béchamel (which is white, or cream, sauce) is most often used simply as a point of departure. To it is added cheese or herbs, even curry, or perhaps a whole other complicated preparation. White sauce is more subtle to my mind when the liquid in it is the water or stock in which a vegetable or meat has cooked.

Hollandaise Sauce, which is simply cooked mayonnaise, is one of the great sauces for vegetables. Made in a blender, it is almost foolproof. Bagna Cauda, a hot creamy dip, is another sauce that should be in the repertoire of every gardener who cooks. Almost any vegetable from asparagus to zucchini can be cut into chunks or strips and served with Bagna Cauda as an appetizer.

BAGNA CAUDA
(Hot Bath)

6 cloves garlic
12 anchovy fillets in oil
1/2 pound (2 sticks) butter

1 cup light olive oil
Black pepper

Mash the garlic and the anchovies to a paste in a mortar. Turn into a fondue dish and heat, stirring until mxture thickens. Stir in butter and oil. Cook for 3 minutes; then lower the flame under the dish as low as possible. Serve with a large plate of iced raw vegetables cut into 3/4- to 1-inch pieces—fennel, celery, crisp salad chunks, green peppers, cucumber, slices of large fresh mushrooms, small quarters of summer squash. In fact, almost anything from the garden. The vegetables are dipped briefly into the bubbling sauce before eating.

Makes about 2 cups.

SAUCE BÉCHAMEL
(White Sauce)

2 tablespoons butter	**2 cups hot milk**
3 tablespoons flour	**1/4 teaspoon salt** ·

1. Melt the butter in an enamel saucepan over low heat. Stir in the flour until the mixture is smooth. (If it overheats, the flour won't absorb the milk, so take care.)

2. Add all the milk at once, and stir vigorously to blend well. Keep stirring as the mixture simmers for another 5 to 10 minutes. Add the salt. This is the basic white sauce recipe.

Makes about 2 cups.

Cheese Sauce. Add 1/4 teaspoon mustard and 1/2 cup of your favorite cheese, grated, to the sauce when it is cooked. Heat and stir until the cheese dissolves.

Curry Sauce. Add from 1/2 teaspoon to 1 tablespoon of powdered curry to the butter with the flour.

Herb Sauce. Add 1 teaspoon or more of minced fresh herbs, or 1/2 teaspoon of dried herbs, after the hot milk is in.

HOLLANDAISE IN A BLENDER
This is a popular sauce for nearly all vegetables, as well as for broiled, grilled, and cold meats, eggs, and delicate fish.

1/4 pound (1 stick) butter	**1/4 teaspoon salt**
3 egg yolks or 2 whole eggs	**Freshly ground black pepper**
2 tablespoons lemon juice	

1. Heat the butter to bubbling but don't brown it. Remove at once from the heat. Set next to the blender.

2. Put egg yolks, lemon juice, salt and pepper into the blender, turn on low. Pour hot butter into the blender in a steady stream. When all the butter has been added, turn off the blender.

Makes about 1 cup. To make a larger quantity, use 1/2 pound of butter and 4 egg yolks.

SAUCE BÉARNAISE

1 cup Hollandaise sauce
1/4 cup wine vinegar
1/4 cup dry white Vermouth
1 tablespoon minced shallot or
  onion

1 tablespoon fresh tarragon or
  1/2 teaspoon dried tarragon
1/8 teaspoon pepper

Follow recipe for Hollandaise, omitting the salt and pepper, and blend until thick. Combine vinegar, Vermouth, shallot, tarragon, and pepper, and simmer until reduced to 2 tablespoons. If desired, you can then add 2 more tablespoons of tarragon or substitute minced parsley, and stir with the vinegar-Vermouth sauce into the Hollandaise.

Makes a little over 1 cup.

LEMON BUTTER SAUCE

2 tablespoons lemon juice
1/8 teaspoon salt
1/4 pound (1 stick) butter

1. In a tiny enameled saucepan, simmer the lemon juice and salt until the liquid is reduced to 1 tablespoon. Remove from the heat.

2. Stir in half the butter until it melts; then return the pan to the heat and beat in the rest of the butter, a lump at a time. During this process take care that the butter doesn't get so hot that it browns. If you are in a hurry, you can simply melt together 1 stick of butter and 2 to 4 teaspoons of lemon juice, but the result isn't quite the same.

Makes about 1/2 cup.

BISCUITS AND PASTRY

Biscuits and pastry obviously are not vegetables, but a few recipes for them belong with vegetable cookery because they are sometimes part of a recipe featuring a vegetable, as Cabbage Pie or Ratatouille, or they are delicious served with a vegetable.

Diane Simrell's Butter Biscuits are pure pastry poetry and deliciously appropriate for any vegetable luncheon. Try the Easy Short Pastry, as effortless as it is good. Papa's Pie Pastry is worth the extra effort for its fine flaky quality; true, it is a little harder to handle than dough made without butter.

Because so many vegetables, and fruits, too, are good in fritters, I am also including my favorite batter recipe.

DI'S BUTTER BISCUITS

2 cups all-purpose flour
2 teaspoons baking powder
2 teaspoons sugar

1/2 teaspoon salt
6 tablespoons butter
1/2 to 1 cup milk

1. Preheat oven to 450 degrees.
2. Sift flour, baking powder, sugar, and salt into a mixing bowl. Cut in the butter as for pie dough. Add milk, omitting the last little bit if the dough is reaching the point where it won't hold shape.
3. Grease and flour a cookie sheet. Drop the dough on it by the tablespoon and shape into little rounds. Bake 12 to 15 minutes, until a golden brown on top.

Makes eight to ten 2-inch biscuits.

EASY SHORT PASTRY

1/2 pound (2 sticks) butter
8-ounce package cream cheese
1/2 teaspoon salt

1 teaspoon sugar (for sweet
pastry only)
2 cups all-purpose flour

1. Beat butter and cream cheese together in an electric mixer until creamed. Beat in the salt, then the sugar (if you are making dessert pastry). Sift the flour over the mixture and work in with a fork. Gather the last crumbs into the ball with your fingers and store in the refrigerator wrapped in wax paper or a plastic bag. Chill for about an hour or until firm. Store in the least cold part of the refrigerator if you plan to leave the dough for a day or two. I find this pastry keeps well three to four days.
2. Bake double-crust pies at 425 degrees for 15 minutes; reduce heat to 375 degrees and bake 30 minutes more, or until done.
3. To make a pastry shell, roll out one-half of the dough to about 1/8 inch thick, place on upper shelf of the preheated oven, and bake for 15 minutes.

Makes two 9-inch pastry shells or one double-crust pie.

MOCK CROISSANTS

Roll out Easy Short Pastry until it is thin. Cover the surface with soft butter. Fold in three like a letter. Roll out again in the direction in which it is narrowest. Repeat the process twice more, then roll and cut into 6- to 8-inch squares; halve to make 2 triangles. Roll each starting from the base. Curve and place on a greased and floured cookie sheet. Bake at 425 degrees for 15 minutes. Lower heat to 350 degrees and bake 10 to 15 minutes more. Let the croissants rest 5 to 10 minutes before serving.

Makes 12 to 15 croissants.

FRITTER BATTER

2 eggs
1 cup flour
1/2 teaspoon salt
1 tablespoon sugar (for fruit only)

1 tablespoon melted butter
2 tablespoons lemon juice
Milk
2 cups vegetables or fruits, sliced

1. Heat deep fat to 365 degrees.
2. Beat the eggs until thick. Add flour, salt, and sugar if the batter is to be sweet. Mix well. Add butter, lemon juice, and enough cold milk to make a batter about as thick as heavy cream. Beat smooth.
3. Dip parboiled vegetables or fresh fruit into the batter, drop into the fat, turn as the fritters rise to the surface. Keep turning until they are a golden brown all over.

PAPA'S PIE PASTRY

2 cups flour
1/2 teaspoon salt
2 teaspoons sugar
1/2 teaspoon baking powder

2/3 cup shortening
1 tablespoon butter
4 tablespoons ice water

1. Sift flour, salt, sugar, and baking powder together. Cut in the shortening and the butter until the mixture looks like oatmeal. Dribble in the ice water, tossing the mixture with a fork so that the water is very evenly distributed. Press the crumbles together with a fork. Then, with your hands, quickly shape into two flattish balls and chill.

2. Roll half the chilled dough on a floured board with a floured rolling pin. Flip it a quarter turn at each rolling until it is the size of the pie pan. Then fold the pastry in four, gently lift it into the pan, and unfold. Let it rest 5 minutes, then pat it to fit the pie plate and flute the edges with a fork.

3. When the pastry shell is to be used alone, bake it at 425 degrees for 15 to 20 minutes. (Rice laid on wax paper in the bottom will keep the pastry from bubbling.) This makes two 9-inch crusts. Bake two-crust pies with filling 15 to 20 minutes at 425 degrees, then 20 to 30 minutes at 350 degrees.

8 Agreeable Herbs to Grow and Use

(see Table V, page 284)

What is a cook without a herb?

Most herbs are natives of the Mediterranean area, and do best under the growing conditions that exist there: poor, well-drained soil and months of hot sunlight.

Some kinds of mint come from more northern latitudes and often do best in rather moist, but not too rich, soil in shade or shade for part of the day, and can be readily grown in any suitable part of the garden. Everyone knows the common spearmint, but there are others worth growing: orange mint, apple mint, pineapple mint, peppermint, and pennyroyal (a flea repellent).

PLANTING

In colder areas many of the perennial and biennial herbs must be treated as annuals and planted every year. Since they tend to germinate slowly, it is best to plant rooted cuttings or root divisions. You can start some of these from seed indoors and transfer the seedlings to the herb garden when they finally appear. Instructions for starting seeds indoors are given in Chapter 3. Potted seedlings and the seeds for annuals to be sown outdoors can go into the ground as soon as the weather has warmed. Sow biennials and perennials when you still have 2 full months of warm growing weather ahead.

Table V at the back of the book lists the best method of propagation for each herb and any peculiarity it may have as well.

SEEDLINGS OF HERBS

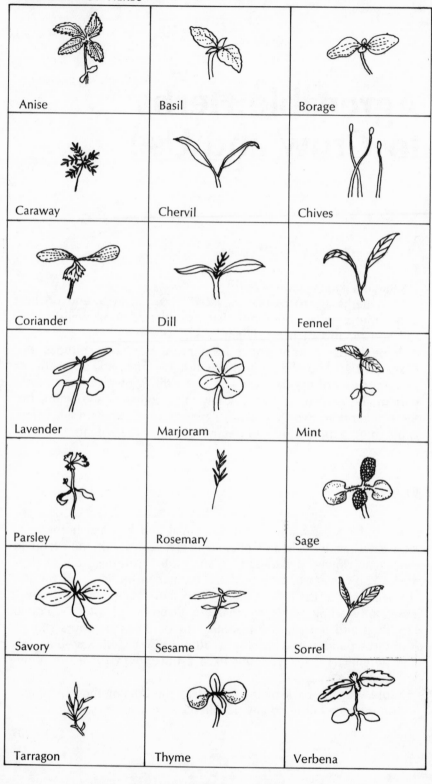

Anise	Basil	Borage
Caraway	Chervil	Chives
Coriander	Dill	Fennel
Lavender	Marjoram	Mint
Parsley	Rosemary	Sage
Savory	Sesame	Sorrel
Tarragon	Thyme	Verbena

GARDENS FOR HERBS

A pot of chives, 2 plants each of tarragon, basil, thyme, rosemary, sweet marjoram, chervil, summer savory, and a short row of parsley and of dill provide enough herbs to enchant any cook. Most of these will fit into a strawberry jar, which can be brought indoors when the weather cools. The jar will be easy to move if you fill the center with a hollow made of rolled hardware cloth, or a roll of chicken wire covered with burlap.

Herbs grown in enough quantity to make a small, formal garden delight the eye and will scent the whole outdoors, but they must be displayed in well-defined spaces or they will look like a tangle of weeds. An easy way to give definition to herbs in a small garden is to plant them between the spokes of an old cart wheel, or between the rungs of an antique ladder. Or within a pattern of parsley: Use parsley for the "black" squares of a checkerboard

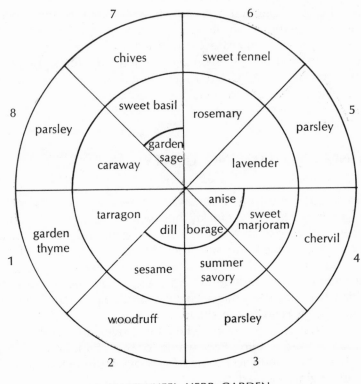

CARTWHEEL HERB GARDEN

pattern, and plant varied herbs for the "white" squares. Protect perennial herbs from cold winters in the same manner as strawberries.

Table V at the back of the book lists the height of each herb at maturity. In planning your herb border, remember to place the taller varieties behind the low-growing ones.

HARVESTING HERB LEAVES

Pick leaves or branch tips at any time after the plant is established. Harvest for drying and storing when the flower buds are just beginning to open. The ideal time is a dry morning when the dew has evaporated and the sun is not yet overhead. Cut perennials down to 1/3 their size. Pull annuals up by the roots, or cut to 1/3 their size if you want to keep some growing until frost.

Although lavender is not used in cooking, I associate it with kitchen herbs because it was grown with them at the château. Lavender is a perennial shrub, easy to grow once it has germinated but easier yet to propagate by root division. The little scented flowers grow in close spikes on a thin stem and should be picked just before opening fully. Dry them as herb leaves, knot into discarded nylons, and use to scent the linen closet.

DRYING AND STORING LEAVES

Discard spoiled foliage, rinse away dirt with a sink spray, or in a little running water, dry quickly between paper toweling, spread between two window screens in a single layer, and place in a dry, well-ventilated place to dry out. They dry well hung from a clothesline in the attic; tie the plant stems upside down with a bit of string and attach to the line. In Westport, where we had no attic, we dried herbs in the garage with the doors open. Sunlight fades herb colors, so keep in the shade.

In ten days or two weeks, when the leaves are crackling dry, strip them from the stems. Pack whole for teas and lotions in tightly capped jars. Rub herbs to be used for cooking through a sieve and pack into tightly capped jars.

HARVESTING THE SEEDS

When the flower stalks have dried late in the season, gather seed heads into a linen-lined basket and spread on clean cloth between two window screens in an airy room. After five days thresh by rubbing between your palms. Do it outdoors so the breeze will carry away the chaff. Spread the seeds on a fresh cloth between screens for another ten days, then store in tightly capped jars. Watch the jars for the first few days for evidence of moisture, and dry the seeds for two hours in an oven at 250 degrees if necessary.

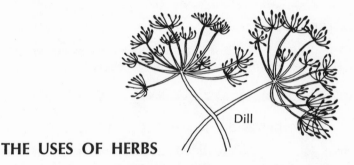

Dill

THE USES OF HERBS

Herbs have been used medicinally and for cooking since ancient times. Few, if any, hold a place in medicine today, except in old-fashioned places like the Vendée, where they are still used for broths to relieve various ailments, and for rubbing lotions. A number are still processed, of course, into moth repellents and perfumes, both commercially and domestically. A few are staple ingredients of candies. For culinary use, however, herbs are increasingly popular. Here, then, are some good reasons for growing herbs in your garden.

If you will turn to Table V at the back of the book, you will find notes on the many other ways each of the herbs, whether fresh or dried, can be used.

Fines Herbes

This famous mixture adds character and savor to omelets, grilled meats, or fish. To make your own, simply mix equal portions of fresh parsley, chives, .tarragon, and chervil.

Herbs for Beef

Mix 1 teaspoon each of the dried crushed leaves of summer savory, basil, sweet marjoram, parsley, and chervil. Test it, then change the emphasis to suit yourself and mix in larger batches for storing.

Herbs for Pork

Mix 1 teaspoon each of the dried crushed leaves of summer savory, basil, sage, rosemary.

Herbs for Lamb or Veal

One teaspoon each of the dried crushed leaves of sweet marjoram, summer savory, rosemary, parsley or chervil.

Herbs for Egg Dishes and Chicken

One teaspoon each of the dried crushed leaves of summer savory, tarragon, chervil, basil, chives, rosemary.

Herb Vinegars

1. Just before the plants flower, cut enough leafy tips of tarragon, mint, basil, marjoram, dill, or caraway to fill 1 cup lightly packed. Press these loosely into a wide-mouthed 1-quart jar. Bruise the leaves with a pestle into the bottom of the jar.
2. Bring 1 scant quart of cider vinegar or white vinegar to the boiling point (do not boil) and pour it over the crushed leaves, allowing 2 inches of headroom.
3. Cap tightly and marinate in a warm room for 10 days, shaking vigorously daily. Taste the vinegar. If you want the herb flavor to be stronger, strain out the herbs, pick and crush a fresh bundle, and add to the vinegar without boiling it. Leave 10 days more. Strain out the leaves, filter the vinegar through a fine strainer or cloth, and store in tightly capped bottles with a single leaf of the herb inside.

Herb Teas

When I was a child and had a stomach-ache, mother made tea with dried mint leaves for me, added a few grains of sugar, and served it in a pretty company teacup. My stomach-ache always went away after I had drunk it. Try it some time. Use not only mint, but any other herb you particularly like. Add a leaf or two of dried or fresh mint to tea for iced teas, and serve with fresh sprigs tucked into the side of the pitcher or glass.

Herb Baths

Pick 4 leafy herb tips from your thyme, lavender, verbena, mint, marjoram, or rosemary plants. Tie into a bit of cloth and boil in 2 cups of water for 15 minutes. Discard the herb bag and pour the herb-scented water into a drawn bath. It is surprisingly refreshing.

Rubbing Lotions

Pick 1 cup of leaves from your thyme, lavender, verbena, mint, marjoram, or rosemary plants, and crush with a pestle in the bottom of a 1-quart glass jar. Pour rubbing alcohol over the crushed leaves, cap tightly, let stand 2 weeks, shake daily. Strain through fine cloth, bottle, cap tightly. Use after baths.

Moth Repellents

In the bottom of a small bowl mix 2 handfuls of dried flowers of lavender, 2 handfuls of dried rosemary leaves, and 1 tablespoon of crushed cloves with a few pieces of dried lemon peel. Mix them hard enough to bruise them a little, knot into toes of discarded nylons, and place in linen closets and woolen chests.

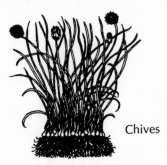

Chives

9 Orchard Fruits and Berries for the Home Garden

(see Table VI, page 286)

Plan your choice of fruits for the home garden so that you will have a continuous supply rather than a periodic deluge. Of each kind of fruit, varieties are available which bear at different times, and are accordingly described by nurseries. With a careful selection of varieties and provision for proper storage you can have fresh fruit through most of the year. The berry fruits freeze easily and well and will round out your fruit-supply year.

Finding varieties that will flourish in your area and provide a succesion of fruits is not difficult. Notify your local Agricultural Extension Service of the general kinds of fruit you want to grow and request their suggestions for suitable varieties. Then select varieties whose crop will overlap. By selection and storage it is possible to have apples from July through winter; pears from late July to March; plums, peaches, and nectarines from July until October; cherries from June until mid-August; strawberries from June to November; raspberries from July to October; grapes from August to Christmas; blueberries from June to September.

Today virtually all fruits, except melons (which are grown in the vegetable garden), are perennials producing crops the second or third year after planting, and bearing for years to come. Not all large standard orchard trees produce fruit in three years, but the dwarf forms do, making them by far the better investment for a small place.

ORCHARD FRUITS

Apples, pears, peaches, nectarines, sweet and sour cherries, and plums are the most popular orchard fruits and are available in the

210

fast-bearing undemanding dwarf and semi-dwarf sizes. In warmer climates plant the trees after they have become dormant in fall, or in late winter or very early spring. North of Philadelphia where winters are colder set them out while still dormant in early spring.

APPLES

There is a bewildering array of apple varieties, some better for eating than others. New varieties are being introduced all the time and among them excellent ones. The old favorites rated excellent for eating are these: Delicious, a winter-keeping apple; Gravenstein, a fall apple; Grimes Golden, a fall apple; Jonathan, a fall apple; McIntosh, a fall apple; Snow, a fall and winter apple; Spitzenburg, a winter apple. Apples rated most suitable for jelly are Northern Spy, Twenty Ounce, and Tompkins, all excellent pie apples as well.

PEARS

Pears are not allowed to tree-ripen: Pick them before they ripen, wrap in soft paper, and store at 65 to 70 degrees for ten days to several weeks, depending upon the variety. The pears are ready to pick when the tree drops one or two, and their color is turning from frankly green toward gold. Those that are ready will come away from the tree easily when tipped from the bottom upward.

To test stored pears for eating readiness, look for those that have softened slightly toward the stem end, and eat one.

Among the best dwarf pears for eating as fresh fruit are the greenish Fame and the Starkrimson, both August-bearing pears, and the Starking Delicious, Magness, Seckel, and Anjou, which are ready in September and are also blight-resistant. The well-known Duchess pear, which produces a large greenish fruit and is self-pollinating, is also ready in September, as is the Bosc pear.

If you want a pear that is good for cooking as well as for eating fresh, try Moonglow or the reddish Bartlett, which ripen in mid-August and are blight-resistant, too. Among the best pears for keeping are Starking Delicious, Magness, Duchess, and Anjou.

CHERRIES

A variety of cherry called Duke, which combines the appearance of sour cherries with some of the sweetness of sweet cherries, was once popular in the home garden. However, improved strains of sour and sweet cherries have made the Dukes almost obsolete. To have lots of cherries for pies and compotes and canning, select a sour-cherry variety that will do well in your area. To have lots of cherries for eating as fresh fruit, select a sweet cherry, or ask the local Agricultural Extension Service to recommend a variety of sour cherry which will be sweet enough to serve as fresh fruit. Or plant one sour cherry, since it will pollinate itself, and a pair of sweet cherries, which will cross-pollinate. Although a sour cherry can pollinate a sweet cherry, the two types do not blossom simultaneously, and so, although they *can* cross-pollinate, they will not.

PLUMS

Plums are ready for picking when they have a "bloom," a dusty, powdery look, and when they come away from the tree easily with a slight twist. To the touch, they will be less than "mushy" soft, though not at all hard. Plums are best completely tree-ripened, but fruit intended for jams or compotes should be picked while still shy of dead ripe.

PEACHES AND NECTARINES

Peaches and nectarines are best when tree-ripened. Fruit intended to make jam should be picked while still rather green; fruit intended for compotes or cooking should be picked just a little less than dead-ripe.

Planting and culture. Fruit trees prosper on good garden loam that is slightly acid. They require full sun and a well-drained location. Avoid planting them in low pockets where frosts settle or in places where they will get the full sweep of north winds.

Plant in a hole large enough to told the roots comfortably, and deep enough to set the tree at the level at which it grew in the nursery. Some dwarf stock has special planting-level requirements, and instructions will be included with your tree. Order 1-year-old whips: My father has proved to me on several occasions that they do better in the long run than more mature trees which suffer from transplanting.

Lack of water is a great killer of new trees. When you have spread the roots comfortably in the planting hole, fill it two-thirds full of soil mixed with humus and a little sand, and with one shovelful of rotted manure, or compost, or else mix in a handful of garden fertilizer. Pour in a bucket of water containing Tre-Pep at half strength. Fill the hole and mound a saucer around the tree to hold future watering. Add half a bucket of water, and wrap the tree in tree tape or cardboard to protect it from sun scald. Give newly planted trees half a bucket every second day for the first two months and once a week after that—more if the summer is dry.

Pruning. Transplanted trees of all sizes suffer some root loss. To compensate for it, prune them back at planting time by removing all but the topmost branch, or leader, and 3 to 5 other well-placed branches. Cut these back to 8 to 10 inches, leaving the leader somewhat longer. Dwarfs will require no more pruning for years to come.

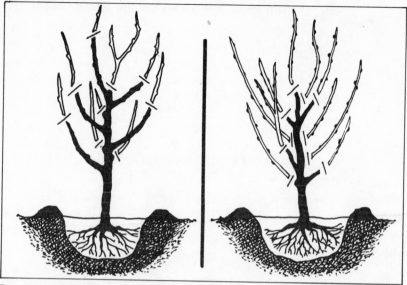

Drawing at left shows how to prune back apple, pear, and cherry trees at planting time. Drawing at right shows planting-time pruning for peach, nectarine, and plum. Circular mound around newly planted trees retains water. Do not plant dwarf or semi-dwarf fruit trees below nursery level unless otherwise instructed, as you may be burying the graft union.

Spraying. At planting time use one of the combination sprays recommended for fruit trees by your garden supply center. When new growth is 1 inch long spray every two weeks for eight weeks. When the tree sets blossoms, switch to the spray schedule listed in Table VI, page 286.

Thinning. Fruit trees produce more fruit than they can mature, and drop a number of them to lighten the load. You can improve the quality of your crop and minimize the likelihood of having trees that produce heavily one year and not at all the next year by thinning fruits to about 6 inches apart. Cherries are the exception: They don't have to be thinned. Never let newly planted fruit trees set any fruit the first year.

Mulching. Keep fruit trees mulched as far as the drip line of the outer branches. Do not plant a ground cover under the trees; it will rob them of moisture and nutrients. Use compost or composted manure if you can, or black plastic, or any organic mulch. This helps new trees preserve moisture, and will cut down on watering chores if the season is dry.

Fertilizing. Trees mulched with manure or compost need no further fertilizing. Feed others in early spring before growth begins with a 45 percent nitrogen fertilizer at the rate of 1/4 pound for each inch of trunk diameter.

Pollination requirements. Most but not all varieties of apples and pears require cross-pollination to set fruit. Many, but not all, varieties of peaches and nectarines are self-pollinating. Plums require cross-pollination, and are particular about which other varieties they need. All sour cherries pollinate themselves, so you can plant just one and have cherries. Most varieties of sweet cherries require cross-pollination. Your local Agricultural Extension Service will send you on request a list of cross-pollinators suitable for varieties that grow well in your area. The safest way to assure cross-pollination is to plant a pair of reciprocal pollinators fairly close together. You can invite the bees to visit, too, by keeping borage in the herb garden. If you are planning to have three trees of one species, make one a variety that can pollinate the other two.

BERRIES

Strawberries, red and black raspberries, and blackberries are wonderful fruit for the home garden, easily established and cared for. Start with small plantings; they will multiply and provide stock for the extension or the renewal of beds.

Red raspberries can be used interchangeably with most strawberry recipes, and black raspberries can be used interchangeably with most raspberry recipes. Both berries make excellent jams, but are likely to be seedy, and should be strained. Do freeze extras. They are so simple to do, and so very good thawed come snow time.

STRAWBERRIES

These hardy plants are available in varieties that produce one crop a year—early, midseason or late—and in everbearing varieties, most of which produce a large crop in late spring, a few berries in midsummer, and a small crop in late summer. Twenty-five to fifty of each of four or five varieties keep a family in berries all season long and takes more space than the average gardener can afford. If you can spare a permanent row 75 by 4 feet, plant fifty berry plants, twenty-five of an early crop and twenty-five of an everbearer whose first crop coincides with that of the other twenty-five plants. Or buy twenty-five of the more ornamental strawberries with showy blossoms, such as the everbearer Geneva, and use them as clumps to edge a flower border and in strawberry jars on the patio. Be aware that some varieties are not self-pollinating and must be planted with other varieties which can pollinate them. Plants set in this spring can be harvested early next spring, and need not be changed for six years.

Planting and culture. Strawberries require a fertile, slightly acid soil; they do badly where lime was recently applied. Dig a covering of 2 inches of well-rotted manure or compost into the bed when preparing the soil, and a good supply of humus. Or dig in 1/2 shovelful of an acid humus for each plant, such as moist peatmoss, or sawdust or cottonseed meal, or leafmold, and add a handful of 5-10-5 or 4-8-4 for each twenty feet of row.

Set plants out in very early spring, as soon as the ground can be worked. If frosts threaten, protect them with plastic canopies or bushel baskets.

There are two hard and fast rules connected with setting out berry plants: Protect roots from any exposure to the sun; plant crowns at the exact level at which they grew before. Make a furrow 1-1/2 inches deep and 4 inches wide. Hold the plant by its center stems level with the surface of the earth, spread the roots out comfortably over a small hump in the trench floor, and cover with 1-1/4 inches of soil. Tamp the soil so that no air pockets are left by the strawberry roots.

Keep all blossoms picked the first season; the size of next year's crop will make it worthwhile. *Newly planted* everbearers are kept

Strawberry plant at left is too far below ground level; the one in center is too far above ground level; the one at right is correctly planted. Tamp soil around planted roots carefully to dispel air pockets.

clear of blooms the *first* spring, allowed to bloom and set fruit later in the summer, and at will after that. The runners the plants send out about six weeks after planting can be rooted in well-worked soil right where they are, then cut from the parent plant and set in new rows. Or they can be left to root themselves. They will soon create a matted row of strawberries. Many growers claim crops from matted rows are inferior, but I know a man who makes his living selling berries grown by the matted-row system. Less work and less space is required in this method. Try it. If it fails to produce satisfactory crops, root and transplant the runners, and keep the rows clean of new runners by chopping them off and discarding.

Whichever system you choose to grow your strawberries, the bed must be dug up every four to six years; two years before the bed must be changed, root as many runners as you want strawberry plants for the new bed and transplant during the following spring. The spring after that, when the old bed must be dug up, your new bed will be producing.

Winter protection. Cover berries with 6 inches of mulch when the temperature goes down to 20 degrees; when the ground freezes hard, add another foot of mulch. Remove most of the mulch in early spring; some of it will mat down and give the berries a clean bed to grow on. Strawberries are best if they are not washed before using.

Fertilizing. Feed established beds in early spring by broadcasting 5-10-5 at the specified rate on a day when the leaves are completely dry. Brush the fertilizer from the leaves at once (I use a feather duster), then water in the fertilizer. Or feed the row a liquid fertilizer that will not harm the leaves.

Harvesting. Never harvest berries into a metal container. Ripe strawberries will be perfect for only a day, so keep ripe berries picked.

Freezing. Hull ripe firm berries, seal into a plastic freezer bag, and freeze. Berries that have soil on them and must be washed had better be dried and coated with granulated sugar at the rate of 1 pound of sugar to 4 pounds of berries. Seal into a freezer container and freeze. Acidulous berries are best packed in syrup. Stir 3 cups of sugar into 1 quart of cold water until the water·is clear and the sugar dissolved. Place washed, hulled, sliced berries in freezer containers, fill with syrup leaving 1/2-inch headroom, seal and freeze.

RASPBERRIES AND BLACKBERRIES

A memory most French country children have in common is that of walks along back roads in August when the towering wild blackberry hedges drip ripening fruit from their topmost branches to the dust of the road. Black raspberries seem more common in America and there is relatively little difference between them, excepting that the core of the blackberry is part of the fruit while black raspberries come away leaving a little white core behind, as do red raspberries. Blackberries prefer a milder climate; raspberries thrive well up into Canada. All three plants prefer a garden loam well supplied with humus, well-drained, and slightly acid, between pH 5.5 and pH 6.5. Avoid nitrogenous fertilizers, which produce lots of leaves but few berries.

Planting and culture. In areas north of Philadelphia, plant in early spring as soon as the soil can be prepared. In warmer areas, plant in late winter or very early spring. Set plants 1 foot apart in trenches that bring crowns to the level they grew at in the nursery. Rows should be 6 feet apart. A permanent mulch to keep weeds down is strongly recommended; if the mulch is rotted manure or compost you won't have to fertilize. Otherwise, early every spring work a small handful of 5-10-5 into the soil around each plant.

Pruning. Many gardeners stake raspberries and claim better yields. Since canes that have just produced must be cut back almost to the ground to keep the bed trim and the fruit of best quality, staking has never seemed to me to be justified or necessary. Instead, keep your berry patches in bounds by picking, then pruning at once. At the time of planting, prune canes back to 6 to 8 inches from the ground. Remove any blossoms the first season. Allow canes to set fruit the following year, then after the harvest cut to ground level the old canes the fruit grew on. The following spring cut the past season's new growth back by one third. This will leave canes 24 to 36 inches tall. Cut away any dead canes, and thin those remaining to stand 3 to 4 inches apart.

Prune everbearing varieties this way: In the spring cut back to live wood the tips of canes that bore last year's late crop. These canes will bear a midsummer crop, after which they can be cut to the ground. The new canes will produce the late crop.

Spraying. Berry fruits have few problems. A well-fed bed, in a

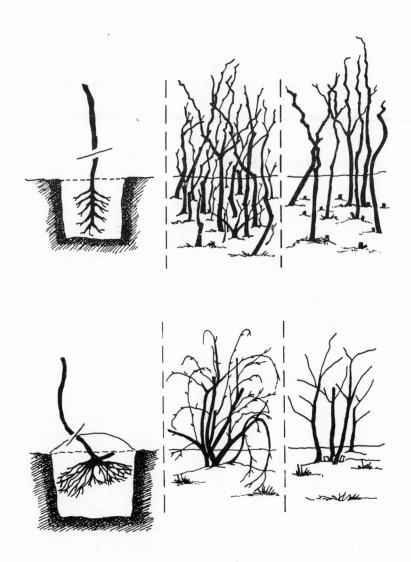

Top strip of drawings shows how to plant red raspberry bushes. Prune back to 2 inches at planting time. Center top shows red raspberry patch before spring pruning; top right shows patch after spring pruning.

Bottom strip shows how to plant blackberry and black and purple raspberry bushes. Mound soil 2 inches high, cut back cane as indicated, and spread mound to ground level as the season progresses. Center bottom shows blackberry and black and purple raspberry patch before spring pruning; bottom right shows blackberry and black and purple raspberry patch after spring pruning.

well-drained location, pruned enough to have good air circulation, will be healthy.

Freezing and harvesting. When berries slip readily from the core they are ripe. Do not wash berries unless absolutely necessary. Spread on a breadboard, sprinkle with sugar, pack and freeze: This is my favorite way to handle raspberries and blackberries. You may prefer them in syrup: see Strawberries: Freezing.

BLUEBERRIES

The blueberries you buy in stores get larger and more tasteless by the year. Unless a variety that is a selection from a wild blueberry will do well in your garden, don't bother with this fruit. The wild strains are smaller but so much better! Blueberries are easy to grow, provided the soil is quite acid, with a pH of 4.4 to 5.1. If your soil tends to be alkaline and you want blueberries very much, add 2 parts acid peat to one part garden loam and grow them in barrels or boxed trenches. Blueberries also require a cross-pollination; any two varieties will cross-pollinate each other.

Planting and culture. In early spring set roots out as for raspberries, and cut upper branches back to 1/2 their length. Wait to fertilize until June 1. Then add 1 ounce of sulfate of ammonia to each plant. As the plant grows older, raise this amount until you are feeding each plant 4 ounces. Every three years apply 2 to 8 ounces of 10-10-10, depending on the size of the bush, and reduce the ammonium sulfate that year to half the amount. Don't let new plants produce fruit the first two years. They will go on bearing for upward of twelve years, so you can afford to be patient. The only pruning required is the removal of excessive small growth and dead branches or twigs. The crop ripens over a six-week period, and will need netting to protect it from birds.

GRAPES

Grapes are undemanding vines that will grow on poor, rocky soil that other fruits balk at. They are newly hardy, too; time was when the only grapes New England gardeners could grow were the Concords, which are fine for jellies, but less appealing than other kinds

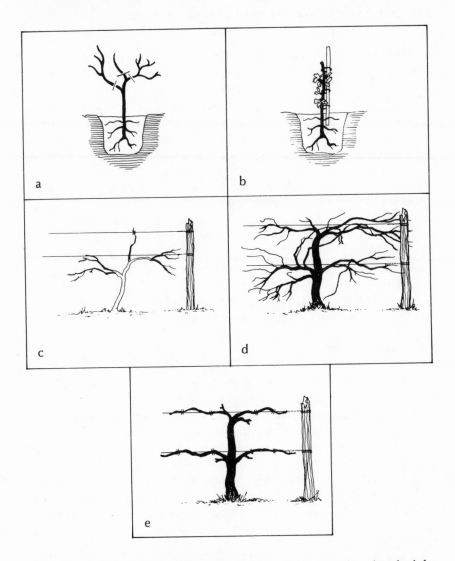

Drawing *a* and *b* show newly planted grape vine pruned and staked for its first season. Drawing *c* shows vine in its second season, with longest vertical shoot trained to the top wire of a two-wire trellis and one cane selected to grow right and left along bottom wire. Drawings *d* and *e* show mature grape vine before and after pruning, using the Four-Arm Kniffin System. Prune in late winter before buds swell, leaving only year-old canes, from ¼ to ⅜ inch diameter, which have 5 to 8 inches between the fifth and sixth buds. Make cuts at least 1 inch beyond the buds. Short spurs near the main stem have been pruned back to 2 buds each to provide wood for renewal of growth. Four-year-old vine should have a total of about 40 buds left after pruning.

for table use. Now three or four fine table grapes are hardy in cold areas. Though the very best are grown in California, many excellent varieties succeed in a great number of states.

Good jams can be made with conventional recipes, but at some time try the Bordeaux Jam. It is a great way to use an overflow crop with little effort. Peeled grapes are elegant in fruit cups.

One of the little-known uses of grape vines in this country is that of the leaves. Before you pickle green cucumbers, line the preserving kettle with grape leaves, turn the cucumbers into it, cover them with boiling water, and let stand until cold. Drain and cover with hot vinegar and water, one part vinegar to three parts water, and let stand until tepid. Then proceed with your recipe for cucumbers. This improves the flavor and texture of the cucumbers. Or add 2 or 3 medium-size grape leaves per quart jar of pickles to enhance the flavor and color.

The large tender leaves of Thompson Seedless are the best grape leaves for wrapping rice and meat mixtures.

Planting and culture. Plant 2- to 3-year-old vines in light, well-drained soil well supplied with organic matter. Set plants 8 to 10 feet apart in early spring while the ground is still moist. Plant as you would a tree, then cut the vine back to above the two lowest buds. Train the vine toward a wire set between two stakes the first year, and in subsequent years prune for maximum production, as in the illustration on page 221. Grapes will produce the second or third year after planting, and will go on bearing for decades. A few varieties require cross-pollination; most do not. Mulch to keep the ground weed-free and preserve moisture. Water the plants when they begin to set fruit, to improve the harvest. In early spring fertilize with a handful of compost, or with 3/4 pound of 5-10-5 per plant.

Spraying. We have never had to spray our grapes, but if you run into trouble, check Table VI.

10 Cooking and Serving Fruits

Fresh fruit, sun-ripened on the plant, hand-picked at the right time, brought with care to the kitchen, and briefly chilled is so good that one wonders why we should ever do much else to it. For variety, for one thing, many fruits having a different taste when cooked. Some people also find certain fruits more digestible when cooked, especially apples, pears, peaches, and berries. And for the interest of combining fruits, or adding their flavor to other food, as in Fruit Compote with a heavenly Custard Sauce, or homemade Refrigerator Fruit Ice Cream made with heavy cream. And what is more attractive and delicious than mixed fruit cups, fruit soufflés, and wonderful purées fluffed with whipped cream or served hot on ice cream? And when you have quantities of fruit, how satisfying it is to make preserves and jams that will recall in the dead of winter the taste of the summer crop.

FRUIT EN COMPOTE
This is a basic recipe for the home-grown fruits. *En compote* fruits can be drained and used with meringues, warmed and set alight with a liqueur, or served in such traditional desserts as Poires Hélène. Some fruits that do not always mix well fresh will blend perfectly when cooked. Excellent combinations can be made of sour or sweet cherries and peaches, of pears and plums, and they can be garnished with ripe berries.

2 cups water
1 cup sugar
Pinch of salt
4 cups fresh fruit

Lemon juice
1/2 teaspoon vanilla extract
Spices or liqueurs, optional

1. Bring water, sugar, and salt to a boil and simmer 5 minutes to make a light syrup.

2. Wash and prepare the fruit, peeling, coring or pitting, and cutting up, as needed.

3. Add to the hot syrup. Add lemon juice if the fruit lacks tartness. Cook until tender, about 6 to 10 minutes. When the fruit pierces easily with a fork, remove from the heat, stir in the vanilla, and chill.

Serves six to eight.

FRUIT PUREE

Prepare Fruit en Compote, drain, force through a sieve, or purée in a blender at low speed. This is good by itself, or mixed with whipped cream and sweetened to taste.

CREAM CUSTARD FOR FRUIT

In France, fruits *en compote* are often served with custard sauce. But this custard is also a delicious dessert served by itself in tall sherbet glasses with a few drops of dark rum.

3 eggs
1/4 cup sugar
Water

1-1/2 cups heavy cream
1 teaspoon vanilla extract
Dark rum, optional

1. Beat eggs until thick. Add the sugar.

2. Bring 2 inches of water to a boil in the bottom of a double boiler. Turn heat very low.

3. Mix 1 cup of the cream in the egg mixture and pour into the top of the double boiler. Cook, stirring, about 15 minutes, or until the mixture thickens. If the eggs begin to curdle, quickly stir in half the remaining cream. Turn off the heat, add vanilla, and chill. Float the remaining cream on top of the custard to keep a skin from forming as it cools. Beat this cream into the custard before serving.

Serves four to six.

FRUIT SOUFFLÉ

1 cup fruit purée, strained
1/2 cup sugar
1 tablespoon lemon juice
1 tablespoon grated lemon rind,
  optional

5 egg whites
1/4 teaspoon cream of tartar
1/4 teaspoon salt

1. To the fruit purée add half the sugar. Heat to boiling and add lemon juice and rind, if desired.
2. Beat egg whites until frothy, sprinkle with cream of tartar and salt, and beat until stiff but not dry. Gradually beat in the rest of the sugar.
3. Fold egg whites into the fruit purée. Turn into a well-buttered 6-cup baking dish and coat the top with sugar.
4. Bake at 325 degrees for 50 to 60 minutes, or until well browned, on a lower shelf of the oven. Serve with a cold sweet berry sauce or whipped cream, or with a sauce made of the same fruit as the soufflé.

Serves six to eight.

SWEET BERRY SAUCE

2 cups washed hulled berries
Sugar to taste
1 tablespoon Kirsch, optional

Purée berries in a blender, or mash through a sieve. Beat in sugar to taste, stir in Kirsch, and chill 2 hours or more, covered, in the refrigerator.

Makes about 2 cups.

FRUIT FOOLS

These are popular in Britain. Frozen as for Refrigerator Fruit Ice Cream, a "fool" becomes an old-fashioned ice.

2 cups cut-up fresh fruit
Sugar to taste
2 cups heavy cream, whipped

Purée or crush the fresh fruit, or put through a blender. Add sugar to taste. Strain off the juice and simmer it until reduced to a light syrup, about 15 minutes. Cool, stir in the fruit, and chill. Fold the cream into the fruit mixture, and serve in tall sherbet glasses. Serves six to eight.

REFRIGERATOR FRUIT ICE CREAM

1 tablespoon (1 envelope) gelatine   **Sugar**
1/2 cup cold milk   **2 cups heavy cream**
Salt   **1 teaspoon vanilla**
2 cups crushed or puréed fresh
** fruit**

1. Soften the gelatine in milk and set over hot water until dissolved. Add a few grains of salt.
2. Add sugar to taste to the fruit. You want this fairly sweet.
3. Whip the cream until it is thick but not quite stiff. Fold in the fruit, then the milk with gelatine, and the vanilla or almond extract. Turn the mixture into shallow bowls so it will freeze more quickly. Place in freezer with indicator at the coldest position.
4. When the cream begins to look like slush in March, turn it into a mixer and beat until smooth and glossy. Then pour it into the refrigerator trays to freeze.

Black sweet cherries, peaches, nectarines, and all the berries make excellent refrigerator ice cream. Add a few drops of lemon juice or liqueur to pick up the flavor if you like.
Serves six.

FRUIT CUP COMBINATIONS

Some fresh fruits go well together; you have only to pick the mature crops, peel or pit, slice or dice, sweeten to taste, and serve in a little orange juice, or perked up with a few teaspoons of lemon juice or Kirsch. Here are a few suggestions for mixing fruits likely to be ready for harvest at the same time.

July. Pears, peaches, plums, cherries, prepared *en compote*, chilled and garnished with ripe sweet strawberries, halved.

June. Cherries, strawberries, blueberries, in a little orange juice, or a semisweet chilled white wine.

August. Pears prepared *en compote* and sliced, fresh peach wedges, and raspberries, in orange juice.

September. Muskmelon wedges, diced apples, ripe pear slices, peach slices, sliced plums *en compote*, raspberries, peeled seeded grapes, and a few blueberries.

FRUIT JAMS

Fruit jams are among the simplest of preserves; all you have to do is weigh fruit and sugar, and cook together until the mixture either thickens or sheets. The jam "sheets" when, instead of running quickly off the spoon in single drops, it slides down the spoon and falls off in a broad sheet, which then becomes slow-falling drops.

For 1 pound of strawberries, use 1 pound of sugar.

For 1 pound of other berries, use 3/4 pound sugar.

To 1 cup of cooked, mashed pulp, use 1 pound of sugar.

To all, add 1 tablespoon lemon juice.

1. Wash, pare, hull, or otherwise prepare fruit. Weigh out amount of sugar according to the fruit you are using.

2. Turn into a large preserving kettle. Heat slowly until the fruit boils, then add sugar and stir until it dissolves.

3. Continue to cook, stirring often, for 10 to 20 minutes, or until syrup sheets or thickens. Pour into sterilized jars, leaving 1/4 inch space at the top. Pour hot paraffin into jars, cool, and cover.

Makes about 1 pint, pound for pound.

APPLES AND PEARS

Apples and pears have a somewhat similar consistency, and they can be interchanged in many recipes. When I use pears for an apple recipe, I add 1/2 tablespoon of lemon juice. Promise the children Candied Apples on a Stick, and they'll be glad to help with the apple harvest. Make Apple Butter when you want to use up lots of apples, Swiss Applesauce when you have no time to fuss with dessert, and Rolled Apple Dumplings when you do have time to make something really delicious. The Pears and Brandied Cheese dessert can be made with tart apples as well. It is for sophisticated palates.

MOTHER'S BAKED APPLES

8 medium apples
3/4 cup brown sugar
1/2 cup white raisins
1/2 cup chopped nuts
1/4 cup butter

1/2 cup brown sugar
1/2 cup boiling water
1 tablespoon lemon juice
Whipped cream, optional

1. Heat oven to 375 degrees.
2. Wash and core the apples, remove stems, but do not peel. Stand in buttered glass baking dish and distribute the 3/4 cup of sugar, the raisins and the nuts evenly among the apples, stuffing well down into the centers. Fill up the cavities with butter, and sprinkle on 1/2 cup of brown sugar. Dab bits of any remaining butter on the tops. Pour boiling water into the bottom of the pan, and set it in the oven. When apples have baked for 20 minutes, baste them with liquid in the pan, and sprinkle lemon juice over. If liquid is disappearing, add 1/4 cup of water. Bake about 15 minutes more, or until the apples are tender. Serve hot or cold, with or without whipped cream. Heavy cream is also good on baked apples.
Serves eight.

APPLE BUTTER

2 quarts sweet cider
1 quart peeled, cored, and sliced
  apples
1-1/4 cups sugar

1/4 teaspoon cinnamon
1/4 teaspoon allspice
1/8 teaspoon ground cloves
1/4 teaspoon salt

1. Boil the cider to reduce it by half. Stir in the apples. Cook rapidly, stirring frequently, until apples are soft. Then cook slowly, stirring constantly.

2. When mixture begins to thicken, add sugar, spices, and salt. Cook, stirring constantly, until mixture is smooth and thick enough to spread.

3. Pour into hot sterilized jars, cover with hot paraffin and cap. If you have a great many apples, double the amounts and make twice as much.

Makes about six 8-ounce jars.

SWISS APPLESAUCE

3/4 cup lemon juice
8 apples

1 cup white or brown sugar
1 cup heavy cream, whipped

1. Strain lemon juice into a medium-size bowl.

2. Core but do not peel the apples. Shred and toss with the lemon juice. Sweeten to taste with sugar. Fold cream into the apple mixture. Serve immediately, as the apples tend to discolor.

Serves six to eight.

PANCAKES À LA POMME

1-1/2 cups flour
Pinch of salt
1 cup milk
4 eggs
2 tablespoons melted bacon fat or
  butter

1 cup peeled, cored, and grated
  apple
Butter and syrup

1. Measure flour into a medium-size bowl. Add salt, milk, eggs, and shortening. Beat until all the flour is moistened.

2. Stir the apple quickly into the mixture. Bake on a hot well-greased griddle, and serve with butter, or butter and corn syrup or maple syrup.

Serves six to eight.

ROLLED APPLE DUMPLINGS

Papa's Pie Pastry
6 medium apples
3/4 cup brown sugar, firmly
    packed
1 teaspoon cinnamon

1/2 teaspoon mace
1/3 cup chopped nuts
1-1/2 tablespoons butter
1 tablespoon grated lemon rind
1/2 cup heavy cream, whipped

1. Heat oven to 375 degrees.
2. Prepare the pastry but omit the butter. Roll out 1/8 inch thick and cut into 6 squares.
3. Peel and core the apples and place one on each square of pastry. Mix the sugar, cinnamon, mace, and nuts. Cut in the butter. Fill the cored centers with the mixture, and sprinkle with lemon rind.
4. Bring the corners of the dough together on top of the apples. Moisten the edges with milk to seal. Prick with a fork all around so steam can escape. Bake 30 to 45 minutes, or until pastry is brown and apples tender. Serve with whipped cream or hard sauce. Serves six.

DAVID'S FAVORITE APPLE STUFFING

3 green cooking apples
8-ounce package cream cheese

1/4 teaspoon salt
1/8 teaspoon pepper

1. Peel and core the apples. Press them through a grater, mince in the blender, or put through a meat grinder.
2. Beat the cheese until soft; beat in the apples and add the salt and pepper. Work quickly so the apples won't discolor.
This fills the cavity of a 6- to 8-pound turkey, which is then roasted as usual.

CANDIED APPLES ON A STICK

2 cups sugar	Pinch of cinnamon
2/3 cup corn syrup	6 medium-size apples
1 cup water	Red food coloring
Salt	6 wooden skewers

1. Combine sugar, corn syrup, water, and salt in the top of a double boiler. Heat, stirring constantly until syrup boils.

2. Cook without stirring until your candy thermometer indicates 280 degrees. Then reduce heat to avoid browning syrup, but let it continue to cook to 300 degrees.

3. Remove from heat and quickly stir in enough food coloring to make syrup bright red.

4. While syrup is cooking, insert a wooden skewer into the stem end of each apple. As soon as the syrup is ready, dip the skewered apples into it, rolling them around to coat completely. Place upside down on a well-buttered cookie sheet. Let them cool. Makes six.

PEARS AND BRANDIED CHEESE

An interesting and excellent dessert for grown-ups. Children show a certain lack of appreciation for it. The cheese and brandy mixture alone makes a great spread for cocktail crackers.

8-ounce package cream cheese	2 tablespoons fine brandy
2-ounce package Danish blue cheese	6 fresh pears

1. Beat the cream cheese and the blue cheese with the brandy for 5 minutes in an electric beater at high speed. Scrape into a bowl, cover, and refrigerate. This is best when it is at least one week old.

2. Wash and halve the pears without breaking off the stems. Scoop out the cores. Dry the cut side of the pears and fill with the cheese mixture. Fit the halves together and arrange in a bowl small enough to pack the pears tightly together, as the pear juice tends to make them come unstuck. Add a pretty garnish, black cherries, for instance, or big raspberries, sugar coated, or seedless green grapes. Serve pears with an asparagus server. Serves six.

POIRES HÉLÈNE

6 pears, en compote
6 thick slices vanilla ice cream
Chocolate Sauce Escoffier

Drain the pears, place beside a scoop of ice cream on a dessert plate, and ladle Chocolate Sauce Escoffier sparingly over them. The great Escoffier added candied violets, but one rarely has these.
Serves six.

Chocolate Sauce Escoffier

8-ounce package semisweet
   chocolate
1 cup water, plus 2 tablespoons

1/2 teaspoon vanilla
3 tablespoons heavy cream
1-1/2 tablespoons sweet butter

Grate chocolate into the water, add the sugar, and simmer 25 minutes. Add the vanilla, stir in the cream, and then the butter. This sauce has a bitter flavor compared to most chocolate sauces, so you had best sample it and sweeten to your taste before serving.
Makes about 1-1/2 cups.

PEAR GARNISH FOR MEAT

4 pears, halved and cored
2 tablespoons butter
3 tablespoons honey

2 tablespoons strained lemon juice
Tart red jelly or sugared
   cranberries, chopped

1. Cook the pears *en compote*.
2. Melt butter in a heavy skillet and melt the honey into it. Add lemon juice and simmer the pears in this mixture, basting frequently, until a glaze clings to the pears.
3. Remove, fill the centers with jelly or cranberries. Excellent with grilled meats or chops.
Serves six to eight.

PEACHES AND NECTARINES

Peaches and nectarines have similar flavor and consistency, nectarines being actually only a smooth-skinned variety of peach. In any recipe they can be interchanged. Try Peaches Sultane for a festive occasion. And do put up a quantity of the Pickled Peaches; they are expensive to buy but easy to make, and much better homemade from your own crop. I add a few very ripe peach slices to an apple pie, and sometimes put a sliced green apple in a peach pie.

PEACH MELBA

2 cups raspberries
Sugar
1 tablespoon Kirsch

4 peaches, en compote
1 quart vanilla ice cream

1. Wash and hull raspberries, purée in a blender, sweeten to taste, stir in Kirsch, and chill.
2. Place peach halves on a layer of ice cream in a crystal dessert bowl and top with raspberry purée.
Serves eight.

FRESH PEACH TART

Papa's Pie Pastry
1/4 cup peach jam
3/4 cup sugar
1/4 teaspoon salt
4 cups peeled sliced peaches

1 egg
2 tablespoons butter
1 tablespoon lemon juice
Milk

1. Prepare pie shell and heat oven to 425 degrees. Cover the bottom of the shell with peach jam.
2. Combine sugar and salt, and toss the peaches in the mixture. Beat egg until thick, blend into peaches. Turn into pie shell, dot with butter, and sprinkle with lemon juice.
3. Roll out the remaining dough 1/8 inch thick; cut into narrow strips. Twist the strips and then attach to the edge of the pie shell to make a lattice top. Bake 30 minutes on a lower shelf of the oven.
Serves six or eight.

PÊCHES FLAMBÉES

Easy Short Pastry   **Confectioner's sugar**
6 to 8 peaches, en compote   **2 tablespoons brandy**
1 pint peach ice cream

1. Roll out the pastry to 1/8-inch thickness, cut into 2-1/2-inch squares, bake, and cool.
2. Prepare peaches *en compote*. Drain and keep warm, or reheat in oven just before serving.
3. At serving time cover the 12 or more pastry squares with ice cream and place a drained peach half on each. Press the fruit down to anchor it.
4. Warm the brandy, pour a little into each warm peach half, and light as you enter the dining room.

    Serves twelve or more.

PEACHES SULTANE

1 quart pistachio ice cream   **Alex's Sabayon Sauce**
6 ripe peaches, en compote   **Pistachio nuts, chopped**

1. Arrange a scoop of ice cream on an individual dessert plate and cradle a cooked peach on top.
2. Cover with Alex's Sabayon Sauce and sprinkle with pistachio nuts.

    Serves six.

Alex's Sabayon Sauce

8 egg yokes
1/8 teaspoon salt
1 cup fine granulated sugar
1 tablespoon lemon juice

1 cup amontillado or any fine
   dry, pale sherry
2 tablespoons brandy
1 cup heavy cream, whipped

1. Beat egg yolks and salt until thick; dribble in sugar and lemon juice. Turn into a double boiler and, still beating, cook until thick. Dribble in the sherry and brandy, beat and cook until thickened again.

2. Cool. Fold in the cream, pour into a serving dish, and chill. Serve, as above, or with a fruit compote.

Alex doesn't add the whipped cream, but the cream holds it better when chilled. Also, the cream will retrieve it if it starts to curdle.

PEACH CRISP

1 cup rolled oats
1/2 cup sifted flour
1/2 cup brown sugar, firmly
   packed
1/4 teaspoon salt

1/2 cup butter
1 teaspoon lemon juice
4 cups peeled sliced peaches
Ice cream, peach or vanilla

1. Heat the oven to 350 degrees.

2. In a medium-size bowl, place the rolled oats, either quick-cooking or standard, and the flour, sugar, and salt. Mix enough to blend.

3. Melt butter and beat into the rolled oat mixture until well mixed. Sprinkle lemon juice over peaches.

4. Arrange the peaches in a glass baking dish, well buttered. Spread the oatmeal mixture on top of the fruit, pressing down lightly. Bake 30 minutes, or until the topping is brown and the peaches tender. Serve hot with a little ice cream on top.

Serves six.

PICKLED PEACHES

3 quarts sugar
2 quarts vinegar
7 2-inch pieces stick cinnamon
2 tablespoons whole cloves
11 quarts small or medium
  peaches

4 quarts water
2 tablespoons salt
2 tablespoons vinegar
Extra stick cinnamon and whole
  cloves, optional

1. Combine the sugar and vinegar in a preserving kettle, and drop in the cinnamon and cloves tied in a small cheesecloth bag. Bring to a boil and let simmer covered, about 30 minutes. Remove the bag.

2. Wash the peaches, and remove the skins. To prevent darkening, as you finish peeling each peach, drop it into a bowl containing the water, salt, and vinegar. Drain just before cooking.

3. Drop the peaches into the boiling syrup, two or three quarts at a time, and simmer each lot for 5 minutes, or until just tender. Pack the peaches into hot sterilized pint or quart jars, as each batch is finished. When all are cooked, pour in the boiling syrup, leaving half an inch of space at the top of each jar. Adjust the jar lids. You can add a piece of stick cinnamon and 2 whole cloves to each jar before sealing if you like.

4. Process in boiling water for 20 minutes. (Count processing time *after* the water in the canner returns to boiling.) Set the jars on a wire rack to cool.

Makes 7 quarts.

MADELEINE'S NECTARINE MERINGUES

5 egg whites
1-1/2 cups sugar
1 cup finely ground roasted
  almonds

6 nectarines, halved, en compote
Peach jam
1 tablespoon lemon juice
1 cup heavy cream, whipped and
  sweetened

1. Heat oven to 250 degrees.

2. Beat egg whites until stiff but not dry. Sift in sugar a little at a time, beating until mixture is dry. Fold in ground almonds. Drop by large spoonfuls onto cookie sheet, making twelve large meringues. Make a depression in the center of each large enough to hold a nectarine half. Place in the oven and let dry out for about 1 hour.

3. Slide each meringue onto a dessert plate with a spatula. Spread the center of each with jam to prevent the fruit juice from soaking in. Place a nectarine half on each meringue, and sprinkle a few drops of lemon juice over it. Cover with the whipped cream. Serves twelve.

PLUMS

Plums are out of favor; very few new home orchards include them and cookbooks have almost literally no recipes for plums. Plum pudding never has plums in it! And this is a pity, because the plum in bloom is one of the loveliest of the fruit trees. Whether dwarfed or full size, it is easy to handle, too. Plums are excellent *en compote* with Custard Sauce, and very good in Plum Turnovers.

PLUM TURNOVERS

Easy Short Pastry	**1 apple, peeled, cored, and**
2 tablespoons water	**quartered**
1/2 cup sugar	**2 tablespoons red raspberries**
6 plums, peeled and pitted	**2 tablespoons butter, melted**
	Sugar

1. Prepare pastry dough and chill.
2. Simmer water and sugar 2 minutes, add plums, apple, and raspberries, and simmer to the consistency of jam. This will require 30 minutes or more, depending on the moisture content of the plums. Cool.
3. Heat the oven to 400 degrees.
4. Roll out the pastry dough 1/4 inch thick and brush with butter. Cut into 3-inch squares. Divide the plum mixture among the squares, heaping it into the center of each. Fold over the dough to form a triangle. Seal the edges with the tines of a fork. Place on a greased cookie sheet, and bake 20 to 25 minutes.
Makes 8 turnovers.

PLUM BUTTER

6 pounds pitted plums
1 green apple, peeled, cored, and
  sliced
1 cup water

Sugar
1 tablespoon lemon juice
1/2 teaspoon mace

1. Simmer the plums and apple in the water until soft, about 15 minutes. Purée in a blender or force through a sieve. Weigh, add half the weight in sugar. If you like jams sweet, add 2/3 as much sugar.

2. In a preserving kettle, simmer the plum pulp, sugar, lemon juice and mace, stirring frequently to prevent scorching, until mixture is thick enough to spread. Turn into hot sterilized jars, seal with melted paraffin, and cap.

Makes about eight 8-ounce jars.

SPICY PICKLED PLUMS

8 pounds purple plums
7-1/4 cups sugar
2 cups vinegar
1 teaspoon nutmeg

1/4 teaspoon ground cinnamon
1 tablespoon whole allspice
1 cup white raisins

1. Prick plums with the end of a sharp knife to prevent bursting when they cook.

2. Boil sugar, vinegar, and spices 5 minutes. Cool, add plums, and simmer 5 minutes more. Let stand overnight.

3. Cook with the raisins 15 minutes over medium heat, or until plums are tender. Pack into hot sterilized jars and seal. Process in boiling water for 5 minutes.

Makes 6 to 7 pints.

CHERRIES AND BERRIES

My favorite pie of all is sour cherry pie, and Sally Erath's recipe is a good one. Sweet cherries hardly ever get as far as the kitchen; and when they do are rarely cooked. The exception is Cherries Jubilation, which isn't quite the same as Cherries Jubilee, but awfully good. Cherries are especially delicious in Fruit en Compote.

SALLY ERATH'S SOUR CHERRY PIE

Pastry for 2-crust 8-inch pie	2 cups pitted sour cherries
1 cup sugar	1 egg
1/4 teaspoon cinnamon	Butter
1/4 teaspoon nutmeg	Milk

1. Heat the oven to 425 degrees.

2. Roll out half the pastry and line an 8-inch pie pan.

3. Combine sugar, cinnamon, and nutmeg. Stem the cherries and toss them in the sugar mixture. Beat the egg until thick, then blend it into the cherries. Turn into the pie shell and dot with butter.

4. Roll out the rest of the pastry and cover and seal the filled shell. Brush with milk so the top will color nicely. Bake 30 to 40 minutes.

Serves six to eight.

CHERRIES JUBILATION

4 cups sweet cherries	1 cup sugar
1 whole clove	4 tablespoons cherry brandy
2 cups dry red wine	Vanilla ice cream, optional
1/2 cup Marsala wine	

1. Wash the cherries, preferably the large, black, sweet ones. Stem and pit them. Stick the clove into one cherry. Crack a handful of the pits with a mallet (I use the rolling pin!) and place the pits with the clove-stuck cherry in a small cheesecloth bag. Put the bag in a kettle and add the red wine, the Marsala, and the sugar. Simmer 5 minutes.

2. Add the cherries and simmer, covered, 10 minutes more. Drain the cherries and place in a serving dish. Strain the syrup into a pan and boil rapidly until it has reduced to about 1-1/2 cups.

3. Just before you serve, heat the cherry brandy (or plain brandy will do), and bring it to the table with the cherries. Set fire to the brandy and ladle it onto the warm cherries. Ladle from the flaming bowl into dessert dishes. You might like to serve ice cream with this.

Serves six to eight.

DEEP-DISH BLACKBERRY-AND-APPLE PIE

2 cups blackberries
4 to 5 medium-size cooking
  apples
4 tablespoons sugar
2 tablespoons lemon juice

1 egg yolk
1/2 recipe Papa's Pie Pastry
Sugar for garnish
1/2 cup heavy cream, whipped
  and sweetened

1. Preheat the oven to 425 degrees.
2. Hull the berries. Wash them only if necessary.
3. Peel, core, and slice the apples. Layer apples and blackberries in a buttered baking dish, sprinkling each layer with the sugar and lemon juice. If the fruit is tart, add more sugar.
4. Top with the pastry. Bake at 425 degrees for 10 minutes, then reduce heat to 350 degrees and bake 45 minutes more. Sprinkle with sugar. Serve warm with whipped cream.

Serves eight.

RASPBERRY MOUSSE

2 cups raspberries
1 cup sugar
1 envelope gelatine

2 tablespoons cold water
3 tablespoons hot water
1 pint heavy cream

1. Wash and hull raspberries, drain, and sprinkle with sugar. Let stand 1 hour. Purée in a blender, or press through a sieve.
2. Soak gelatine in the cold water and dissolve in the hot water. Stir into the raspberry purée. Refrigerate until mixture begins to thicken.
3. Whip the cream and fold into the berry mixture. Pour into a mold and let set for 4 hours.

Strawberries and blackberries can be prepared the same way, but they may require a little more sugar.

Serves four to six.

MINTED RASPBERRIES IN SYRUP

4 cups raspberries
1 cup sugar

1 cup water
Fresh mint leaves, chopped fine

Wash the raspberries. Make a heavy syrup by boiling sugar and water together for about 10 minutes. Pour the warm, not hot, syrup over the berries and chill. Garnish with a sprinkling of the mint. Serves four.

BLUEBERRIES

Fresh blueberries are unquestionably best uncooked and served with heavy cream and just a sprinkling of sugar. However, nothing makes quite such a good breakfast as blueberry pancakes or muffins, when the berries are fresh from the garden. And do try combining late-bearing blueberries with vine-ripened cantaloupe! Marinated in a cup of semisweet white wine, like Barsac, and chilled for 2 to 3 hours, this is a marvelous fruit cup. Blueberry pie is, of course, a great American favorite. Adapt Sally Erath's Sour Cherry Pie by omitting the spices and sweetening only to taste.

JOHN MORRIS'S BLUEBERRY PANCAKES

3 eggs
1 cup milk
1/3 cup melted butter
2 cups flour
3 teaspoons baking powder

3 teaspoons sugar
1/2 teaspoon salt
1 cup blueberries
Maple syrup

1. In a large mixing bowl, beat the eggs, add milk and butter. Combine flour, baking powder, sugar, and salt, and add to the egg mixture. Beat with a fork or a whisk to blend well. Allow to rest while griddle is heating. Don't try to get all the lumps out, however. They make pancakes taste better, John says.

2. Carefully blend in the blueberries, taking care not to mash them.

3. Bake on a hot griddle well buttered for each pancake, and serve with real maple syrup, which is very light and much less sweet than the commercial kind.

John serves these pancakes with small sausages grilled to perfection.

Serves six.

TEN-MINUTE BLUEBERRY MUFFINS

1 egg	1/3 cup sugar
4 tablespoons butter	3 teaspoons baking powder
1 cup milk	1/2 teaspoon salt
2 cups flour	1 cup blueberries

1. Grease muffin pans and preheat the oven to 425 degrees.

2. Beat the egg until thick. Melt the butter, and add it to the milk. Beat both into the egg.

3. Combine flour, sugar, baking powder, and salt in a sifter. Sift into a bowl, pour in the egg mixture, and mix with about 15 strokes. Shake a little flour over the blueberries, and fold them into the batter.

4. Fill the muffin cups two-thirds full, and bake 20 minutes.

When I make blueberry muffins for breakfast, I measure the dry ingredients into the sifter the night before, and send the children out to pick the berries while I make the batter and heat the oven.

Serves six to eight.

BLUEBERRY JAM

4 cups blueberries	1/2 cup water
4 medium-size apples	2 teaspoons lemon juice
6 cups sugar	

1. Wash and drain blueberries. Pare, core, and chop the apples and measure 2 cupfuls.

2. In a preserving kettle, combine the sugar, water, and lemon juice. Stir and heat slowly to a simmer. Stir in the blueberries and apples and bring to a boil. Cook until thick and syrupy, about 20 minutes.

3. Pour into hot sterilized jars, cover with hot paraffin, and cap.

Makes five to six 8-ounce jars.

STRAWBERRIES

Some desserts may be better than Strawberry Shortcake, but few are more popular! Try this old-fashioned recipe, using thickened but not whipped cream, and the baking-powder type of biscuits that made shortcake famous. Use the recipe for your other berry crops as well. The Strawberry Tart Chimney Hill resembles the strawberry tart we make in France, but you will have to find wild strawberries to serve the true Fraises des Bois Crème Fraîche. A delicate and quick way to turn strawberries into a gourmet dessert is to marinate cut halves in a delicate semisweet white wine, like Barsac, for several hours in the refrigerator.

OLD-FASHIONED STRAWBERRY SHORTCAKES

2 cups all-purpose flour
3 teaspoons baking powder
2 tablespoons sugar
1/2 teaspoon salt
3/4 cup milk

3 tablespoons melted butter
Sweet butter, softened
Strawberries or peaches
Heavy cream

1. Preheat the oven to 450 degrees.
2. Mix flour and baking powder; add sugar and salt, and stir in the milk. This may require a tablespoon more of milk to make dough light and soft. Mix the butter into the dough. Turn onto a floured board and roll or pat into 1/2-inch thickness. Cut into biscuit-sized rounds and bake 12 to 15 minutes, or until lightly browned.
3. Split the shortcakes with two forks and spread with the sweet butter to keep juice from soaking the biscuits. Fill with mashed strawberries, sweetened mashed peaches, or whatever fruit is ripe in the garden. Top with whole slices of fruit and cream, whipped, or simply somewhat thickened by beating a little.
   Serves six to eight.

STRAWBERRY FRITTERS ESCOFFIER

An elegant garnish for plain vanilla ice cream

2 cups large firm strawberries	**Fritter Batter (page 201)**
1/2 cup sugar	**Fat for deep frying**
1/4 cup Kirsch	

1. Wash the berries quickly under running water, but only if you must. Dry them well, hull, arrange on a plate, and sprinkle with sugar, and then with Kirsch. Refrigerate for 1 hour.
2. Heat the fat to 375 degrees.
3. Drain the berries well, coat with the thin sweetened Fritter Batter. Using a basket, lower the berries a few at a time into the deep fat. As soon as they are golden, lift out. You have to work quickly or the berries will become jam. Drain, sift with confectioner's sugar if you like, and serve on a lace-paper doily.
Serves six.

TARTE AUX FRAISES CHIMNEY HILL

1/2 recipe Easy Short Pastry	**1 tablespoon sugar**
4 cups strawberries	**1/2 teaspoon vanilla extract**
1 tablespoon Cointreau, optional	**1-ounce jar red raspberry jelly**
2 8-ounce packages cream	**2 tablespoons sugar**
** cheese**	**1 cup heavy cream, whipped and**
Light cream	** sweetened, optional**

1. Bake a 9-inch pastry shell.
2. Wash the berries under running water, dry, hull into a bowl. Sprinkle with Cointreau.
3. Beat the cream cheese until fluffy, then beat into it enough light cream to make it soft but not runny. Beat in the 1 tablespoon of sugar and the vanilla.
4. Boil raspberry jelly with the 2 tablespoons of sugar until it has a sticky look and dribbles from the spoon. Cover the inside of the pie shell with this glaze, and brush it over the edges. Sprinkle a little sugar over the glaze.
5. Spoon the cream-cheese mixture into the crust, smooth, arrange the berries decoratively on it, halving the largest. Reheat the raspberry glaze and spoon it over the berries to coat them. Serve this with whipped cream if you like.
Serves eight.

STRAWBERRIES WILHELMINA

4 cups strawberries	2 cups heavy cream
1/2 cup Kirsch	1/4 cup sugar
1/2 cup fine granulated sugar	1/2 teaspoon vanilla

1. Wash berries quickly under running water, dry, hull, layer in a glass serving bowl, right side up, with the largest berries on top. Sprinkle each layer with Kirsch and sugar. Cover and chill 3 hours.

2. Just before serving, whip the cream with the sugar and the vanilla. Serve with the berries in a silver bowl, chilled in the freezer so that it will frost as it warms. You can substitute Curaçao, Maraschino, or Grand Marnier for the Kirsch.

Serves six to eight.

STRAWBERRY AND RHUBARB PIE

2-1/2 cups diced rhubarb	1/8 teaspoon salt
3/4 cup granulated sugar	2 cups ripe strawberries
2-1/2 tablespoons Minute tapioca	1 tablespoon butter
1/2 teaspoon lemon juice	Easy Short Pastry
1 teaspoon grated lemon rind	

1. Preheat oven to 425 degrees.

2. Toss the rhubarb with sugar, tapioca, lemon juice, lemon rind, and salt. Marinate for 15 minutes.

3. Wash the berries under running water, dry, and hull. Mix gently with the rhubarb. Pile into a well-buttered baking dish, dot with butter, and top with pastry rolled 1/4 inch thick. Pinch the edges of the pastry over the lip of the dish and slash in 3 places to let steam escape. Bake at 425 degrees for 10 minutes, then reduce heat to 350 degrees and bake 30 minutes more.

Serves six.

CALIFORNIA STRAWBERRY PRESERVES

You can increase the amounts given to suit the number of berries you have, but keep the proportions exactly the same.

1/4 cup strawberry juice	**2 cups strawberries**
2 cups sugar	**1 teaspoon lemon juice**

1. Make strawberry juice by crushing small imperfect berries, and cooking at moderate heat 3 minutes, stirring constantly. Strain. Measure 1/4 cup of juice.
2. Combine sugar and strawberry juice. Heat slowly, stirring constantly until sugar dissolves. Add the whole berries and simmer gently 3 or 4 minutes. Remove berries from the syrup and space them an inch apart in shallow enamel pans.
3. Boil the syrup until it is very thick, about 10 minutes, or to 220 degrees on a candy thermometer. Add lemon juice and pour over the berries in a thin coat. Cover the pans with glass, keeping at least 1/2 inch between glass and pans. Set in hot sun for 2 to 4 days, but take the pans indoors at night. Turn the berries once a day. When the syrup around the berries has jelled, pack the fruit and syrup into hot sterilized jelly glasses. Cover with hot paraffin and seal.

Makes two 8-ounce glasses.

STRAWBERRIES WITH RASPBERRY SAUCE

1 quart large strawberries	**3 tablespoons Kirsch**
3 cups fresh raspberries	**Mint leaves**
Sugar	

1. Rinse the strawberries under running water, dry, hull, and chill.
2. Rinse the raspberries, hull, and purée in a blender or mash through a stainless-steel sieve. Sweeten with sugar to taste. (How sweet the sauce should be depends on the tartness of the berries, as this is the only sweetening in the recipe.) Add Kirsch to the purée and chill.
3. About 2 hours before dinner, turn the berries into a glass serving bowl, pour the sauce over them, and chill again. Finally, garnish with a few mint leaves. (I am always tempted to add whipped cream to this recipe but that would ruin it!)

Serves six to eight.

MELONS, CANTALOUPES, AND GRAPES

My father and Adolphe, the gardener at l'Enardière, used to grow "Chartreuse cantaloupes." They pierced the skin of ripening melons, inserted a small tube which drew liqueur from a stoppered vial, taped it all together, and harvested the incomparable melon in about ten days. Try it some time, or achieve a similar effect this simpler way: Cut an opening in a melon, large enough to fit a tablespoon, remove the seeds, spill in an ounce of a sweet liqueur, plug the hole, and chill the melon for several hours. In France we eat cantaloupe with a fork and knife, and salt it lightly. Try that sometime, too.

For a festive dessert, scoop out small balls from cantaloupe halves. Press a 2-inch layer of vanilla ice cream into the shell half, and refreeze. At serving time fill with the cantaloupe balls marinated in a fiery liqueur like brandy or Benedictine.

To make melon balls, scoop out the meat with a rounded teaspoon or melon scoop.

To make melon baskets, first pencil a circle crosswise around the melon. With a thin, sharp pointed knife, mark a sawtooth pattern with the penciled circle as the center. Then pull the halves apart gently. To make "handles" for the baskets, cut a second melon in half crosswise, scoop out the seeds, and slice a 1-1/2-inch round from an open end of a half. Cut through the middle; this will make a handle for each sawtoothed half-melon.

Delicious Melon and Fruit Combinations

To serve with ice cream, preferably vanilla, or alone in tall chilled compotes, the edges rimmed with sugar as for champagne cocktails, combine:

1. strawberries, halved, with raspberries, red currants, slices of ripe peaches, and melon balls—all sprinkled with sugar
2. diced pineapple, stemmed-and-pitted black cherries, peeled seedless green grapes, and melon balls, topped with a mint leaf
3. mixed cantaloupe and honeydew melon balls marinated in 1 tablespoon of lime juice, with a sprinkling of sugar.

CANTALOUPE-PEACH MARMALADE

3 oranges, halved and seeded

2 lemons, halved and seeded

4 cups finely diced cantaloupe

4 cups peeled diced peaches

6 cups sugar

6 to 8 maraschino cherries, halved

1. Put oranges and lemons through a food chopper.

2. Simmer cantaloupe and peaches in a preserving kettle for 2 minutes; add oranges and lemons, and stir in the sugar. Simmer over moderate heat until mixture thickens, stirring frequently to keep sugar from burning.

3. When mixture sheets a spoon, pour into hot sterilized jelly jars. Drop a cherry half in each, cover with melted paraffin, and seal.

Makes six to eight 8-ounce jars.

CANTALOUPE RIND PRESERVES

I save this recipe to use for those melons that obviously aren't going to ripen before the first frost.

8 pounds cantaloupe rind

1/2 cup salt

2 tablespoons powdered alum

8 pounds sugar

1 tablespoon cinnamon

1 pineapple, shelled and sliced

1. Remove green skin and pink flesh from cantaloupes and weigh out the rind. Cut into 1-inch squares. Cover with cold water to which the salt has been added. Let stand for a day and a night. The next morning, drain the rind and cover with fresh cold water to which the alum has been added. Let stand another day and a night.

2. Next morning put the rind into a preserving kettle, cover with fresh cold water, boil until you can pierce the rind with a food pick. Drain the rind and add the sugar and the cinnamon to the kettle with the pineapple. With heat very low, simmer the rind until it looks clear, about 45 minutes. If the rind begins to turn white and opaque, add a little more water. Ladle the rind into hot sterilized jars, then fill up with syrup. Wipe edges of jars and seal with jar lids. Process in boiling water for 5 minutes. Cool on racks.

Makes 5 to 6 pints.

MELON BEVERAGE DESSERT

1 ripe cantaloupe or honeydew
  melon
1/2 cup cream
2 tablespoons Cointreau

1 teaspoon lime juice
1 tablespoon sugar
Pinch of salt
1 pint vanilla ice cream

1. Seed, peel, and coarsely chop the melon.
2. Put into a blender with everything but the ice cream, and stir at low speed until smooth. Remove half the mixture and add half the ice cream; turn on the blender at low speed. Repeat the process with the rest of the melon mixture and the ice cream. Stir into a chilled crystal pitcher, serve at once. This makes a delicious combined beverage and dessert for a sandwich luncheon.

Serves four to six.

WATERMELON DESSERT COCKTAIL

4 cups watermelon balls
1/4 cup B&B or Cointreau
2 tablespoons strained lemon juice

2 tablespoons confectioner's sugar
2 cups heavy cream, whipped

1. Put the watermelon balls in a small bowl. Mix B&B with the lemon juice. (If you use Cointreau, omit lemon juice.) Pour over the melon balls and toss gently. Chill well.
2. Serve in tall glass compotes with a sprinkling of half the sugar, and a dollop of whipped cream to which the rest of the sugar has been added.

Serves six.

PICKLED WATERMELON RIND

1 large watermelon
1/2 cup salt
3 quarts cold water
1-1/2 quarts water
Peel of 1 lemon
3 cups white vinegar

6 cups sugar
3 tablespoons whole allspice
3 tablespoons whole cloves
1 tablespoon whole mustard seeds
5 cinnamon sticks 3 inches long

1. Remove the pink meat from the watermelon and peel off the green rind. The melon should be slightly underripe. Cut rind into 1-inch squares, and measure. There should be 3 quarts.

2. Prepare a brine of the salt and 3 quarts of water. Put the rind in a crock and pour the brine over it. Cover, let stand overnight.

3. Drain the rind and rinse with fresh water. Place in a deep kettle, cover with cold water, and bring to a boil. Simmer until tender, about 10 minutes. Drain.

4. Bring 1-1/2 quarts of water to a boil and add the lemon peel and all other ingredients. Bring to a boil again. Add rind and simmer until it becomes transparent, about 45 minutes.

5. Pour into hot sterilized jars and seal at once. Process in boiling water for 5 minutes. Cool on racks.

Makes 4 to 5 pints.

CANTALOUPE AND GRAPES IN WINE

3 ripe cantaloupes
Seedless green grapes
1 cup Château d'Yquem

1. Halve the melons, scoop out seeds, and chill a little.

2. You will want enough grapes to fill the centers, so the quantity depends on the size of the melons. Wash the grapes and dry well. Fill the center of each cantaloupe half.

3. Shortly before you serve, place the melons on dessert plates and pour a little of the wine into each half. This is a simple yet subtle dessert. Serve the rest of the wine with the melons, but don't chill it so much that the flavor is lost. A good, not-too-dry white wine, a Barsac or a Sauterne, for instance, can be used instead of Château d'Yquem.

Serves six.

CRYSTALIZED GRAPES

A delicious way to eat fresh grapes, and a striking garnish for a party dish of ice cream

2 cups red or purple grapes	1 cup sugar
1/2 cup water	Crystalized or granulated sugar

1. Wash the grapes, dry, and separate into small clusters.
2. Combine water with sugar and simmer 5 minutes.
3. With tongs, dip each bunch of grapes into the syrup. Let excess syrup drip off. Sprinkle grapes at once with the sugar crystals. Place on a cake rack and let harden.

DI'S GRAPE DESSERT

2 tablespoons cognac	2 cups (1 pound) sweet seedless
1 teaspoon lemon juice	green grapes
1/4 cup honey	1 cup thick sour cream

1. Combine cognac, lemon juice, and honey. Wash the grapes, toss them in the honey mixture, and marinate overnight, covered, in a refrigerator.
2. Serve in tall glass compotes with sour cream on top.
Serves four.

BORDEAUX GRAPE JAM

Here is a good way to turn a big grape harvest into tart jam. Any amount of grapes can be used since no other ingredients are called for.

10 pounds of sweet grapes

1. Wash grapes and crush in blender; discard skins and seeds. Turn into a preserving kettle and simmer over very low heat until mixture has the consistency of thick jam. It will take between 10 and 20 minutes, depending on the amount of grapes and how juicy they are.
2. Pour into hot sterilized jars, seal with melted paraffin, and cap.

The Greeks have a way of reducing the jam even further, in sunlight I believe, and rolling it in crushed nuts, but I have never been able to find a recipe for this heavenly dessert.

Makes about five 6-ounce jelly jars, less if the grapes are not very juicy.

11 Bounty from Nut Trees

In rural France many people have some kind of nut tree to help stock the winter larder. At the Bertrand's Riviera farm the walk was peppered with almonds every fall. A hazelnut grows in Aunt Louise's garden; and at l'Enardière we had chestnuts. The only time Daniel and Serge and I got to stay up late was when the chestnut crop was ready; we had to wait until the fire in the library had burned to coals after dinner so the nuts could be roasted without charring, and that always took longer than Mother expected.

In America the closest I have come to home-grown nuts were some excellent pecans friends sent me (shelled!) from the South, and the wild butternuts we lovingly gathered our first autumn in Sharon, dried on screens (while we fought off squirrels every inch of the way), and then threw out in disgust. They were uncrackable, impossible to wrestle from the shell once cracked, and not very good to boot. They are, unfortunately, typical of most kinds of nuts that grow wild in New England.

It is sad but true that nuts grow to their best only in the mild central regions of the United States, or rather, the best-known nuts do—pecans, almonds, chestnuts, English walnuts. In spite of this, at least one species well worth growing will flourish in every state. Exotics, such as the pistachio and the macadamia nut, need very warm climates as in southern California. The coconut grows only in southern Florida and on the Keys. In chilly New England, improved forms of hickory, butternut, and black walnut are making these trees increasingly desirable for the home garden. There are now hardy forms of hazelnut, of filbert, its close relative, and even pecan.

As a rule, named and grafted varieties of nut trees bear in 2 to 3 years instead of the 5 to 10 years formerly required by the self-rooted types. Much depends on the particular variety. In general, the following list is reliable.

252

Almonds .... 3 to 5 years	Black walnuts
Butternuts ...... 4 to 6 years	(new vars.) ... 4 to 5 years
Chinese chestnuts 3 to 4 years	Carpathian
Filberts .... 2 to 3 years	walnuts ...... 3 to 5 years
Hickory .... 5 to 6 years	English walnuts .. 4 to 7 years
Early-bearing	Cultivated
pecans .... 3 to 5 years	coconuts .... 5 to 10 years

Planting and culture. Plant nut trees in early spring while dormant, in cooler areas. Fall planting is preferable for warmer regions. Buy the best stock available locally, and ask for 5-foot trees. Plant as you do fruit trees, but take particular care that the roots are not exposed to the sun during transplanting. When the hole contains the roots comfortably and has been filled two-thirds full of earth, tamp in around all the roots with a small blunt stick to make sure all air pockets are gone.

Give the tree a bucketful of water every day for the first 2 weeks after transplanting, and every second day after that for 4 weeks. Do not let the soil dry out in summer. A mulch to the drip line of the branches is advisable, preferably a mulch of rotted manure or compost, or a non-acid mulch such as buckwheat hulls or black plastic.

Fertilizing. Nut trees, with the exception of the walnut and the chestnut, prefer non-acid soils, which means liming the ground at regular intervals. Time this job to coincide with the liming of your vegetable garden to make it easier to do and to remember. Fertilize in early spring annually with the formula recommended by your local Agricultural Extension Service, or with 5-10-10 at the rate of 1/2 pound per inch of trunk diameter.

Pollination. Although there is a lot we do not know about nut-tree culture, experts are beginning to suspect that more species than was once believed require cross-pollination to produce really good crops. It seems safest, therefore, to plant two varieties, whatever the kind of nut tree.

Harvesting. Allow nuts to mature fully on the trees and to fall naturally to the ground. Beating the branches is seldom justified. If you have children who want to climb and pick, that is all right, but don't pound at the branches of young trees. Gather the nuts as soon as possible after they have fallen. Old sheets spread beneath the tree to catch the crop will make it easier to collect daily. Prolonged exposure to the humidity of the earth discolors nuts, particularly walnuts. Husk nuts soon after the harvest, and spread in thin layers on screens to dry.

Pests and diseases. Nut trees growing in good loam and a healthy environment run into few problems. Give them the same care you would give to any shade tree.

The Almond

This is one of the smallest and probably the loveliest of all the nut trees. It blooms as lavishly as a flowering peach, its close relative, and usually grows no taller than 20 feet. While almost as hardy as the peach, it blooms earlier, between late January and early April, and in areas subject to frosts during this period the frostbitten blooms are lost and with them the crop.

California exports almonds, and they grow well in Utah, parts of Texas, Idaho, Arizona, and New Mexico. Areas where similar climates exist are worth trying almonds in, particularly if you can place the tree in a protected corner.

In choosing a variety, be sure a suitable cross-pollinator is growing nearby, or else ask your nursery to recommend a pair of trees that will cross-pollinate.

Almonds are among the most versatile of nuts, culinarily speaking. Try them in mayonnaise, and cooked with shrimp, as well as in the sweet Dutch Almond Slices.

The Butternut

This is the hardiest of any of the northern-growing nuts; it belongs to the walnut family and is hardier even than the black walnut. Native from New Brunswick to Arkansas, it is a good choice for the garden in cooler areas.

Trees reach a height of 50 to 75 feet, and love rich soils and stream banks. Although the shells are rather hard to crack, some new named varieties have less tough shells.

The butternut is a beautiful tree and long-lived and self-pollinating as well. In early summer the pioneers harvested half-grown nuts and pickled them. "As long as a pin goes into the nut without resistance, it is ready to 'relish.'" The nuts were soaked in brine for three weeks, then scalded. The hairy outer skin was rubbed off, and the nuts, hull and all, were put into a jar and covered with a syrup of water, vinegar, sugar, and spices.

Butternuts are excellent chopped into cream-cheese sandwiches, in cake and pastry fillings, and in sweets.

The Chestnut

Chinese chestnut is the blight-resistant species most of us must plant since the magnificent American chestnut forests were destroyed at the turn of the century by a disease no plant pathologist has yet defeated. Recently the blight has appeared in Italy, where chestnut forests cover many mountainsides. The Chinese chestnut is less hardy than were our native giants, but is usually successful in areas where peach trees will thrive. It grows to about 40 feet tall, produces slightly smaller nuts than the American and European chestnuts, and must be planted in two varieties, as it requires cross-pollination. Named varieties have been bred to greater blight resistance; make sure to buy two different named varieties.

At home we boil chestnuts in the shells until soft, peel them, mash slightly, melt sweet or salt butter over them, and serve as a vegetable de luxe. But you may prefer chestnuts in desserts. The chestnut desserts given in Chapter 12 are typically French and are favorites among chestnut fanciers.

The Coconut

Coconuts require the kind of humidity and heat that exist on the southern Florida coast and in many subtropical regions. They grow near the sea. Farther north they have been successfully grown in greenhouses, primarily as ornamental trees, but do not live long. Reaching 100 feet or more at maturity, the coconut palm requires an average annual temperature of 72 degrees or higher. The trees produce their first crops in five to ten years; when the nuts are ripe they fall. Although most Americans cannot hope to grow their own, they can obtain coconuts much of the year at supermarket counters, and serve grated fresh in desserts or main courses. Pat Gill Murphy, who has lived most of her life south of the border, makes a wonderful South American variation of Boston cream pie (see Chapter 12). Coconut is a staple of much Far Eastern as well as Caribbean cuisine.

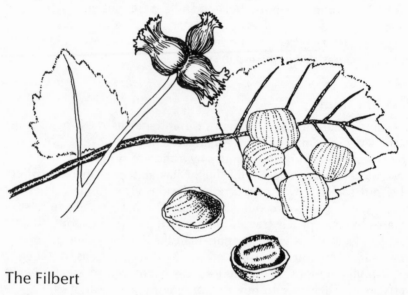

The Filbert

The hazelnut and the filbert belong to the same genus. The distinctions between the two are so minor as to cause much confusion. The true filbert of southeastern Europe has oblong nuts in long husks, and the hazelnuts—several species of Europe, Asia, and North America—have roundish nuts in short husks. Popularly the two names are synonymous. Improved hybrid forms are now becoming available. They grow well wherever peaches succeed, and extremely well in the Northwest. They are small trees, easily fitted into suburban landscapes, and will flourish as far south as southern Pennsylvania.

A rich, well-drained soil is suitable for the hazelnut-filbert. Protect trees from north winds if possible. Prune as you do peaches, but not too severely or the tree may suffer winter damage. Two or more filbert trees, not necessarily different varieties, should be planted to effect good pollination. Filberts are delicious in any recipe requiring a crisp, compact nut.

The Hickory

Pecans are a species of hickory, and the shagbark hickory produces nuts almost as good as the best pecans. It succeeds as far north as Brunswick, Maine, but is not often raised in nurseries because its long taproot makes it difficult to transplant except when young. But it is a most excellent nut tree for the garden in cooler climates, and self-pollinating, so only one is needed. Slow-growing, it may reach towering heights of up to 130 feet at maturity. Shagbarks prefer hillside locations, need 60 to 90 feet of space all around, and do well on rather poor soil. Incidentally, all hickories, and their cousin, the butternut, attract the beautiful Nile-green lunar moth (whose caterpillars seem to do little harm).

Hickory nuts can be used for most pecan recipes. Some popular hickory-nut specialties are given in the next chapter.

The Pecan

Although a few varieties of paper-shell pecans have been developed which will produce nuts north of Washington, D.C., this is primarily a tree for Southern growers. The flavor of pecans is improved if the nuts are stored for two weeks after they have fallen. Hang them in a mesh or burlap bag in a dry airy place. The trees grow to a height of 120 feet at maturity, and require lots of breathing room, 60 to 80 feet of it, in fact. Plant trees in the fall in the South. Pecans produce when they are six to eight years old.

Everybody knows about hot caramel sauce with pecans over ice cream, but have you ever tasted homemade pralines? They're worth waiting for! Of course, you can always buy a few pecans while you are waiting for your tree to produce.

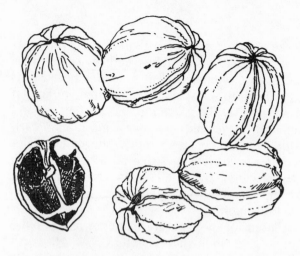

The Walnut

English walnuts actually came from Persia, and are close kin to the winter-hardy black walnut and the butternut, which pioneers named "white walnut." Walnuts reach a height of 100 feet at maturity, and grow anywhere peaches grows, but aren't quite as hardy as the little fruit tree and can be killed by a severe winter.

Several new varieties are hardy, among them the much advertised Carpathian walnut from Poland, which is only 50 feet tall at maturity. Walnuts thrive on rich, well-drained soil, but should not be fertilized too enthusiastically in cooler areas. The heart nut, or Japanese walnut, is somewhat less hardy than the Carpathian variety, but has better shelling qualities. Black walnuts are hardier than English walnuts, but are in danger in areas where winter temperatures fall below 20 degrees. Nuts from wild black walnuts are hard to crack and not very meaty. Some of the cultivated varieties are improved, and worth a try if black walnuts grow wild in your area.

Cross-pollination is a requirement of the walnut; if no other walnut tree grows nearby, nut production may fall off severely.

When walnuts fall, gather and remove the husks at once. Wash the shells, and layer the nuts in an airy room until dried.

Try the Walnut Pie Crust recipe with any kind of walnuts you can grow; it is truly delicious with airy fillings and tart fruit.

12 Cooking with Nuts

When you have a generous supply of nuts growing in your own backyard, the cookies, candies, cakes, and desserts that you can make with them are almost endless. You can fry nuts, and glacé them, too. Of course you can salt them, and they are a delicious ingredient in many recipes. They even make a fast, and deliciously crisp, pie crust!

Learn to use nuts for texture as well as flavor, and as accessories to a main dish; salads, sandwich fillings, stuffings, as well as cakes, cookies, and sweet breads, textured with broken or chopped nut meats are more interesting. Slivered almonds, sautéed in butter, enhance green beans and many other vegetables, as well as filet of sole; try them, too, in Chantilly Mayonnaise, or ground, in the more exotic Shrimp with Almond Sauce. Fresh grated coconut is a traditional side dish for Indian curries; used as described in the Lobster Curry, coconut adds enormous subtlety to many Oriental dishes.

Skinning Nuts

Cover the shelled nuts with boiling water for 3 minutes, or until the skins wrinkle. Drain, spray with cold water to cool, then rub off skins with your fingers or between towels, or scrape them off with a small, pointed knife. Dry between paper towels and set in a low oven, 250 degrees, for 10 minutes.

French-Fried Nuts

Skin the nuts, dry carefully. Heat fat for deep frying to 360 degrees and lower the nuts into the fat in a frying basket or a colander. When they are *slightly* browned, they are done. Drain on paper towels, and sprinkle with salt.

Salted Nuts

Skin the nuts. Heat the oven to 350 degrees. Place a cupful of nuts in a bowl and sprinkle with 1 teaspoon melted butter or oil. Stir the nuts until all have a sheen. Then spread out on a cookie sheet in a single layer. Sprinkle with salt lightly, and bake 10 minutes, or until *lightly* browned.

Glacéed Nuts

Blanch and skin nuts. Prepare the same glacé syrup as for Candied Apples on a Stick. While the syrup is cooking, butter a cookie sheet. When the syrup is ready, pour it into the top of a double boiler and set over boiling water to keep it from hardening. Dip the nuts into the syrup one at a time with tongs or a slotted spoon, and drop onto the buttered cookie sheet.

For storage, crush some of the glacéed nuts into small bits, hammering them between sheets of wax paper or in a plastic bag, and keep, tightly capped, and in a cool, dry place, to use as garnish for ice cream, whipped cream, in custard, or on pastry.

SHRIMP WITH ALMOND SAUCE

2 pounds fresh or unshelled frozen shrimp
1 teaspoon salt
1-1/2 cups water
1 stalk celery
1 bay leaf
1/2 teaspoon thyme
5 slices white bread
1-1/2 cups milk
4 tablespoons butter

2 onions, finely chopped
2 cloves garlic, minced
1/2 teaspoon freshly ground black pepper
1 teaspoon paprika
Dash of chili powder
1 teaspoon salt
1/2 cup olive oil
1 cup ground almonds

1. Place shrimp in a shallow saucepan with salt, water, celery, bay leaf, and thyme. Bring to a simmer and cook for 5 to 6 minutes; cool and drain, reserving 1 cup of stock. Peel and devein the shrimp.

2. Soak the bread in the milk and pull into bits with two forks. Melt butter in a large skillet; stir in the onions, garlic, pepper, paprika, chili powder to taste, and salt. Simmer 15 minutes.

3. Add the bread and milk mixture and simmer 5 minutes more, stirring. Add the oil, a few drops at a time, stirring continually.

Stir in almonds and the shrimp. Thin the mixture with the reserved stock. Simmer, stirring, until the mixture is smooth and thick, about 5 minutes more. Serve hot with plain boiled rice.

Serves six.

DUTCH ALMOND SLICES

3/4 cup flour
1/2 teaspoon baking powder
2 eggs
1/2 cup sugar
1/2 teaspoon almond extract

1/2 teaspoon lemon extract
2 tablespoons ice water
3/4 cup sliced almonds
2 tablespoons sugar

1. Heat oven to 350 degrees.
2. Sift flour and baking powder together.
3. Cream eggs and 1/2 cup of sugar, and beat in the almond and lemon extracts and the water. Fold the nuts, flour, and baking powder into the egg mixture and beat lightly until smooth.
4. Turn the batter into a 9-inch-square greased cake pan, sprinkle with the 2 tablespoons of sugar, and bake until brown, 25 to 35 minutes. Cool in the pan. Cut into 3-inch squares and serve with whipped cream.

Makes 9 squares.

BUTTERNUT FUDGE

2 squares unsweetened chocolate
1 cup brown sugar, firmly packed
1 cup granulated sugar
2/3 cup condensed milk

2 tablespoons corn syrup
2 tablespoons butter
1 teaspoon vanilla extract
1 cup chopped butternuts

1. Grate the chocolate or cut into small pieces, and place in the top of a double boiler with the brown and the white sugar, condensed milk, and corn syrup. Stir until sugar dissolves. Place over boiling water and simmer, stirring, until the candy thermometer reads 240 degrees or until a few drops of the mixture dropped into a glass of cold water forms a soft ball.
2. Remove from the heat, add butter, and let stand until cooled a little. Beat until the mixture loses its glossy appearance. Stir in the vanilla and the nut meats, then turn into a shallow, buttered, 8-inch-square cake pan. Cut into 1-inch squares when the candy has set.

CHOCOLATE BUTTERNUT CLUSTERS

1/2 pound milk chocolate
1/8 teaspoon salt
2 cups coarsley chopped butternuts

Melt chocolate and salt in the top of a double boiler over hot water. Stir in the chopped nuts, mixing until they are well coated with chocolate. Then drop from a fork onto a buttered cookie sheet. Set in a cool place to harden.

Makes 15 to 20 clusters.

MOTHER'S BUTTERNUT COOKIES

2/3 cup butter
1-1/2 cups sugar
2 eggs
1 cup dark raisins, or 1/2 cup
   dark, 1/2 cup white
1 cup butternuts
1-1/2 teaspoons mace

1 teaspoon ground cloves
2 teaspoons cinnamon
Pinch of salt
1/2 pint sour cream
2-1/2 cups flour
1 teaspoon soda

1. Heat oven to 375 degrees.
2. Cream the butter and sugar. Beat eggs until thick, and beat into the creamed butter and sugar. Mix in raisins, butternuts, mace, cloves, cinnamon, and salt.
3. Add the sour cream to the egg mixture alternately with the flour and soda sifted together. Beat until smooth. Drop from a teaspoon onto a greased and floured cookie sheet. Bake until the cookies look firm and dry, 12 to 15 minutes. Test with a food pick.

Makes 5- to 6-dozen cookies.

BUTTERNUT TORTE

3 eggs
1 cup granulated sugar
1 cup flour
1 teaspoon baking powder

1 cup chopped dates
1 cup chopped butternuts
Confectioner's sugar

1. Heat oven to 350 degrees.
2. Beat eggs until thick, then beat in the granulated sugar. Sift flour with the baking powder. Toss the dates and nuts in the flour mixture until all are well coated. Combine flour, dates, and nuts with the eggs and sugar, and beat smooth.
3. Turn into a buttered and floured square cake tin, and bake for 20 minutes. With a spatula turn out onto a cutting board and cut into squares. Sift confectioner's sugar over the torte, cool, and serve. Or serve hot with melting vanilla ice cream over it.
Serves six to eight.

CHESTNUT PUREE DESSERT

4 cups chestnuts
2 cups milk
1/2 teaspoon vanilla extract
1 cup corn syrup
1 tablespoon dark rum

1/2 cup heavy cream, whipped, sweetened and chilled
1 tablespoon grated semisweet chocolate

1. Shell the chestnuts, boil in water to cover for 3 minutes, cool, and peel off the inner skins. Turn into a small saucepan, and cover with the milk and vanilla. Simmer until soft, 30 to 45 minutes. Drain, mash through a strainer, and set aside.
2. Simmer corn syrup in a small saucepan until it makes a fine thread. Stir in the rum (light rum will do) and quickly mix this into the mashed chestnuts. The mixture should look a little like mashed potatoes. Spoon small mounds onto dessert plates, top with dollops of the chilled cream, and garnish with grated chocolate.
Serves six to eight.

CHESTNUT-AND-ORANGE DESSERT

4 cups chestnuts
2 tablespoons sugar
Pinch of salt

1/2 cup heavy cream, whipped
  and sweetened
1 orange, peeled and sliced thin
1/4 cup glacéed walnuts

1. Gash the chestnut tops and boil in water to cover for 45 minutes. Shell, peel off the inner skins, and mash through a strainer or through a ricer. Add sugar and salt; taste and add more sugar if desired.

2. Fold half the cream into the purée when it has cooled. Press gently into a mold, first rinsed in cold water, and turn out onto a serving plate. Chill, covered, for 2 hours.

3. Smother in the remaining whipped cream, garnish with orange slices and walnuts.

Serves six to eight.

CHESTNUT STUFFING CHIMNEY HILL

3 cups chestnuts
1/4 cup (1/2 stick) butter
1/4 cup finely chopped onion
1/2 pound ground pork

1/4 teaspoon sage
1/4 teaspoon thyme
2 tablespoons finely chopped
  parsley

1. Gash the chestnut tops, boil 35 minutes, shell, peel off inner skins, and crumble the nuts lightly with a fork.

2. Melt butter in a heavy skillet, Simmer onions in it for 5 minutes, sauté the ground pork until slightly browned. Stir in sage, thyme, and parsley. Fold in the chestnuts and mix well. Pack lightly into the fowl.

Makes enough for an 8-pound bird.

LOBSTER CURRY WITH COCONUT

2-1/2 cups milk
2 cups freshly grated coconut
1/4 pound (1 stick) butter
3 onions, chopped
2 cloves garlic, minced
2 teaspoons powdered ginger
Dash of cayenne
Salt

2 tablespoons curry powder
3 tomatoes, chopped
2 tablespoons potato or other
   flour
1 cucumber, peeled and cubed
1-1/2 pounds lobster meat, cubed
2 tablespoons lemon juice
1 tablespoon plum jam, optional

1. Combine milk and coconut in a saucepan, bring to a boil, remove from the heat and let cool.

2. Melt butter in a saucepan, add onions and garlic, simmer for 10 minutes. Add the ginger, cayenne, salt to taste, curry, and tomatoes. Cover, simmer 10 minutes more, stirring occasionally. Stir in the flour, smoothing the mixture, and remove from heat.

3. Drain the pulp from the milk and coconut. Return the butter sauce to the heat, stir in the coconut milk until the mixture is smooth, bring slowly to a boil. Add the cucumber and lobster cubes, and simmer 15 minutes more. Serve with boiled rice.

Serves six.

PAT'S SOUTH AMERICAN COCONUT TART

1-1/4 cups sifted flour
Pinch salt
2/3 cup butter
3 eggs
1 tablespoon cold water

1/4 cup sugar
1 cup milk, scalded
1/2 cup heavy cream
1-1/2 cups cottage cheese
1 cup freshly grated coconut

1. Sift flour and salt into a medium-size bowl. Cut in the butter as for pastry. Beat 1 egg with the water and add to the flour mixture, tossing lightly until it forms dough. Chill 1/2 hour or until firm enough to roll out.

2. Heat oven to 350 degrees.

3. Beat the 2 eggs in a small bowl until thick, beat in sugar, and gradually beat in milk and cream, scalded together. Stir in the cottage cheese, and fold in the coconut.

4. Roll out the dough and line a 9-inch pie pan. Pour the milk and coconut mixture into it. Bake 45 minutes, or until a knife inserted in the center comes out clean. Pat sometimes serves this tart with sweetened peaches or berries.

Serves six to eight.

COCONUT KISSES

6 egg whites
1/4 teaspoon salt
1/4 teaspoon cream of tartar

1-1/2 cups sugar
1 teaspoon vanilla extract
1-1/2 cups freshly grated coconut

1. Heat oven to 275 degrees.

2. Beat the egg whites until thick. Sprinkle salt and cream of tartar over egg whites, and beat until stiff but not dry. Beat in the sugar, a *sifting at a time* until the meringue holds. Beat in the vanilla. Fold in the coconut.

3. Drop a dessertspoonful at a time onto an ungreased cookie sheet. Bake for about 40 minutes. Let the meringues cool inside the oven with the heat turned off and the door open. I use this recipe for egg whites left over from making mayonnaise. When only 2 egg whites are available, use 1/3 of the other ingredients.
Makes 5- to 6-dozen kisses.

FILBERT CRISP

Filberts and hazelnuts are so alike, being species of the same genus, or hybrids from these species, that the names are interchangeable and largely a matter of local usage.

1 cup sugar
1 cup chopped toasted filberts

1. Melt the sugar in a heavy saucepan over very low heat, stirring constantly until it reaches the hard-crack stage, 310 degrees on a candy thermometer, or until the syrup begins to thread as drops fall back from a spoon into the boiling liquid. Remove from the heat and stir in the nuts.

2. Butter a cookie sheet and two kitchen knives. Turn the candy out onto the cookie sheet, shape into squares 1/2 inch thick with the knives. Cool partially and cut into strips.
Makes about 3/4 pound.

FILBERT AND FRUIT CANDY

7-ounce package pitted dates
1/4 cup dried figs
1 cup filberts
1 cup white raisins

Confectioner's sugar
1 tablespoon dark rum or bourbon
  whiskey, optional

Put the dates, figs, raisins, and nuts through a food chopper, adding a few at a time of each so ingredients will blend. Shape the resulting paste into small balls with your hands. Roll in the powdered sugar. If fruits seem dry, mix in up to 1 tablespoon dark rum or bourbon.

Makes about 15 balls.

CHERRY-FILBERT SALAD

4 cups (2 pounds) sweet cherries
1 cup filberts

1 cup Mayonnaise Chantilly
2 lettuce hearts, halved

Pit the cherries and stuff with whole filberts. Arrange on lettuce halves with a dollop of the mayonnaise.

Serves four.

HICKORY-NUT CAKE

1-1/2 cups sugar
1/2 cup (1 stick) butter
2 cups flower
Pinch of salt
2 teaspoons baking powder

3/4 cup cream
4 egg whites, beaten stiff
1-1/2 teaspoons vanilla extract
1 cup hickory nuts, chopped

1. Heat oven to 350 degrees.
2. Cream the sugar and butter. Add flour, salt, and baking powder sifted together, alternately with the cream. Beat well. Fold in egg whites, vanilla, and nuts. Bake in two 9-inch layer pans for 35 to 40 minutes, or until the cake springs back when you press it with your finger.

HICKORY-NUT FROSTING

1 cup sweet cream
2 tablespoons strained lemon juice

2 cups sugar
1 cup finely ground hickory nuts

Combine cream, lemon juice, and sugar in a small saucepan. Simmer, stirring until mixture reaches 240 degrees on a candy thermometer, or until a few drops form a soft ball in cold water. Cool to lukewarm. Beat until creamy. Add the nuts and frost the cake.

Makes one 9-inch two-layer cake.

HICKORY-NUT BRITTLE

3/4 cup chopped hickory nuts
1 cup white sugar
1/2 cup brown sugar, firmly
  packed
1/4 cup light corn syrup

1/2 cup water
2 tablespoons butter
Pinch of baking soda
Pinch of salt

1. Turn the oven to 275 degrees and warm the nuts.
2. Combine white sugar and brown sugar, corn syrup, and water in a medium-size saucepan, and stir over low heat until the sugar dissolves. Raise the heat and cook without stirring until the candy thermometer registers 300 to 310 degrees, or until drops thread when falling from a spoon.
3. Remove from the stove, add butter, soda, salt, and the warm nuts, stirring as little as possible. Turn at once onto a buttered baking sheet. Do not scrape the pan. Press the candy into a thin layer with a spatula. As soon as it cools enough to handle, grasp the edges with your fingers, lift lightly, and stretch to make the sheet as thin as possible. When the candy is cold, crack it into irregular pieces.

HICKORY-NUT DROPS

4 egg whites
2 cups confectioner's sugar
2 cups ground hickory nuts

1 cup ground filberts
Pinch of salt

1. Heat oven to 350 degrees.
2. Beat egg whites until stiff but not dry. Beat in the sugar, a sifting at a time until the whites stand in stiff peaks. Fold in the nuts. Let the mixture stand one hour.
3. Drop by the teaspoonful onto a greased baking sheet. Bake 10 minutes, no more.

Makes 3 to 4 dozen.

PECAN PIE

9-inch pie shell, unbaked
2 eggs
1 cup brown sugar, firmly packed
1 cup heavy cream
Pinch of salt
1 teaspoon vanilla extract
1 teaspoon flour
2 tablespoons melted butter
1 cup pecan halves
1 cup heavy cream, whipped and sweetened

1. Heat oven to 325 degrees.
2. Beat eggs until thick. Beat in sugar, cream, salt, vanilla extract, flour, and butter. Pour into the pastry shell and cover with the pecans. Bake until firm, about 45 minutes. Cool. Cover with chilled whipped cream, and serve.

Serves six to eight.

PRALINES

4 cups brown sugar, firmly packed
1/2 cup cream
2 tablespoons butter
2-1/2 cups (1 pound) whole pecans

1. Combine sugar, cream, and butter in a saucepan; stir over medium-high heat until sugar dissolves. Bring to the boiling point and boil 3 minutes, or until candy thermometer reads 240 degrees, or a few drops form a soft ball in cold water. Remove from the heat and let stand 5 minutes without stirring.
2. Add the nuts and stir until the syrup thickens and begins to look cloudy. Drop from a tablespoon to make patties on a buttered cookie sheet. Let stand until cold.

Makes 2 to 3 dozen.

CHRISTMAS WALNUT CHOCOLATE BALLS

1 cup coarsely ground walnuts
2/3 cup confectioner's sugar
1 egg yolk, well beaten
3 ounces semisweet chocolate,
 grated

1 tablespoon bourbon
2 egg whites
1/2 cup ground walnuts

 1. Mix together the 1 cup of walnuts, sugar, egg yolk, chocolate, and bourbon. Form into balls the size of a walnut.
 2. Beat the egg whites until foamy, and roll the chocolate balls in the whites, then roll in the ground walnuts. Let dry 2 hours before serving.
Makes 20 to 24 balls.

WONDERFUL WALNUT PIE CRUST

1 cup finely ground walnuts or hickory nuts
2-1/2 tablespoons sugar
1/4 teaspoon salt

Blend nuts, sugar, and salt. Press with a spoon on the bottom and sides of a buttered 8-inch pie pan. Bake at 400 degrees for 6 to 8 minutes.

BLACK-WALNUT COOKIES

4 eggs
2 cups brown sugar, firmly packed
1/2 cup flour
1/2 teaspoon salt

1/2 teaspoon baking powder
1-1/2 cups (1 pound) black-walnut
 meats, finely chopped

 1. Heat oven to 375 degrees.
 2. Beat eggs until thick; beat in the sugar.
 3. Sift the flour, salt, and baking powder together, and stir into the egg-and-sugar mixture. Stir in the nuts. Drop from a teaspoon onto a greased cookie sheet, and bake 12 minutes.
Makes 3- to 4-dozen cookies.

BURNT WALNUT BISQUE

3 egg yolks
1/3 cup sugar
2 cups milk, scalded
2/3 cup sugar

2/3 cup finely chopped walnuts
1 cup heavy cream
3/4 teaspoon vanilla extract

1. Beat egg yolks until thick. Beat in the 1/3 cup of sugar, and then the scalded milk. Pour into the top of a double boiler and cook over simmering water, stirring until the mixture thickens into a custard. Remove from the heat at once. Chill.

2. Put 2/3 cup of sugar into a heavy skillet. With heat on low, cook slowly until the brown of caramelizing sugar bubbles up through the white sugar on top. Stir until all sugar is caramelized and the color is reddish brown. Add the walnuts, remove at once from the heat, and scrape onto a buttered cake pan. Cool.

3. When the sugar has hardened, place in a plastic bag, or between sheets of wax paper, and pound until the sugar is pulverized enough to sift through a coarse strainer.

4. Stir into the cooled custard. Beat heavy cream with vanilla until stiff, stir into the custard. Turn into a mold and freeze.
Serves six.

BROWNIES

3 ounces (squares) unsweetened
  chocolate
1/3 cup butter
2 eggs
1 cup sugar
1/2 teaspoon vanilla

1 tablespoon bourbon (optional)
1/2 cup flour
1/2 teaspoon baking powder
1/4 teaspoon salt
1 cup chopped walnuts, pecans,
  black walnuts, or filberts

1. Heat oven to 375 degrees.

2. Place chocolate and butter in the top of a double boiler and melt, stirring, over boiling water. Remove from heat.

3. Beat eggs until lemon colored, then beat in sugar, vanilla, and bourbon. Stir the egg mixture into the chocolate mixture.

4. Sift flour, baking powder, and salt together. Stir into the egg and chocolate mixture. Fold in the nuts. Spread the dough in a greased and floured 8-inch square cake pan. Bake 20 to 25 minutes. Cool slightly in the pan, then cut into 2-inch squares. Serve cold.
Makes 16 squares.

Appendix

State Agricultural Extension Services Addresses

A gardener's best friend can be his local Agriculture Extension Service. The Service will test your soil, in most states for a nominal charge, and give good advice on varieties most likely to be successful in your area. It will recommend possible solutions for any trouble that besets you. The Service is not, as is often supposed, interested in helping only the professional farmer; it is also designed to help you, the tax-paying home gardener. Look below for the address of the Extension Service nearest you.

Alabama Polytechnic Institute, Auburn, Alabama
University of Alaska, College, Alaska
University of Arizona, Tuscon, Arizona
College of Agriculture, University of Arkansas, Fayetteville, Arkansas
College of Agriculture, University of California, Berkeley, California
Colorado State University, Fort Collins, Colorado
College of Agriculture, University of Connecticut, Stors, Connecticut
Connecticut Agricultural Experiment Station, New Haven, Connecticut
School of Agriculture, University of Delaware, Newark, Delaware
University of Florida, Gainesville, Florida
College of Agriculture, University of Georgia, Athens, Georgia
University of Hawaii, Honolulu, Hawaii
University of Idaho, Moscow, Idaho
College of Agriculture, University of Illinois, Urbana, Illinois
Purdue University, Lafayette, Indiana
Iowa State College of Agriculture, Ames, Iowa
Kansas State College of Agriculture, Manhattan, Kansas
College of Agriculture, University of Kentucky, Lexington, Kentucky
Agricultural College, Louisiana State University, Baton Rouge, Louisiana
College of Agriculture, University of Maine, Orono, Maine
University of Maryland, College Park, Maryland
College of Agriculture, University of Massachusetts, Amherst, Massachusetts

College of Agriculture, Michigan State University, East Lansing, Michigan
Institute of Agriculture, University of Minnesota, St. Paul, Minnesota
Mississippi State College, State College, Mississippi
College of Agriculture, University of Missouri, Columbia, Missouri
Montana State College, Bozeman, Montana
College of Agriculture, University of Nebraska, Lincoln, Nebraska
College of Agriculture, University of Nevada, Reno, Nevada
University of New Hampshire, Durham, New Hampshire
Rutgers University, New Brunswick, New Jersey
College of Agriculture, State College, New Mexico
College of Agriculture, Cornell University, Ithaca, New York
State College of Agriculture, University of North Carolina, Raleigh, North
   Carolina
State Agricultural College, Fargo, North Dakota
College of Agriculture, Ohio State University, Columbus, Ohio
Oklahoma A. and M. College, Stillwater, Oklahoma
Oregon State College, Corvallis, Oregon
Pennsylvania State University, University Park, Pennsylvania
University of Puerto Rico, Box 607, Rio Piedras, Puerto Rico
University of Rhode Island, Kingston, Rhode Island
Clemson Agricultural College, Clemson, South Carolina
South Dakota State College, College Station, South Dakota
College of Agriculture, University of Tennessee, Knoxville, Tennessee
Texas A. and M. College, College Station, Texas
College of Agriculture, Utah State University, Logan, Utah
State Agricultural College, University of Vermont, Burlington, Vermont
Virginia Polytechnic Institute, Blacksburg, Virginia
State College of Washington, Pullman, Washington
West Virginia University, Morgantown, West Virginia
College of Agriculture, University of Wisconsin, Madison, Wisconsin
College of Agriculture, University of Wyoming, Laramie, Wyoming

Table I / Vegetables to Plant in Early Spring

(As soon as the ground can be worked*)

Vegetable	Plants 50' row	Yield 50' row	Space between rows	Space between plants	Depth to plant	Approximate days to maturity
Asparagus perennial	35 plants	25 lbs.	4'	18"	5"-6"	second season
Beets	½ oz.	1 bushel	12"-18"	2"-3"	½"	early, 45 days late, 65 days
Broccoli	25 plants (1 pk. seed)	25-40 heads	20"-24"	18"	¼"-½"	plants, 50-60 days seed, 80-100 days
Brussels sprouts	25 plants (1 pk. seed)	1-2 bushels	20"-24"	18"	½"	plants, 60-70 days seed, 95 days
Cabbage	25 plants (1 pk. seed)	25 heads	20"-30"	18"	½"	early, 40-50 days late, 70-90 days
Carrots	¼ oz.	1 bushel	20"	1"-2"	¼"	75-80 days
Cauliflower	25 plants (1 pk. seed)	25 heads	20"-30"	18"	½"	plants, 65-75 days seed, 80-100 days
Chard, Swiss	½ oz.	2 bushels	18"	4"-6"	¼"	55 days
Chicory	½ pk.	30 lbs.	12"	4"	¼"	112 days
Cress, Garden	1 pk.	20 lbs.	24"	12"	¼"	20 days
Dandelion (perennial)	½ pk.	30 lbs.	18"	4"	¼"	second season
Endive and escarole	½ pk.	50 lbs.	12"	4"	¼"	65-90 days

Garlic (cloves)	½ lb.	¾ bushel	8"	3"	1¼"	125 days
Horseradish (perennial)	25 roots	¾ bushel	24"	15"	12"	120 days
Jerusalem artichoke (perennial)	2-3 lbs.	2 bushels	3'-4'	18"	2"	second season
Kale	½ pk.	125 lbs.	12"-18"	10"	½"	56-75 days
Leeks	2 pk.	100 plants	10"-12"	2"-3" later 6"	¼"	130 days
Lettuce	1 pk.	50 lbs.	12"	2"-3"	¼"	40-90 days
Onion sets	½ lb.	1 bushel	12"	8"	1"	110 days
Parsnips	2 pk.	1½ bushels	12"	3"-4"	½"-1¼"	95-150 days
Peas	½ lb.	1 bushel	20"-30"	3"	1"-2"	early, 58 days late, 80 days
Potatoes, Irish	2-3 lbs.	2 bushels	2'-3'	18"	trench 4"-6" cover 2"	80-100 days
Radishes	2 pk.	50 bunches	12"	1"-2"	¼"	early, 20 days late, 60 days
Rhubarb (perennial)	17 roots	too much	3'	3'	10"	second season
Spinach	½ oz.	1 bushel	12"	4"	¼"-½"	40-50 days
Strawberries (perennial)	35 plants	½-1 quart	4'	18"	1½"	second season
Turnips	1 pk.	1 bushel	18"	6"	½"	early, 35 days late, 60 days
Watercress	200	too much	4"	3"	root level	second season

*"As soon as the ground can be worked" means as soon as a handful of soil squeezed into a ball in your fist crumbles readily under pressure from your thumb.

275

Table II / Vegetables to Plant in Mid-Spring

(As soon as the ground has warmed*)

Vegetable	Plants 50' row	Yield 50' row	Space between rows	Space between plants	Depth to plant	Approximate days to maturity
Artichokes (perennial)	17 plants	2 bushels	36"	36"	5"-6"	second season
Beans						
bush, snap	¼ lb.	25 quarts	20"-30"	3"-5"	1"-1½"	55-65 days
pole	¼ lb.	2 bushels	30"-36"	4-6 per pole	1"	65 days
limas, bush	¼ lb.	7 quarts	30"-36"	4"	1"-1½"	75 days
limas, pole	½ lb.	10 quarts	30"-36"	4-6 per pole	1"	12-14 weeks
Celeriac	¼ pk.	100 roots	20"	6"	¼"	120 days
Celery	¼ pk.	100	20"-24"	6"	¼"	120 days
Corn						
sweet	¼ lb.	75 ears	36"	8"	½"-1"	75 days
Indian	¼ lb.	75 ears	24"-36"	10"-12"	½"-1"	105 days
popcorn	¼ lb.	12-15 lb.	24"-36"	10"-12"	½"-1"	90-105 days
Cucumbers	½ pk.	75 lbs.	48"	4"-6"	½" in peat pot	50 days
Gourds	½ pk.	Too much	36"	5'	1" in peat pot	100 days
Kohlrabi	¼ oz.	30 lbs.	18"	6"-8"	½"-1"	48-60 days
Parsley (biennial)	½ pk.	25 lbs.	18"	6"-8"	¼"	120 days
Peppers	35 plants	2 bushels	20"-24"	18"	¼"	60-80 days

Vegetable	Plants 50' row	Yield 50' row	Space between rows	Space between plants	Depth to plant	Approximate days to maturity
Pumpkins	½ pk.	150 lbs.	5'	5'	1"	100-120 days
Rutabaga	1 pk.	1 bushel	18"	8"	½"	85-90 days
Salsify	2 pk.	1 bushel	12"	3"-4"	¼"-½"	120 days
Shallots	½ lb.	½ bushel	12"	3"	1"	80-100 days
Spinach, New Zealand	½ oz.	1 bushel	18"	6"	¼"-½"	70 days
Squash summer winter	½ pk. ½ pk.	60-70 lbs. 150 lbs.	24"-36" 6'	6" 5'	1" 1"	45-50 days 90-110 days
Tomatoes	17 plants	75 pounds	3'-4'	2'-3'	¼"-½"	70-80 days

*"As soon as the ground has warmed" is about three to four weeks after the ground has become workable.

Table III / Vegetables to Plant in Late Spring

(When the temperature stays above 70 degrees)

Vegetable	Plants 50' row	Yield 50' row	Space between rows	Space between plants	Depth to plant	Approximate days to maturity
Eggplant	½ pk.	150 fruit	20"-30"	18"	½"	60-75 days
Melons cantaloupe watermelon	½ pk. 1 pk.	40-60 fruit 150 lbs.	4' 6'	8"-10" 3'	1" in peat pot 1"	70 days 70-85 days
Okra	2 pk.	30 quarts	20"	15"-24"	½"	56 days
Sweet potatoes	2-3 lbs.	2 bushels	24"-36"	18"	5"	120-150 days

Table IV / Vegetable Troubles and What to Do

Vegetable	What it looks like	What it probably is	How to control or prevent
Asparagus	Ferns yellow, have spiky look.	Rust	Plant resistant varieties.
	New shoots eaten.	Beetle	Rotenone during harvest; Methoxychlor after harvest.
Beans	Round, dark, sunken area on pods, pink in center.	Anthracnose	Use Western seed. Do not touch plants when moist.
	Brown area on leaves, red-brown spots on pods.	Bacterial blight	As above.
	Yellow mottling of leaves; stunted plants.	Mosaics	Plant resistant varieties. Control aphids that spread disease with Malathion.
	Skeletonized leaves.	Mexican bean beetle	Control with rotenone dust.
	Round holes in dried, stored beans.	Been weevil	Use treated seed.
Lima beans	White mold on pods.	Downy mildew	Treat weekly with Maneb or Zineb.
Beets	Brown spots that dry and leave holes.	Leaf spot	Bordeaux mixture; Ziram or Zineb.
	Small green lice on leaves, which become dwarfed.	Aphids	Nicotine dust or spray.
Brassicas cabbage cauliflower Brussels sprouts	Plants yellow, brown, then die.	Black rot	Use 4-year crop rotation.
	Plants wilt; roots are malformed.	Club root	As above. Keep soil pH between 6.0 and 7.0.

278

Vegetable	Symptom	Problem	Control
broccoli	Plant dwarfed; yellowed lower leaves drop.	Yellows	Plant resistant varieties.
	Foliage eaten by green caterpillar.	Cabbage worms	Rotenone.
	Stems of seedlings eaten by pale brown caterpillar.	Cutworms	Use prepared poison bait.
Carrot	Yellow or brown spots on leaves. Top may die.	Leaf blight	Maneb or Zineb, 4 to 5 times at 10-day intervals, starting when plants are 6" tall.
	Yellowing of center leaves.	Yellows	Control leafhopper that spreads disease with Malathion or Carbaryl.
Celery	Leaves show small yellow spots that turn gray.	Early blight	Use treated seed. Use Maneb or Zineb every 7 days.
	Older leaves have small brown spots that develop black dots.	Late blight	As above.
	Stalks eaten by mottled brown bug.	Tarnished plant bug	Control with Malathion or rotenone.
Corn	Plants show silver or gray swellings that puff black spores at maturity.	Corn smut	Burn swellings before maturity. Use 3-year crop rotation, and resistant varieties.
	Light green or yellow streaks on leaves. Plant stunted or wilted.	Bacterial wilt	Control flea beetles that spread disease with Carbaryl before seedling appears. Use resistant varieties.
	Holes bored into ears.	Corn borer	Use Carbaryl when half the tassel can be seen.
	Silk and tips eaten.	Corn earworm	Treat emerging silk with Carbaryl. Repeat 3 times at 2-day intervals.

Table IV / Vegetable Troubles and What to Do (continued)

Vegetable	What it looks like	What it probably is	How to control or prevent
Cucurbits cucumber squash melons	Sunken spots on fruit, pink at first, then black.	Anthracnose	Use treated seed. Rotate crops. Use Captan or Maneb at 7- to 10-day intervals starting when plants appear.
	Grayish purple fungus on underside of leaves.	Downy mildew	Use resistant varieties. Treat at 7- to 10-day intervals with Maneb.
	Powdery gray-white growth on leaves. Defoliation.	Powdery mildew	Spray with Karathane when mildew appears. Repeat 10 days later.
	Leaves turn dull green and wilt; plant dies.	Bacterial wilt	Rotenone dust.
	Foliage devoured.	Striped cucumber beetle	Control with Carbaryl, Malathion or Methoxychlor.
Eggplant	Leaves turn yellow, then brown; plants stunted.	Verticillium wilt	If garden is infected, change location.
	Young plants covered with brown spots. Seedlings rot at soil level, and die.	Phomopsis blight	Use treated seed. Use Maneb or Captan weekly.
	Tiny holes in leaves.	Flea beetle	Use Carbaryl or rotenone at weekly intervals.
Lettuce	Rot at plant base spreads to top.	Bottom rot, drop rot	Change planting to well-drained location. Use 4-year crop rotation. Omit mulch.
	Chewed leaves. Badly formed heads.	Leafhoppers	Use Carbaryl, Malathion, or Methoxychlor as soon as seedlings appear.

Melon	See **Cucurbits.**	
Onions	Plants stunted, then die. Roots turn pink, then black.	Pink root	Use resistant varieties. Do not plant onions where disease exists.
	Plants turn yellow; tops of leaves have pale green spots.	Downy mildew	Maneb or Zineb.
	Leaves at neck of bulb eaten.	Thrips	Several applications of Malathion.
Parsley	Soft rot that spreads.	Crown rot	Crop rotation.
Peas	Stems decay; plant dies.	Root rot	Resistant varieties. Crop rotation; plant only in well-drained soil.
	Dwarfed leaves; small green lice.	Aphids	Nicotine dust.
	Gray areas, with brown dot, on pods and leaves.	Ascochyta blight	Resistant varieties. Crop rotation.
Peppers	Raised yellow spots on leaves.	Bacterial leaf spot	Use treated seed. Control disease with fixed copper spray.
	Water-soaked areas which enlarge and blacken.	Phoma rot	Crop rotation.
	Dark brown sunken area on fruit bottom.	Blossom end rot	Avoid excessive use of nitrogen fertilizer. Maintain even moisture supply.
	Soft-bodied insects on undersides of leaves.	Aphids	Malathion.
	Small white spots on leaves where minute pale or reddish insects have fed.	Mites or red spider	Malathion.

281

Table IV / Vegetable Troubles and What to Do (continued)

Vegetable	What it looks like	What it probably is	How to control or prevent
Potato	Dark brown circular spots on foliage.	Early blight	Zineb; plant only healthy tubers.
	Water-soaked areas.	Late blight	As above.
	Dark fungus on tuber.	Rhizoctonia	Use disease-free seed.
	Scabs with corky ridge on tuber.	Scab	Plant only in soil with acid pH.
	Reddish larvae on leaves; striped beetles with brown markings.	Potato beetle	Rotenone.
Pumpkin	See **Cucurbits.**		
Spinach	Yellow spots on leaf tops, gray mold on underside.	Downy mildew	Maneb or Zineb; several applications.
	Mottled yellow on inner leaves spreading to outer foliage.	Yellows	Control aphids which spread disease with Malathion.
Squash	See **Cucurbits.**		

Tomato

Symptom	Problem	Remedy
Dark brown sunken area on fruit bottom.	Blossom end rot	Avoid excessive use of nitrogen fertilizer. Maintain even moisture.
Lower leaves wilt, yellow and die.	Fusarium wilt	Plant resistant varieties. Use 5-year crop rotation.
Rolling of leaves.	Leaf roll	Does not affect yield.
Abnormal fruit formation at lower end. Cause unknown.	Catface	Grow locally recommended varieties.
Brown irregular target-pattern spots.	Early blight	Maneb every 5 to 7 days during growing season.
Dark, water-soaked greenish-black blotches.	Late blight	As above.
Round water-soaked spots on fruit.	Anthracnose	Stake plants. Apply Maneb weekly, starting when plants bloom.
Leaves and fruit eaten by large hideous green caterpillar.	Horn worm	Control with Carbaryl; or pick off by hand.
Small white spots on leaves.	Mites or red spiders	Apply Malathion to underside of leaves.
Tiny holes in leaves.	Flea beetle	Carbaryl or rotenone at weekly intervals.

P.S. Report troubles hard to identify to your Agricultural Extension Service.

Table V / Herb Planting and Use

Herb	Height	Propagation method	Remarks and uses
Anise (annual)	2'-3'	Seed	Licorice flavor; fresh leaves in salads; seed in breads; cakes; dried leaves for teas; powdered flower flavors wine or alcohol.
Basil, sweet (annual)	1'-2'	Seed; seedlings	Keep top pinched out; fresh leaves for vinegar, soup, salad, tomatoes.
Borage (annual)	18"-2'	Seed	Attracts bees. Won't transplant. Cucumber flavor. Fresh leaf in cool drinks, salads, pickles.
Caraway (biennial)	2'	Seed	Harvest seeds second season. Sows itself. Use seeds in breads, sauerkraut, with cheese.
Chervil (annual)	6"-12"	Seed	Flavor like fine parsley. Use fresh leaf in sorrel salad, spinach soup, egg dishes, salads. Dry for winter.
Chives (perennial)	10"-12"	Seed; bulbs	Mild onion flavor. Use fresh in soups, salads, cheese, fish and meat sauces.
Coriander (annual)	18"	Seed	Won't transplant. Ripe seeds are fragrant. Dried powdery seeds in breads, baking, with baked apples, vinegar. Crush seeds for demi-tasse.
Dill (annual)	2'-3'	Seed	Won't transplant; prefers rich soil. Use fern fresh in salads, with vegetables, meats. Dried seed for winter. Dried seed head for pickles.
Fennel, sweet (annual)	6"-10"	Seed	Faint licorice flavor. Use as celery, raw or cooked.
Lavender (perennial)	2'-3'	Seed; root cutting; root division	Very slow to germinate. Keep top pinched out first year. Harvest second season. Dig in wood ashes in fall. Moth deterrent, insect repellent; lovely scent.

Mint (perennial)	Root cuttings	2'-3'	Apple and orange mints are most delicate; pineapple is the prettiest. Contain the root, it spreads like a weed. Leaf fresh or dried for teas, lamb sauces, pea soup, jellies, vinegar.
Marjoram, sweet (annual)	Seed; cuttings	1 1/2'	Bring indoors in cold climates. Fresh leaf in vinegar, soups, salads, meats, stock, egg dishes, vegetables. Dry for winter.
Parsley (biennial)	Seed	8"-12"	Fresh or dried in salads, vegetables, soups, stocks. Dry for winter.
Rosemary	Seed; cuttings	3'-6'	Slow to germinate. Bring indoors for winter. Leaf in stews, soup, Italian recipes. Add to deep fat for frying potatoes.
Sage, garden (perennial)	Seed cuttings	2'-3'	Replant every 3 to 4 years. Dried leaf for tea, stuffings, soft cheese.
Savory, summer (annual)	Seed	12"-18"	Likes rich soil. Fresh leaf in salads, sauces, meats, stuffings. Dry for winter. Fresh crushed leaf relieves bee sting. Nice in baths.
Sesame (annual)	Seed	2'	Dried seeds in breads, pastries.
Sorrel, French (perennial)	Seed: root divisions	3'	Requires staking, and heavy moist soil. Tasteless in early spring, acid later. Leaf in salads, soups.
Tarragon (perennial)	Cuttings	3'	Winterkills easily. Fresh leaves with steaks, chops, salads, fish sauces, mustard, mayonnaise, pickles. Dry for winter.
Thyme (perennial)	Seed; cuttings	6"-8"	Very slow to germinate. Fresh leaves in vinegar, meats and fish stocks, chowders. Dry for winter. Dried leaves in sachets to deter moths.
Verbena, lemon (perennial)	Seed; cuttings	4'-5'	Lemon-scented. Half-ripe wood cuttings root well. Dried leaves in sachets.

Table VI / Fruit Planting and Spraying

Fruit	Yield	Height	Distance between rows	Distance between plants	Pollination	Use combination spray
Dwarf Apple	1-2 bushels	8'-10'	Allow 10' x 10'		Cross-pollination required.	1. When buds show pink but before blossoms open.
Semi-dwarf Apple	2-3 bushels	12'-15'	Allow 10' x 20'		As above.	2. As soon as petals have fallen.
						3. Ten days later.
Dwarf Pear	1-2 bushels	8'-10'	Allow 10' x 10'		Cross-pollination required.	4. Two weeks later.
						5. Two weeks later (omit for early varieties).
Semi-dwarf Pear	2-3 bushels	12'-15'	Allow 10' x 20'		As above.	6. Two weeks later.
Dwarf Peach	1-2 bushels	8'-10'	Allow 10' x 10'		Most are self-pollinators.	1. In very early spring while plant is still dormant.
Semi-dwarf Peach	2-3 bushels	12'-15'	Allow 10' x 20'		As above.	2. As soon as petals have fallen.
						3. Ten days later
Nectarine	As above.		As above.		As above.	4. One week later.
						5. Two weeks later.
						6. Six weeks later (omit for early varieties).
Semi-dwarf Plum	1-2 bushels	12'-15'	Allow 10' x 20'		Most require cross-pollination.	1. As soon as petals have fallen.

Standard Plum	2-4 bushels	20'-25'	Allow 16' x 16'		As above.	2. Ten days later.
Standard Sour Cherry	1-2 bushels	20'-25'	Allow 16' x 16'		All are self-pollinators.	3. One week later.
Semi-dwarf Sweet Cherry	1-2 bushels	12'-15'	Allow 10' x 20'		Cross-pollination required.	4. Two weeks later (omit for early varieties of cherry).
Straw-berry	1 qt.	6"	3'-4'	18"	A few require cross-pollination.	Protect from birds with netting.
Rasp-berry	1 1/2 qt.	6'-8'	6'-7'	3'		As above.
Black-berry	1 1/4 qt.	6'-7'	6'-7'	3'		As above.
Blue-berry	4 qt.	10'-15'	8'-10'	4'-5'	Cross-pollination improves yield.	As above.
Grapes	15-30 pounds	up to 50'	7'	7'	Some require cross-pollination.	1. When new growth is 12' long. 2. When shoots are 12". 3. One week after bloom. 4. Three weeks later. 5. Four weeks before harvest.

Index

Acidity, soil, 11, 12, 15
Acorn squash, 81, 174
Agricultural Extension Service, 12, 13, 15, 20, 215
Aioli, 55, 134, 193
Alex's Sabayon Sauce, 235
Alfalfa, 13
Alice Schrier's Potato Latkes, 160
Alkalinity, soil, 11, 15
Almond Mayonnaise, 194
Almonds, 5, 194, 252, 253, 254, 260, 261
Ammonium sulfate, 15
Anita Westsmith's Sukiyaki, 189
Apple and Beet Puree for Pork, 105
Apple-and-Blackberry Deep-Dish Pie, 240
Apple Butter, 229
Apple Dumplings, Rolled, 230
Apple mint, 203
Apple Stuffing, David's Favorite, 230
Apple trees, espaliered, 6
Apples, 4, 228–231
    Baked, Mother's, 228
    Candied, on a Stick, 231
    varieties, 211
Applesauce, Swiss, 229
Artichokes, 33–34, 94–96
    globe, 6, 33
    Jerusalem, 57, 136
    marinade of, 34, 96
    Puree of, au Beurre Noire, 33, 95–96
    Seraphina's Way, 94–95
    Shrimp-Dressed, 33, 95
Asparagus, 1, 3, 6, 34–36, 96–99
    Bruxelles, 98
    au Naturel, 96–97
    rust-resistant varieties, 35
    Soup, Cream of, 98
    Stir-Fried, 99

Tips in Cream, 97–98
Aspics, 90
Aunt Andrée's Celeriac Hors d'Oeuvre, 120
Avocado and Watercress Salad, 182

Bagna Cauda, 58, 79, 197
Baked Mushrooms, 146
Baking, 88
Barbro's Cold Rhubarb Soup, 167
Basil, 4, 205
Beans, 5, 36–37, 100–103
    beetle repellent for, 36
    bush snap, 3
    dried white shell, 103
    fusarium wilt inhibitor for, 36
    green, 3, 100, 121
    lima, 102–103
    pole, 3
    varieties, 36
    wax, 102
Beef
    Cauliflower, and Snow Peas, 44, 119
    herbs for, 208
    and Parsnips, Boiled, 153
    with Radishes, Chinese, 76, 167
    with Turnips, Walter's Chinese, 181
Beet and Apple Puree for Pork, 105
Beet Greens, 105–106
Beet Relish, Gabrielle's, 38, 104
Beet Salad Escoffier, 106
Beets, 3, 38, 104–106
    Lily's Polish, 106
    Mother's Way, 104
Belgian fence espalier, 6
Berries, 215
    See also Blackberries; Blueberries; Raspberries; Strawberries
Beurre Sablais, 66, 145

Biscuits, 199
Blackberries, 4, 218—220
Blackberry-and-Apple Deep-Dish Pie, 240
Black-Walnut Cookies, 270
Black walnuts, 252, 253, 258
Bloody Marys, 83
Blueberries, 4, 6, 220, 241—242
Blueberry Jam, 242
Blueberry Muffins, Ten-Minute, 242
Blueberry Pancakes, John Morris's, 241
Boiled Beef and Parsnips, 153
Boiled Dinner with a Difference, 190
Boiled Dressing, Old-Fashioned, 195
Boiling
    American way, 88, 89
    French way, 88—89
Bordeaux Grape Jam, 222, 251
Borscht, 38, 104—105
    Green, 172
Brassica genus, 39, 44, 58, 59, 78, 85
Bread
    Potato, 162
    Pumpkin Nut, 165
Bread-and-Butter Pickles, 128
Broccoli, 3, 5, 39, 106—108
    with Chestnuts, 108
    au Gratin, 107
    à l'Italienne, 106—107
Brownies, 271
Brussels sprouts, 3, 39, 40, 61, 108—110
Brussels Sprouts in Cream, 109
Brussels Sprouts Milanaise, 40, 109
Burnt Walnut Bisque, 271
Butter Biscuits, Di's, 99, 101, 199, 200
Butternut Cookies, Mother's, 262
Butternut Fudge, 261
Butternut Squash Pie, Sadie Agnes's, 175
Butternuts, 252, 253, 254—255, 258, 261—263

Cabbage, 3, 5, 39, 41—42, 61, 68, 110—115
    celery, 41
    Chinese, 41
    Pie, 110, 199
    red, 41
    Savoy, 41

Soup
    l'Enardière, 111
    with Potato Dumplings, 111
    Stuffed, 112—113
California Strawberry Preserves, 246
Canard aux Navets, 180
Candied Apples on a Stick, 231
Candy
    Butternut Fudge, 261
    Filbert and Fruit, 267
    Hickory-Nut Brittle, 268
    Pralines, 269
Cantaloupe and Grapes in Wine, 250
Cantaloupe-Peach Marmalade, 248
Cantaloupe Rind Preserves, 248
Cantaloupes, 42, 62, 247—250
Carrot and Raisin Salad, Didi's, 43, 116
Carrot and Turnip Mélange, 179
Carrot Cookies, 43, 117
Carrot Marmalade, Mrs. Bartlett's, 43, 116
Carrots, 3, 43, 115—117
    in Cream, 115
    Glazed, au Citron, 43, 116
Casaba melons, 42, 62
Casseroles, 120—121, 131, 137
Cauliflower, 39, 44, 117—119
    Gratinée of, with Watercress, 117—118
    Salad, 118
    and Shrimp Salad, 118
"Caviar," Turkish, 132
Celeriac, 45, 119—121
    Casserole, Madame Malraux, 120—121
    à la Française, 119
    Hors d'Oeuvre, Aunt Andrée's, 120
    Soup, Green, 121
Celery, 46, 121—123
    cabbage, 41
    à la Chinoise, 123
    Guacamole, 121—122
    root, 45
    Soup, Lazy-Day, 122
Chapman, Maro, 23
Chard, 47, 123—124
    Swiss, 47, 80
Cheese
    Brandied, and Pears, 231
    Ravioli and Otto's Spinach, 172—173

Cherries, 4, 238–239
  Jubilation, 239
  varieties, 212
Cherry-Filbert Salad, 267
Cherry Pie, Sally Erath's Sour, 239
Chervil, 205
Chestnut-and-Orange Dessert, 264
Chestnut Puree Dessert, 263
Chestnut Stuffing Chimney Hill, 264
Chestnuts, 252, 255, 263–264
  Broccoli with, 108
  Chinese, 253
Chicken
  Brunswick Stew with Okra, 65, 149
  herbs for, 208
  Stock, 94
Chicory, 48, 54, 61
Chinese Beef with Radishes, 76, 167
Chinese cabbage, 41
Chinese Cabbage with Crabmeat
    Sauce, 113
Chinese cooking method, 88, 89–90
Chives, 4, 66
Cichorium endivia, 54
Chocolate
  Balls, Christmas Walnut, 270
  Butternut Clusters, 262
  Sauce Escoffier, 232
Chouans, 110
Christmas Walnut Chocolate Balls, 270
Clarified Butter for Sautéing, 92, 125
Clay soil, 12
Clover, 13
Coconut, 252, 253, 255–256, 265–266
  Kisses, 266
  Lobster Curry with, 265
  Tart, Pat's South American, 265
Coffee grounds, 36
Companion planting, 3
Compost pile, 14
Cookies
  Black-Walnut, 270
  Butternut, Mother's, 262
  Carrot, 43, 117
Cooking methods, five basic, 88–89
Cool-season crops, 21
Corn, 3, 5, 48–49, 124–126
  on the Cob, the Right Way, 124
  Fritters, Easy, 124–125
  Pudding, 125

sweet, 48
  varieties, 48
Cover crops, 13
Crab Gumbo, New Orleans Fresh, 65,
    148
Crabmeat Sauce, 113
Crackerjack Popcorn, 125–126
Cream Custard for Fruit, 224
Cream of Asparagus Soup, 98
Cream of Brussels Sprouts Soup, 40,
    110
Creamed Kale Casserole, 137
Creamed Turnip Cups, 180
Cresses, 61
Croissants, Mock, 201
Cross pollination, 4, 5
Crystallized Grapes, 251
Cucumber and Veal Scallops, 126
Cucumber Soup, 51, 127
Cucumbers, 3, 5, 50–51, 61, 126–127
Cucurbils, 51, 56, 75, 81
Culture, *see* Planting, and culture

Dandelion and Lettuce Salad, 130
Dandelion Flower Omelet, 129, 152
Dandelion Wine, Old-Fashioned, 52,
    130
Dandelions, 52, 129–131
David's Favorite Apple Stuffing, 230
David's Tomato Breakfast, 176
Deep-Dish Blackberry-and-Apple Pie,
    240
Didi's Carrot and Raisin Salad, 116
Digging, 25
Dill, 4, 205
Dill Pickles, Kosher, 128
Dilled Green Beans, 100, 121
Dilled Radishes, 166
Di's Butter Biscuits, 199, 200
Di's Gazpacho, 187
Di's Grape Dessert, 251
Dressings, cold, 194–197
  Aioli, 193
  Almond Mayonnaise, 194
  Boiled, Old-Fashioned, 195
  Fresh Mayonnaise, 193
  Fruit Mayonnaise, 194
  Garlic, 194
  Mayonnaise Chantilly, 193

Dressings, cold (*cont.*)
New York Green Goddess, 194
Oil-and-Vinegar, 192, 195
Roquefort, 195
Russian, 194
Sour Cream, 196
Duck with Turnips, 180
Dumplings
Apple, Rolled, 230
Potato, with Cabbage Soup, 111
Dutch Almond Slices, 261
Dutch Dandelion Salad, 131

Early Spring Salad, 140
Easy Corn Fritters, 124–125
Easy Short Pastry, 199, 200
Egg dishes, herbs for, 208
Eggplant, 53–54, 131–132
Casserole, 131
Salad, Gay's, 53, 132
Elegant Mushroom Soup, 145
Enardière, l', 252
Endive, 48, 54, 61, 133
Belgian, 54, 133
English walnuts, 252, 253, 258
Escarole, 54, 61

Fertility, soil, 11, 13–14
Fertilizer, complete, 13
Fertilizing
fruit trees, 214
nut trees, 253
strawberries, 217
Filbert and Fruit Candy, 267
Filbert Crisp, 266
Filberts, 252, 253, 256, 266–267
Fine Garlic Butter, 92–93
Fine Garlic Soup, 134
Fines Herbes, 207
Flageolets, 103
Flats, 21
Food plants
aesthetics, 6
essentials, 5
in your landscape, 1–10
Forsythia, 6
Francesca Morris's Marinade, 96
Fran's Fine New Potato Salad, 159
Fresh Mayonnaise, 193

Fresh Mint Sauce, 196
Fresh Peach Tart, 233
Fritter Batter, 201
Fritters
Corn, Easy, 124–125
Strawberry, Escoffier, 244
Frost-tolerant vegetables, 21
Fruit crop, 4–5, 6
Fruit-cup combinations, 227
Fruit en Compote, 223–224
Fruit Fools, 226
Fruit jams, 227
Fruit Mayonnaise, 194
Fruit Puree, 224
Fruit Soufflé, 225
Fruit trees, 4, 210–215
dwarf, 4, 6
espaliered, 6
fertilizing, 214
mulching, 214
thinning, 214
Fruits
cooking and serving recipes, 223–251
orchard, 210–215

Gabrielle's Beet Relish, 38, 104
Garden
diary for, 18–19
digging, 25
fruit crop, 4–5, 6, 210–215
herb crop, 4, 6, 20, 203
nut crop, 5, 252–258
planting plan, 20–21
size, 1–3
soil, 11–15
tools, 24
vegetable crop, 1–3, 33–87
when to plant, 20–21
where to plant, 5–10
Garden cress, 50, 61
Garden log, 18–19
Garden tools, 24
Garlic, 4, 55
Garlic Butter, Fine, 55, 92–93
Garlic Dressing, 134, 194
Garlic Soup Paysanne, 55, 135
Garnishes
Beurre Sablais, 66, 145

parsley, 67, 151
pear, 232
Gay's Eggplant Salad, 53, 132
Gay's Rhubarb Jam, 169
Gazpacho, Di's, 187
Giant Zucchini, 184
Glazed Carrots au Citron, 116
Globe artichoke, 6, 33
Good Braised Celery, 122–123
Gorgeous Soufflé of Peas, 155
Gourds, 51, 56
Grape Dessert, Di's, 251
Grape Jam, Bordeaux, 222, 251
Grapes, 4, 220, 250–251
    Crystallized, 251
    as hedge or arbor, 6
    leaves, 222
Gratine dishes, 90
Gratinée of Cauliflower with Water-
        cress, 117–118
Green Bean Salad, 100–101
Green Beans Fukien, 101–102
Green Borscht, 172
Green Celeriac Soup, 121
Green Leek Soup, 139
Green or Yellow Tomato Preserves, 177
Green Parsley Soup, 151
Green Pepper Relish, 72, 158
Greens
    Beet, 105–106
    Mess of, 129
    Radish, with Sour Cream, 166
    salad, 48, 54, 60–61
Gumbo, 65, 148

Ham and Asparagus Rolls, 99
Hamburgers, Special, 146
Harvesting, 32
Hasty-Tasty Rhubarb Mousse, 168
Hazelnuts, 5, 252, 266
Heart nut, 258
Helenium, 6
Herb baths, 209
Herb crop, 4, 6
Herb teas, 209
Herb vinegars, 208
Herbs, 4, 6, 20
    agreeable to grow and use, 203–209
    drying and storing leaves, 206

Fines, 207
    gardens, 205
    harvesting leaves, 206
    harvesting seeds, 207
    planting, 203
    strawberry jar planting, 4, 205
    uses of, 207
Hickory-Nut Brittle, 268
Hickory-Nut Cake, 267
Hickory-Nut Drops, 268–269
Hickory-Nut Frosting, 268
Hickory nuts, 252, 253, 257, 267–269
Hills, seed-planting, 27
Hollandaise in a Blender, 198
Homemade Sauerkraut, 113–114
Honeydew melons, 42, 62
Hors d'oeuvres, 120, 121
Horseradish, 56–57
    Iced, 136
    Pickled, 135
    Sauce, Hot, 135
Hot Bath (Bagna Cauda) Sauce, 197
Hot Green Tomato Relish, 177
Hot Horseradish Sauce, 135
Hot Watercress and Mushrooms, 183
Humus, 12
Hunter, David Marvin, 52, 176, 230

Iced Horseradish, 136
Icy Summer Salad, 127
Intercropping, 3, 16
Irene's Vegetable Curry, 189–190

Jam
    Blueberry, 242
    Bordeaux Grape, 222, 251
    Rhubarb, Gay's, 169
Jams, fruit, 227
Jane Yamamoto's Summer Squash, 81,
        174
Jan's Spring Lettuce Soup, 141
Jansson's Temptation, 161
Japanese walnuts, 258
Jerusalem artichokes, 57
Jerusalem Artichokes Béchamel, 136
John Morris's Blueberry Pancakes, 241
John Morris's Zucchini Salad, 183

Kale, 47, 58, 80
  Bohemian Style, 137
  Creamed, Casserole, 137
  Stir-Fried, 136
Kentucky Wonder Appetizer, 101
Kidneys with Pat's Gorgeous Peppers,
    157
Kohlrabi, 58–59
  in Cream, 138
  l'Enardière, 138
Kosher Dill Pickles, 128

Lamb
  herbs for, 208
  with Lima Beans and Endive—for
    Garlic Lovers, 102–103
Landscape, food plants in, 1–10
Larousse Gastronomique, 43
Lazy-Day Celery Soup, 122
Leafy vegetables, 5
Leek Soup, Green, 139
Leeks, 59–60, 139–140
Lemon Butter Sauce, 91, 94, 97, 104,
    199
Lettuce, 3, 60–61, 140–142
  Bibb, 61
  Boston, 61
  cos, 61
  iceberg, 61
  Melbourne, 142
  à la Normande, 141
  romaine, 61
  Soup, Jan's Spring, 141
  Sour-Cream, 142
Lily's Polish Beets, 106
Lima Beans with Lamb and Endive—
    for Garlic Lovers, 102–103
Lime, 15
Loam, 12
Lobster Curry with Coconut, 265

Macadamis, 252
Madame Paquet's Turnips and Pork,
    181
Madeleine's Nectarine Meringues, 236
Manure, 12
Marigolds, 36, 68

Marmalade
  Cantaloupe-Peach, 248
  Carrot, Mrs. Bartlett's, 43, 116
  Rhubarb, Mrs. Wetmore's, 169
Mayonnaise
  Fresh, 193
  Chantilly, 193
Melon and fruit combinations, 144
Melon balls, 144
Melon baskets, 144
Melons, 4, 5, 42, 51, 62, 144, 247–250
Mess of Greens, 129
Mexican Chili, 71, 157
Mild Salsify Salad, 171
Mint Sauce, 196
Minted Raspberries in Syrup, 240–241
Mints, 203
Mrs. Bartlett's Carrot Marmalade, **116**
Mrs. Friedlander's Spinach Mold, 171
Mrs. Wetmore's Rhubarb Marmalade,
    169
Mixed Mustard Pickles, 158
Mock Croissants, 201
Mock Oyster Soup, 79, 170
Moth repellents, 209
Mother's Baked Apples, 228
Mother's Butternut Cookies, 262
Muffins, Ten-Minute Blueberry, 242
Mulches, 31
Mulching, 30–31
  fruit trees, 214
  strawberries, 217
Mushroom Soup, Elegant, 145
Mushrooms, 63–64, 145–147
  Baked, 146
  Hot Watercress and, 183
  Rice with, 146–147
Muskmelons, 42, 62
My Favorite All-Purpose Stock, 93–94
My Favorite Pumpkin Pie, 164

Napolean I, 110
Nectarines, 4
  See also Peaches, and nectarines
New Orleans Fresh Crab Gumbo, 65,
    148
New Orleans "Pain Patate," 162
New Potato Salad, Fran's Fine, 159
New Potatoes in Cream, 159

New York Green Goddess Dressing, 194

New Zealand spinach, 64, 80

Nitrogen, 13

Nut crop, 5, 6

Nut trees
bounty from, 252–258
fertilizing, 253

Nuts, cooking with, 259–271
French-fried, 259
glacéed, 260
salted, 260
skinning, 259

Oil-and-Vinegar Dressing, 100, 192, 195

Okra, 65, 147–149
and Shrimp Vinaigrette, 147
-Stuffed Peppers, 147

Old-Fashioned Boiled Dressing, 195

Old-Fashioned Dandelion Wine, 52, 130

Old-Fashioned Strawberry Shortcakes, 243

Omelet
Dandelion Flower, 129, 152
Salsify, Uncle Marc's, 170

Omelette les Sables, 152

Onion Soup les Halles, 150

Onions, 3, 61, 66–67, 149–150
Bermuda, 3, 66, 150
bunching, 66
Southern Style, 149
Spanish, 3, 67

Orange mint, 203

Orchard fruits, 210–215

Otto's Spinach and Cheese Ravioli, 172–173

Painless Borscht, 104–105

Pancakes
Blueberry, John Morris's, 241
à la Pomme, 229
Potato, 160

Pan-Fried Peppers, 156

Papa's Petits Pois, 154

Papa's Pie Pastry, 199, 201–202

Parsley, 4, 67–69, 151, 205
Garnish, Sizzled, 151
Soup, Green, 151

Parsnip Cakes, Sadie Agnes's, 152

Parsnips, 69, 152–153
and Boiled Beef, 153
à l'Orange, 153

Pastry, 199–202
Papa's Pie, 201–202
Ratatouille, 190–191
Walnut Pie Crust, Wonderful, 270

Pat's Gorgeous Peppers with Kidneys, 157

Pat's South American Coconut Tart, 265

Pea Soup à l'Anglaise, 154

Peach Crisp, 235

Peach Melba, 233

Peach Tart, Fresh, 233

Peaches, 4
and nectarines, 213, 233–237
Pickled, 236
Sultane, 234

Pear Garnish for Meat, 232

Pears, 4, 211, 228, 231–232
and Brandied Cheese, 231
varieties, 212

Peas, 3, 70–71, 154–155
snow (or sugar), 70
Soufflé of, Gorgeous, 155

Peat pots, 21

Pecan Pie, 269

Pecans, 252, 253, 257

Pêches Flambées, 234

Pennyroyal, 203

Peppermint, 203

Peppers, 3, 6, 71–72, 156–158
with Kidneys, Pat's Gorgeous, 157
Okra-Stuffed, 147
Pan-Fried, 156
Stuffed, Provençale, 156
varieties, 71

PH, see Potential of hydrogen

Phlox, 6

Phosphorus, 13

Piccalilli, 178

Pickled Horseradish, 135

Pickled Peaches, 236

Pickled Plums, Spicy, 238

Pickled Watermelon Rind, 143

Pickles
  Bread-and-Butter, 128
  Kosher Dill, 128
  Mixed Mustard, 158
Pie
  Butternut Squash, Sadie Agnes's, 175
  Cabbage, 110, 199
  Deep-Dish   Blackberry-and-Apple,
    240
  Pecan, 269
  Pumpkin, My Favorite, 164
  Sour Cherry, Sally Erath's, 239
  Strawberry and Rhubarb, 245
Pineapple mint, 203
Piselli al Prosciutto, 155
Pistachio, 252
Planting
  companion, 3
  and culture
    berries, 218
    fruit trees, 213
    helping plants prosper, 30–31
    nut trees, 253
    strawberries, 216–217
  intercropping, 3, 16
  plan for, 16–19
  succession, 3, 16
  temperature for, 21
  timing, 16
  when to plant, 20–21
  where to plant, 5–10
Plastic
  black, for mulching, 30
  clear, for frost protection, 25
Plum Butter, 238
Plum Turnovers, 237
Plums, 4, 212, 237–238
  Spicy Pickled, 238
Poires Hélène, 232
Pollination requirements
  cross pollination, 4, 5
  fruit trees, 215
  nut trees, 253
Pommes de Terre Sautées, 72, 161–
  162
Popcorn, Crackerjack, 48, 125–126
Pork
  Beet and Apple Puree for, 105
  herbs for, 208
  and Turnips, Madame Paquet's, 181

Potash, 13
Potato Bread, 162
Potato Dumplings, 112
Potato Nests, 72, 160
Potato Pancakes, 160
Potato Salad, Fran's Fine New, 159
Potatoes, 5, 72–73, 159–162
  Fried, 72, 161–162
  in Cream, New, 159
  Irish, 74
  See also Sweet potatoes
Pot-au-Feu Aunt Andrée, 140
Potential of hydrogen (pH)
  definition of, 15
  reaction, of soil, 11, 12, 15
  testing kits, 15
Pralines, 269
Preserves
  California Strawberry, 246
  Cantaloupe Rind, 248
  Green or Yellow Tomato, 177
Prosciutto, 62
Pruning
  fruit trees, 213
  raspberries and blackberries, 218
Pumpkin Nut Bread, 165
Pumpkin Pie, My Favorite, 164
Pumpkin Soup, 163
Pumpkin Wedges, 164
Pumpkins, 3, 75, 163–165
Puree of Artichokes au Beurre Noire,
  95–96

Quackgrass, 25
Quiche aux Endives, 133
Quick Bermuda Onion Rings, 150
Quick Remoulade Sauce, 196

Radish Greens with Sour Cream, 166
Radishes, 3, 76, 165–167
  au Beurre, 165
  with Chinese beef, 76, 167
  Dilled, 166
Raspberries, 4, 6, 218–220
  Minted, in Syrup, 240–241
Raspberry Mousse, 240
Raspberry Sauce, Strawberries with, 246
Ratatouille Pastry, 190–191, 199
Refrigerator Fruit Ice Cream, 226

Relish
Beet, Gabrielle's, 38, 104
Green Pepper, 72, 158
Hot Green Tomato, 177
Rhubarb, 1, 3, 6, 77, 167–169
Jam, Gay's, 169
Marmalade, Mrs. Wetmore's, 169
Mother's Way, 168
Mousse, Hasty-Tasty, 168
Soup, Barbro's Cold, 167
and Strawberry Pie, 245
Risotto con Funghi, 146–147
Rolled Apple Dumplings, 230
Romaine, 61
Root vegetables, 3, 5
Roquefort Dressing, 195
Rosemary, 205
Rosy Lettuce Soup, 141
Rototiller, 12, 13, 25
Rubbing lotions, 209
Rudbeckia, 6
Russian Dressing, 194
Rutabaga, 78, 85
Rye, 13

Sadie Agnes's Butternut Squash Pie, 175
Sadie Agnes's Parsnip Cakes, 152
Salad
Beet, Escoffier, 106
Carrot and Raisin, 43, 116
Cauliflower, 118
and Shrimp, 118
Cherry-Filbert, 267
Dandelion and Lettuce, 130, 131
Early Spring, 140
Eggplant, Gay's, 53, 132
greens, 48, 54, 60–61
Icy Summer, 127
Potato, Fran's Fine New, 159
Salsify, Mild, 171
Tomato, Madame Bertrand, 179
Watercress and Avocado, 182
Zucchini, John Morris's, 183
Sally Erath's Sour Cherry Pie, 239
Salsa Bianca, 173
Salsify, 79, 170–171
Omelet, Uncle Marc's, 170
Salt hay, 31

Sand, 12
Sauces, 192–199
Béarnaise, 66, 91, 199
Béchamel, 91, 136, 198
Berry, Sweet, 205
Chocolate, Escoffier, 232
cold, 192–197
Hollandaise in a Blender, 91, **94**, **97**, 198
hot, 197–199
Lemon Butter, 91, **94**, **97**, 104, 199
Mint, Fresh, 196
Raspberry, Strawberries with, 246
Remoulade, Quick, 192, 196
Sabayon, Alex's, 235
Vinaigrette, 91, **96**, **106**, 192, 196
White, 198
Sauerkraut, 113–114
Dinner Chimney Hill, 114–115
Savory, 36
Savory Brussels Sprouts, 108
Savoy cabbage, 41
Scallions, 66
Scalloped Vegetables au Gratin, 91–92
Seedlings, 21–22
transplanting, 22
Seeds
disease resistant, 20
insect resistant, 20
sowing, 27
starting indoors, 21
Shallots, 66, 79
Sherried Sweet Potatoes, 163
Shrimp
with Almond Sauce, 260
and Cauliflower Salad, 118
-Dressed Artichokes, 95
Simrell, Diane, 199
Sizzled Parsley Garnish, 67, 151
Soil
fertility, 11, 13–14
improvement program for, **11**
pH reaction, 11, 12, 15
structure, 11, 12–13
testing kits, 15
for top production, 11–15
Soufflé, 90
Fruit, 225
of Peas, Gorgeous, 155

Soufflé (*cont.*)
  Vegetable, 91
Soup
  Cabbage
    l'Enardière, 111
    with Potato Dumplings, 111
  Celery, Lazy-Day, 122
  Cream of Asparagus, 98
  Cream of Brussels Sprouts, 40, 110
  Cucumber, 51, 127
  Garlic, Paysanne, 55, 134, 135
  Gauloise, 59, 139
  Green Celeriac, 121
  Green Leek, 139
  Green Parsley, 151
  Lettuce, Jan's Spring, 141
  Mock Oyster, 79, 170
  Mushroom, Elegant, 145
  Onion, les Halles, 150
  Pea, à l'Anglaise, 154
  Pumpkin, 163
  Rhubarb, Barbro's Cold, 167
  Too-Many-Tomatoes, 83, 175
  Vegetable
    Summer, 186
    Winter, 187
  Watercress, Walter's Chinese, 182
Soupe Gauloise, 59, 139
Sour Cream
  Dressing, 196
  Lettuce, 142
Southern Sweet Potato Balls, 162
Spearmint, 203
Special Hamburgers, 146
Sphagnum moss, 21
Spicy Pickled Plums, 238
Spinach, 47, 80, 171–173
  and Cheese Ravioli, Otto's, 172–173
  Mold, Mrs. Friedlander's, 171
  See also New Zealand spinach
Spraying
  berries, 218
  fruit trees, 214
  grapes, 222
Squash, 3, 51, 81–82, 174–175
  varieties, 81
Starter solution, 22
Stir-Fried Asparagus, 99
Stir-Fried Kale, 136
Stir-frying, 88, 89–90

Stock, 93–94
Storing, 32
Strawberries, 1, 4, 215–217, 243–246
  climbing, 10
  with Raspberry Sauce, 246
  Wilhelmina, 245
Strawberry and Rhubarb Pie, 245
Strawberry Fritters Escoffier, 244
Strawberry jar, 4, 205
Strawberry Preserves, California, 246
Strawberry Shortcakes, Old-Fashioned,
    243
Stuffed Cabbage, 112–113
Stuffed Chard Ribs Paysanne, 123–124
Stuffed Peppers Provençale, 72, 156
Stuffing
  Apple, David's Favorite, 230
  Chestnut, Chimney Hill, 264
Succession planting, 16
Succotash, 188
Sukiyaki, Anita Westsmith's, 189
Summer Porch Supper, 133
Summer savory, 4, 205
Summer Vegetable Soup, 186
Sunflower, 57
Superphosphate, 13
Sweet Acorn Squash, 174
Sweet Berry Sauce, 225
Sweet marjoram, 4, 205
Sweet Potato Balls, Southern, 162
Sweet potatoes, 74, 162–163
Sweet vetch, 13
Swiss Applesauce, 229
Swiss chard, 47, 80

Tarragon, 4, 205
Tarte aux Fraises Chimney Hill, 244,
Temperature, planting, 21
Ten-Minute Blueberry Muffins, 242
Thinning, fruit trees, 214
Thyme, 4, 205
Timing, 16
Tomato Breakfast, David's, 176
Tomato Chutney, 178
Tomato Rarebit on Toast, 176
Tomato Salad Madame Bertrand, 179
Tomatoes, 3, 5, 6, 82–85, 175–179
Too-Many-Tomatoes Soup, 83, 175
Tools, 24

Topinambours, 57
Transplanting, 22
Turkish "Caviar," 53, 132
Turnip and Carrot Mélange, 179
Turnip Cups, Creamed, 180
Turnips, 3, 78, 85–86, 179–181
   with Chinese Beef, Walter's, 181
   and Pork, Madame Paquet's, 181
   varieties, 78, 85

Uncle Marc's Salsify Omelet, 170

Veal
   herbs for, 208
   Scallops and Cucumber, 126
   Stock, 94
Vegetable Chop Suey, 188
Vegetable crop, 1–3
   cool-season crops, 21
   frost-tolerant, 21
   harvesting and storing, 32
   how to grow, 33–87
   leafy, 5
   perennials, 1
   planting plan, 16–19
   root, 3, 5
   for starting indoors, 21, 22
   warm-season crops, 21
Vegetable Curry, Irene's, 189–190
Vegetable Soufflé, 91
Vegetable Soup
   Summer, 186
   Winter, 187
Vegetables, combined, recipes for, 186–190

Vegetables in Aspic, 90–91
Vendée, 100, 139
Vetch, sweet, 13

Walnut Chocolate Balls, Christmas, 270
Walnut Pie Crust, Wonderful, 270
Walnuts, 258, 270–271
Walter's Chinese Beef with Turnips, 181
Walter's Chinese Watercress Soup, 182
Warm-season crops, 21
Watercress, 86, 182–183
   and Avocado Salad, 182
   and Mushrooms, Hot, 183
   Soup, Walter's Chinese, 182
Watering, 30
Watermelon Dessert Cocktail, 143
Watermelons, 62, 143
Wax Beans in Cream, 102
Weeding, 30
White Sauce, 198
Wilson, Helen Van Pelt, 185
Winter Vegetable Soup, 187
Witchgrass, 25
Wok, 89
Wonderful Walnut Pie Crust, 270

Yams, 74

Zucchini, 81, 87, 183–185
   Appetizer, 185
   with Meat Sauce, 87, 185
   Salad, John Morris's, 183

Jacqueline Hériteau (Mrs. David M. Hunter) was born in France at the Château de l'Enardière in the Vendée. Her mother was Scotch-Canadian; her father French. She lived in Paris in winter and Canada in summer, and after World War II she attended the Sorbonne. In 1955 she married an American and came to live in the United States. In her father's village, Les Sables d'Olonne, the family was famous for its cuisine, for which all the vegetables and fruits were gathered, of course, from the home garden—so Jacqueline came naturally by her interest in both gardening and cooking. Through the years she has had food gardens in France, Sweden, and in this country in Cape Cod (Mass.), in Plainfield (Vt.), and in Westport and Sharon (Conn.), where she now lives with her husband, daughter, and two sons. Professionally, she has been Women's Editor for a newspaper in Montreal and for Station CJAD there, for two New York public-relations publications, for *Precis* magazine, and for Central Feature News. Her articles and short stories have appeared in the Canadian *Week End, Chatelaine,* and *Mayfair* magazines; and in the United States in *Parent's Magazine, Compact, Better Homes & Gardens,* and *House Beautiful.*